Bible-365

Discovering God in the Ordinary
Through a Lifetime of Journaling

STEPHEN J. ROBIN

Seshat Press
211 Pauline Drive #513
York, PA 17402
www.seshatpress.com
Send questions to: support@seshatpress.com

Paperback ISBN: 979-8-9920502-9-5
eBook ISBN: 979-8-9996544-0-3
Library of Congress Control Number: 2025917761

Printed in the United States of America

Seshat Press is proud to be a part of the Tree Neutral® program. Tree Neutral offsets the number of trees consumed in the production and printing of this book by taking proactive steps such as planting trees in direct proportion to the number of trees used to print books. To learn more about Tree Neutral, please visit treeneutral.com.

Dedicated to both my parents and grandmother,
Peter and Vera Robin, and Agnes Webb.

Their love and understanding has been core to
my very being for over seventy years.

When all else failed me, their love stayed constant
as my North Star.

Introduction

When a friend first suggested that I write a book about my life's journey and experiences, I was skeptical. I could not imagine anyone would find my story compelling, especially when compared to the weighty tomes by theological giants that had filled my bookshelves since seminary. Yet, my friend persisted, urging me to draw from the thoughts and stories recorded in my journals, which I had kept frequently each year—chronicling my daily pilgrimage with the Bible, and spanning over fifty years.

As I delved into these journals once more, I found myself retracing the contours of my life, rediscovering the memories and challenges that have shaped my understanding of purpose. Capturing these experiences on paper—descriptive scenes, vivid sights, resonant sounds, and evocative scents—initially felt disjointed, incomplete. However, as I completed my writings and revisited 365 daily entries, I was struck by the depth and authenticity of what I had shared. Maintaining truthfulness throughout the process was crucial, helping me confront both the perceptions of others and my own lingering imposter syndrome. Writing demanded compassion, particularly when recounting moments of personal trauma, and some pages were harder to face than others.

I remember sitting at the feet of my grandmother, who, having started working in service at the age of seven, had never attended school. So, she taught herself to read the Bible, one word at a time. To her, the Bible was more than literature; it was life itself. Reading together, when the text seemed dull or repetitive, she would seamlessly weave in tales of her own life—mundane struggles and profound reflections. Her narratives brought the scriptures to life, contrasting sharply with the scholarly environment I later encountered in seminary. There, esteemed professors and colleagues advocated for a scholarly approach: exploring highlights, commentaries, translations—even foreign languages—without taking the text literally.

Combining these diverse influences—my grandmother's heartfelt interpretations and the academic rigor of seminary—deepened my appreciation for the Bible's universal reach. This perspective shaped my leadership of a small Bible study group, in which a dozen of us embarked on a transformative journey, reading the Bible cover to cover over the course of a year. Through weekly discussions, each person shared their unique encounters with the scriptures, revealing a collective yearning to be understood and affirmed in our shared humanity. In our safe space, vulnerability became our currency as we unearthed our deepest fears and aspirations, the very essence of who we were and whom we strived to become.

As our group flourished, others took notice, forming their own gatherings to explore the Bible's relevance in their lives. Witnessing this burgeoning community, I observed a profound evolution—from seeking external guidance to recognizing the intrinsic wisdom within each individual's journey. This shift underscored a fundamental truth: the greatest teacher resides within us, shaping our understanding and guiding our spiritual growth more profoundly than any external authority.

My pilgrimage through life has been a tapestry woven with diverse experiences and encounters that have imparted invaluable lessons. Journaling daily alongside my Bible readings provided a crucial anchor, enabling me to distill these lessons and acknowledge the transformative impact of each day's reflections. This practice—challenging, yet enriching—fostered mindfulness and self-awareness, helping me navigate personal brokenness and support healing in others.

Embracing the daily discipline of reading, meditating, and journaling has been far from easy. Yet, I hear the echoes of my grandmother and mother, whose voices remind me, *If it was easy, God would not have asked you to do it.* Their wisdom underscores the importance of perseverance, urging me to continue fostering spiritual growth not only within myself but within those I meet along the way.

This journey led me to Ferguson, Missouri, to a small Episcopal church where I found a calling to provide solace, support, and spiritual guidance to those in need. Here, amid seekers striving for clarity and connection with their souls, I continue to draw on the lessons of my pilgrimage. This spiritual autobiography is a personal narrative—moving in and out of chronological order, inviting you to embark on your own journey of self-discovery and spiritual growth through the practice of journaling and reflection.

As you delve into my story, pick up a copy of the Bible—one you like to read—pull out a journal or a notebook to write in, and on each new day, start anew to jot down your thoughts, feelings, and understandings of how this amazing book can affect your life.

Kingdoms come and go. Even the great empires of Greece and Rome collapsed with time. Somehow the community, who was one of the smallest in its time, a community defeated and scattered to the four winds, managed to reinvent itself.

What I found in the process of reading the Bible and sitting with the text for a while each day, were ways to survive in my life that I have taken for granted. Even more than that, I continue to find strategies waiting for me to discover within its pages each day as my life and circumstances change.

Even on days when I could not write anything, I could pick up the story in the Bible from where I left off, and that, too, added meaning to my journey. I grew up with the Bible present daily in our home and lives. My father would read aloud to me as a child, and I followed in my own children's version, complete with paintings summarizing the storyline. No question was too simple. Yet my father would often answer with a question back to me, challenging me to think about what I had heard. I hope that as you read my story, you will feel how reading the Bible every day has guided me and helped me through the changes and challenges in my life.

I pray you experience this too. Write powerfully.

—Stephen J. Robin, Ferguson, Missouri, 2025

Day 1

Read: Genesis 1–3

Then God said, "Let there be light;" and there was light.

—Genesis 1:1

I curled up as tightly as I could, and then just a little bit tighter—like the bud of a flower, folded up inside of a warm, soft place. A deep rhythmic sound ebbed and flowed around me, through me, beyond me. A roaring, rushing sound began to rumble beneath me, and suddenly, I was being sucked down into a tunnel and squeezed toward the light—a light so bright I couldn't see. And then, the glow was gone, the warmth was gone, but someone wrapped me up and laid me back near the deep, throbbing sound. And so, like a stone dropped into still waters, I arrived, causing ripples to spread far and wide. And so began a rhythm of breathing in the air and sensing the breezes rustling the nearby trees, which could stir me from my sleep as I lay on my back in the pram on the front porch of the house. This would be my world. All I could see hovered above me. The sun stretched fingers of light through the clouds into the pram, and I opened my eyes to a glorious new world, a new day. There were new things to see, new things to explore. Wonders I will never take for granted. In that moment, I could see God's world planned through the eyes of a child, a child of God.

I continue to see God's presence in everything and everyone around me, even in life itself.

Day 2

Read: Genesis 4–7

Now Abel was a keeper of sheep, and Cain a tiller of the ground.

—Genesis 4:2

A face peered over the edge of the pram and looked down at me. This was the first time I remember seeing my brother who is five years older than me. To him, I must have just been a helpless, vulnerable little thing who came to disrupt his life. As I looked up at him, I thought how sad he looked, how hurt, how disappointed. I tried to speak to him, but all he heard was a gurgle. Even at that moment, I realized his world was going to change in many ways, and things would never be the same for him again. Someone called out to him, and he left, leaving me alone again where I lay.

Within moments, a pair of birds flew down and perched on the handle of the pram. They looked at me, turning their heads from side to side, listening as they chirped. I smiled up at the birds, listened to them, and tried to copy their sounds, and the birds spoke back, encouraging me—the first of many conversations. They visited two by two, sharing their thoughts and lives with me. It rained gently. I looked up out of the pram and saw the clouds drifting away. The sun came out, and after the rain, came a rainbow. I could feel warmth in the sun and joy in the rainbow, and everything seemed to be calm in the world, refreshed and renewed.

Day 3

Read: Genesis 8–11

Come, let us go down, and confuse their language there, so that they will not understand one another's speech.

—Genesis 11:7

As I lay there, I was aware of a powerful scent in the air, a scent I would recognize for the rest of my life. I would come to know it was a beautiful white flower, a lily of the valley, which my mother had planted by the path in and out of our house. I associated this scent with my mother for the rest of her life.

At first, I didn't understand when anyone spoke to me. Everyone made such strange sounds, believing I would understand them, believing they were communicating with me. They were searching for a way to relate with me, seeking a response from me. *Couldn't they hear me?* I listened to all the different sounds—the birds, the dogs, the cats, the rain. I listened as our neighbors leaned over my pram to say *Hello.* I listened to the sounds of their different voices, the sounds of a North London suburb in the 1950s: Hebrew, Chinese, Japanese, Hindi, Pashtu, Sinhalese, French, German, Dutch, and English. I heard not just one sound, but many as the neighbors visited, welcoming me in their languages from countries, which I would find out later, were originally far, far away.

And then there was my grandmother, who cooed over me with her soft cockney accent, so different from the others, even my parents. So different from the others, yet in her sing-song style, somehow comforting and safe. She shared her dreams, her hopes, and her love, all for me.

Day 4

Read: Genesis 12–15

Now the Lord said to Abram, "Go from your country and your kindred and your father's house to the land that I will show you."

—Genesis 12:1

As the weeks rolled on, I sensed a change in the weather every day as I lay in my pram. I lay there looking up as the sun gradually disappeared into the fog, leaving a cold chill of autumn on my face. As dusk rolled in, my father reached down and scooped me up in his arms, taking me inside to sit by the open fire in our family gathering room. He talked softly to me about where he had grown up in the foothills of snowcapped mountains, and fast-flowing icy rivers, far, far away. He told how he and his little sister had traveled with his father and mother to a hot and barren land where men wrenched silver out of the ground with their bare hands.

Suddenly, in the middle of a celebration, his mother died. He spoke sadly of the long journey by boat to England. Of meeting his aunt for the first time, who separated him from his sister. Of saying goodbye to his father and being taken to Marseilles by train, put on a boat on his own as a very young boy, and traveling to the land where his mother had come from. Of his mother's family, who kept him safe, placed him in boarding school, and taught him all he needed to know to grow into the man he became. Of his travels to another land where he attended university. Of meeting and marrying my mother, of starting a family, of the war, of my brother and sisters who would show me how to live and grow up and become everything I could be.

I listened to his words, storing them up.

Day 5

Read: Genesis 16–18

Throughout your generations every male among you shall be circumcised when he is eight days old.

—Genesis 17:12

I cried out for the second time that day. I cried out earlier when the doctor cut away my foreskin. In seconds, I was smiling again. My mother's close friend shared with her how painful it was when she circumcised soldiers as a nurse in the desert during the war. She shared with my mother that a child recovers in moments with a bottle of milk, but the soldiers took longer and needed a bottle of beer.

This second time, my cry was almost a song as water splashed over my head while I was held by several different people: A man's deep voice incanted words over me. Another friend of my mother received me from the deep-voiced man, and I could smell the woman's husband's smokey smell—new to me, a nice smell. They all gathered around the hearth, keeping warm and sharing food my mother and her friends had prepared.

Several others gathered, people I had never seen, or heard, or smelled before, their voices louder, yet friendly. Soon I was drifting in and out of dreams as the voices told stories of people far away, people I might meet some day. They told stories of lives living and lives past. Stories of great achievements and fleeting moments. Stories of challenging authority, of making a difference in the world, of righting wrongs. A lot of the conversations around and over me were deep and sad, laced with the language of suffering, of wars, of people long gone, and of people missed. The women cried, consoling each other. My father spoke in a soft voice, praying for those they'd lost.

I didn't know then the people they talked about, but I felt the pain and the love they shared.

Day 6

Read: Genesis 19–21

Sarah conceived and bore Abraham a son in his old age,
at the time of which God had spoken to him.

—Genesis 21:1

My mother was sitting with the group of women in the clinic. She was older than the other women, and though they knew she had other children, the younger women sitting around her wondered at her conception at her mature age. She would just smile patiently and hold me close, knowing I was the bonus child she had longed for but not expected, believing she was too old to be with a child again. My mother calmed the young mothers and helped the midwives as they checked all the babies, helped the babies latch on to feed, and changed their diapers easily.

She held me closely on her hip, knowing in her heart I was the post-war gift, bringing her family's life and home full circle. Several days a week, my mother would take me, and we would travel on buses and the underground, visiting churches all over London. She would sit and talk with groups of women in these churches about caring for their children and how to shop and make the most of rations, which, post-World War II, still limited what we could buy in England. She shared how they could take care of themselves as well as their children, and she taught them about God, Jesus, and the Holy Spirit—how God was all around us so we were never alone, and how she prayed all day, every day, while she did the most ordinary things that it meant to be a mother and wife.

She taught them a breathing exercise: *Breathe in, God within me. Breathe out, God around me.* Repeat.

Day 7

Read: Genesis 22–24

Abraham weighed out for Ephron the silver that he had named in the hearing of the Hittites, four hundred shekels of silver, according to the weights current among the merchants.

—Genesis 23:16

After Sunday lunch, my father placed me in my pram and the whole family—all seven of us—went out for an *after-lunch walk* around our neighborhood. We came to a street where all I could see was an avenue of trees, large trees, whose branches reached like fingers into the sky. There was a strange smell though, a smokey smell that hung in the air. We turned in through some huge old wooden gates, through a tall brick wall, and suddenly we entered a beautiful, peaceful, hidden garden with a soft sound of water flowing and bubbling from a fountain in a courtyard.

My parents' talk drifted over me, and I was aware of lots of different scents from different flowers, roses, and trees—all mixed with the smell of newly-cut grass. My mother walked away across the freshly cut grass with my brother and sisters, leaving me on my own with my father. He scooped me up and crossed to a doorway where he had to stoop to go inside. It was like entering a tomb—a cool dark atmosphere. Before us were rows upon rows of white and grey boxes, each on shelves, and each engraved with names and dates. My father gently touched one box with writing on its side, a name and date, and his eyes gently wept. He raised me up and placed my tiny hand on the box, and I patted it gently. Then, I turned to him and patted the tears from his cheek. My father knew then my life would be different from his other children, and he stored those thoughts for another day.

Day 8

Read: Genesis 25–26

There Abraham was buried, with his wife Sarah.

—Genesis 25:8

How do you know when an angel walks with you? I think it's because you chat with them and share your life with them, and they are all around you. At least, that is what I felt as I grew bigger and could begin to sit up and look around. I was still placed in the pram on the front porch to rest and get *fresh air*, but now I could see people who passed by on the street, who sometimes stopped at the gate to *pass the time of day* in a one-sided conversation. The birds still flew down and settled on the handle of the pram and sang and talked with me, sharing their news of what they saw happening in the world.

When did I realize someone had died? Someone important to my father's life? I sensed it rather than knew it. It was in the wind. I felt it through the trees. The plants swaying in the breeze whispered it. The birds sang softly with the news of it.

My father was quiet as he kept rereading the airmail letter, rereading it as if to make sure he had read it correctly. He picked me up, holding me tight to his chest, gently breathing, and walked with me—sighing and crying. The person far away had gone even further away now, and I would never know her as my father had done. I would not know her love for my father, her story, her life, her sadness when my father's mother died, or her grief when my father's father died. I would not know her story and her life until I was much, much older. I simply knew she mattered to him.

Day 9

Read: Genesis 27–29

And he dreamed that there was a ladder set up on the earth, the top of it reaching to heaven; and the angels of God were ascending and descending on it.

—Genesis 28:10

My mother placed me on a blanket on the ground in the yard at the back of the house. It was safe for me to play there. I could crawl, but did not walk or run yet, so I was safe. A tall wooden fence surrounded the small garden, keeping out danger. It was nothing much more than a postage-stamp sized yard, including a World War II *Anderson* shelter built ten years previously, still sitting in the corner of the garden. Rocks and dirt had been placed over it and against it. Plants and flowers grew up in the cracks between the rocks.

As I grew up, I played out my dreams on that rockery for hours, moving little plastic soldiers around, intermixed with cars and other toys, creating adventures and stories of great escapades and bravery. Dreaming dreams as a child can. As Easter approached, my mother and godmother shared the stories of Easter with me, so I created my own Garden of Gethsemane among the rocks and flowers with a small cave and its own rock to roll in front of it, though I'm not sure anyone but me knew what it was.

As a child, I dreamed and struggled with voices in my dreams because my dreams were full of the voices of people I had never known but whose lives had touched my parents, their friends, or neighbors.

As Easter grew closer, the stories of people I had never known intermingled with the stories read each day by my parents from the big book in the front room. All the stories felt real, and they all rolled together into one.

Day 10

Read: Genesis 30–31

> *Early the next morning Laban kissed his grandchildren and his*
> *daughters and blessed them. Then he left and returned home.*
>
> —Genesis: 31:55

My siblings told stories to each other every night, sharing their lives, their daily *goings on*. My sisters seemed to have the stories my parents reacted to the most, bringing my father's calming influence to bare almost every day. I would listen with nobody really noticing me being there, listening to everything.

We were going to have to make space for a visitor. My sisters would have to move into different rooms for the duration of his visit, and they weren't happy. The old man stayed with us for several days. He sat with my father, talking long into the night, my father holding me in his arms, gently rocking me. The man had travelled from the place of snowcapped mountains and rushing rivers. He smelled different than my father—of smoke, wind, snow, cold, and aspen trees. My father took the old man, with me in my pram, to visit the place with the memories of his father. They both stood in the cold, dark space, placing their hands on the white box with writing on its side, praying together for a man I never knew but would grow to understand as I grew up.

Again, I reached up to wipe a tear from my father, and he held me close. The old man gave us all gifts brought from afar, gifts of jewelry, clothes, and toys. He left lots of papers with my father when he travelled back to the place far away. My father hugged him awkwardly for a long time as he was leaving. He wrote regularly to us all, and we wrote back to him irregularly, but we never saw him again in our home. My sisters moved back into their own rooms, and peace was restored, at least for a little while.

Day 11

Read: Genesis 32–34

When Jacob heard that his daughter Dinah had been defiled, his sons were in the fields with his livestock; so, he did nothing about it until they came home.
—Genesis 34:5

My mother was crying. We had all been at church and come home for Sunday lunch. My parents went upstairs and closed the door to their bedroom, and all we could hear was sobbing and muffled voices. The youngest of my sisters held me and read to me. My brother sat and pretended to read. My middle sister and oldest sister went into the garden and talked in hushed voices. Things changed.

My oldest sister came in and went up to my parents' room. The muffled voices grew louder. I didn't know what was happening, but the pain and anguish in my mother poured out. My sister put me down on the floor, and that is where I stayed for the rest of the day until my father picked me up and sat me down to eat some food with my sisters and brother, but not my mother. He took me upstairs, bathed me, and put me in my crib, then sat with me quietly reading from the big book for a while until I almost fell asleep, still not knowing what had changed or what would change tomorrow. My dreams were busy and complex that night—lots of voices crying out for answers but none coming, and dawn seemed a long way away.

Day 12

Read: Genesis 35–37

When he told his father as well as his brothers, his father rebuked him and said, "What is this dream you had?"

—Genesis 37:10

I was still little, maybe four or five. My father came into my room early and helped me get up and dressed. I told him I had had strange dreams during the night. Dreams I didn't understand. He asked me to describe them, and I told him what I had seen. "Two birds built a nest and laid four eggs. The first bird to hatch fell from the nest and, though able to fly, kept falling to the ground. The next egg that hatched died after a few minutes. The next flew away, and the last one never hatched. The parent birds watched, then the mother bird stayed with the first baby bird, and the father bird flew away."

My father looked at me, held me close, and gently cried. My mother was downstairs going through the motions of getting my sisters and brother out of the house and off to school. My father whispered to her, and she looked at me emptily. After my father, sisters, and brother had gone, she settled me down with a building toy. Before she went into another room, she told me not to dream so much. I could hear her talking on the phone to her mother, my grandmother. She was angry and sad at the same time, her grief pouring out in her voice.

All I could do was sit, watch, and wait until she came back and held me—rocking and sobbing at the same time.

Day 13

Read: Genesis 38–40

*We both had dreams," they answered, "but there is no one to interpret them."
Then Joseph said to them, "Do not interpretations belong to God? Tell me
your dreams."*

—Genesis 40:8

I could read more than books with pictures; words now made sense.
Something changed, it was quiet at home, and there was little joy. My parents
moved into a different bedroom, and my eldest sister and her husband moved
into their bedroom. My mother went through the motions, taking me out
in my stroller since I had graduated my pram, but without the same love
and care. We walked to the library, stopping at the house of an older lady
from our church, and my mother left me with her for a while.

The old lady was formidable; she had been widowed in the Great War,
the First War, and lived alone with a female companion. She wrote for a
London newspaper reviewing books and always had a big pile of books
waiting to be read. She magically always had a book for me to look at or to
read to her from. Her pile of books never seemed to get any smaller each
time I visited.

Even though I was little, she asked me questions about what I read:
Did I like what I read, and why? She challenged me. Sometimes my brother
joined us after school, and he would read to her in a strange language, an old
language. She would correct him and challenge him too. My mother spoke
with her about my dreams, so she asked me to tell her what I dreamed about.
She gave me a copy of a book to take home with me, a book a friend of hers
had written, Mary Norton's book, *The Borrowers*. That night, I dreamed
dreams of being inside the walls of our house, of being safe, yet having
adventures, too, of being small and vulnerable and yet not seen by anyone.

Day 14

Read: Genesis 41–42

We told him our dreams, and he interpreted them for us, giving each man the interpretation of his dream.

—Genesis 41:12

The old lady made notes of what I shared with her as I told her my stories, my dreams of building houses, of talking with people in different languages, of traveling to places I saw in my father's stamp album, visiting with people in hospitals, singing in church, to planting flowers, trees, and vegetables, to having children of my own. She wrote it all down and smiled. Over tea, she shared new books with me to read to her: stories of animals like *The Tales of Peter Rabbit* by Beatrix Potter, *The Adventures of Winnie the Pooh* by A. A. Milne (who had grown up near us in London), and books of children's adventures, like *Swallows and Amazons*, written by her friend, Arthur Ransome, which he set also set in Beatrix Potter's magical place of the English Lake District.

She saw my love of being at church and encouraged me to read to her from *The Chronicles of Narnia* by C.S. Lewis, which she was reviewing in the newspaper, asking me what I thought of Aslan. She always linked my dreams to stories in books from authors she knew, like many of the different books by H. G. Wells, who had lived near us in Regent's Park, from *Kipps: The Story of a Simple Soul* to *The Time Machine*. Each time she challenged me, asking why I liked the book and what its story meant to me. It would be years before I realized what a gift her friendship and help was to me in my life. She helped me not be afraid of my dreams, but rather to understand them. This helped me be a ripple, helping heal my family much as Joseph healed his.

Day 15

Read: Genesis 47–50

*And Israel said, "I'm convinced! My son Joseph is still alive.
I will go and see him before I die."*

—Genesis 45:28

My family noticed me less and less, and I would disappear into reading a book, drawing, or building another house from a kit. All the time, I would listen as my mother shared with my father her broken heart over my eldest sister's marriage—her disappointment, her fears, her hopes as my sister and her husband moved out into their own home.

Another change was that the trips my mother and I had made to churches around London had stopped. We no longer visited groups of young mothers my mother would help, helping heal their fears and anxiety while bringing prayer into their lives. My mother struggled with being able to help them as she had shut down and couldn't help herself. She would sit for hours at a time, looking out the window. My father helped her as much as he could, but he was traveling for work a lot and seemed more distant than he had been.

It was as if I was living through a famine, and my experience was *feast or famine*, as my other sisters compensated me by hugging me more—or ignoring me more—and my brother seemed to be invisible most of the time. My saving grace was starting school. Our neighbor's daughter would walk with me to and from school. My brother was supposed to be taking me—as he was five years older than me—but the neighbor's daughter, who was only two years older than me, would hold my hand all the way there and all the way back. School became a place outside of home that was safe. A place I could grow again, at least that is what I thought at the beginning.

Day 16

Read: Genesis 46–48

As soon as Joseph appeared before him, he threw his arms around his father and wept for a long time.

—Genesis 46:29

School, however, was different than I expected. I was overwhelmed by going from being on my own all day, every day, to being with other children all day—a complete sensory overload. Not only did I have to do whatever they were doing, but *with* them, at the *same time*. I couldn't just pick up a book when I wanted, or draw when I wanted, or build a model house when I wanted. I had to do what the school wanted.

At first, I cried or looked for somewhere to hide or just pretend I was doing what they wanted me to do. During recess, I would look for my neighbor or my brother, but quickly realized they didn't want to be seen with me at school. So, I would find a place to sit, pretend to read, as I secretly watched and listened to the other children. I could read well, but pretended not to, so as not to stand out. I thought it would be better if I was average, just average.

When I got home most days, I found my mother had dark rings around her eyes. Then one day, my father met my brother and me as we left school. Instead of going home, he took us on the underground into town to a large old Victorian building that echoed as we walked through it and smelled of bleach. He kept saying over and over again that there was nothing to worry about, but like in scripture when the angels said not to fear, it usually meant something was about to happen. The more he said it, the more I was scared. We went up several floors in the building and came to a double door. It was locked. My father rang a bell, and then holding our hands on each side of him, we went in.

Day 17

Read: Genesis 48–50

All these are the twelve tribes of Israel, and this is what their father said to them when he blessed them, giving each the blessing appropriate to him.

—Genesis 49:28

Two of my sisters were sitting on either side of my mother's bed. She was sitting up in bed, forcing a smile when she saw us. My father brought us over to her, lifting me on to her bed so I could be nearer to her. My brother stood next to her, close to my middle sister. My mother didn't look sick, though her eyes were dark and circled from crying. My father kept reassuring us she just needed rest and would be home soon.

After only a few minutes, we were ushered out by a nurse saying we were tiring out my mother. She looked sad to see us go. My youngest older sister took my hand and brought me out into the empty corridor as the door echoed and banged locked behind us. My father came out a few minutes later and took us all home on the underground.

The next few weeks, my sisters took on the role of nagging on my brother and me to get things done so as not to trouble our father. To make our beds. To bathe and brush our hair or our teeth—sometimes one, sometimes the other, and constantly telling me to grow up and act my age. What did that mean? How was I supposed to act? I was only five. I found a special place to hide—a closet under the stairs—and I hid there a lot: out of the way, staying out of trouble, alone. When my mother came home after several months, my father asked us to be quiet and not disturb her as she continued to heal. It was as if she came back from the dead. Gradually, she was present with us again, but never in the same way.

Day 18

Read: Exodus 1–3

So, they put slave masters over them to oppress them with forced labor.

—Exodus: 1:11

My mother seemed to be ever more distant. No longer did we receive hugs. In fact, any hug seemed forced, goodnight kisses empty. No longer did she tuck us in at night. It was as if there was a strange, different person in the house. My mother took to sitting in a chair by the cold empty hearth a lot, and my father got us a television for the first time so that we could all just sit around the cold flickering light in the evenings. It had none of the warmth the hearth used to have when it crackled as a fire burned.

I would sneak away to my special place under the stairs, curl up, and read a book. Never for long, though, as my sisters had taken over most of the chores, which meant they would drag me from my space and set me to do the tasks they felt a five-year-old could manage! They became the overseers—keeping the house clean, clothes clean, meals cooked, and homework done. They enjoyed doing it, especially making my brother and I pull our weight, always with that phrase, *You must act your age!* I learned quickly that it was better to make my bed as I got up in the morning, before I had even dressed or bathed. Then, there was less to beat me up about.

I stopped telling anyone what I dreamed about as no one seemed to care about what I dreamed about or, in fact, anything I said. No one wanted to hear my dreams of people far away, of a man who was called by God who would come to our home, who would show us how to live our lives, the true meaning of our faith, of how he would show us *The Way*.

Day 19

Read: Exodus 4–6

So, Moses put his hand back into his cloak, and when he took it out, it was restored, like the rest of his flesh.

—Exodus 4:7

My home room teacher at school noticed the rash first, sending a note home. Then my godmother noticed it at church one Sunday, pulling my mother to one side to tell her. I had some sort of rash on my arms at first, then my knees, and then on my head. I couldn't tell them that I had dreamed about the rash and that I would have the rash for the rest of my life.

I knew that rash would humiliate me. It would be a badge of honor. It would keep me apart from others. It would drive a wedge between me and the people I loved. More than anything, though, as I grew to understand it, I knew it was a gift from God to teach me how to live my life. My own *mark of Cain.*

My mother and godmother talked at church about what to do about my rash. My mother turned from talking about my rash to tell me the older woman from church was very sick and had asked for us to visit her. When we got there, she was sitting in her chair with the pile of books by her, and I sat down on the window seat next to her. My mother talked and poured out tea, but I just sat, reached out, and held her hands. We looked into each other's eyes, and I remember saying, "It will be okay," though I didn't say it out loud, just through my thoughts and eyes. She squeezed my hand tight, and a tear rolled down her cheek that I gently wiped away.

My mother told me the next day that our friend had died, and it was good that we had seen her. I still hold her in my thoughts, seeing her still.

Day 20

Read: Exodus 7–9

So, Pharaoh's heart was hard, and he would not let the Israelites go, just as the Lord had said through Moses.

—Exodus 9:35

After the death of our older friend from church, my mother took me to the library and let me wander alone in the children's library while she picked books in the adult library. It felt strange to not have my friend's guidance anymore, and at first, I could only look at the books I knew through her.

The following Sunday, I saw her companion at church and ran over to her and gave her a long hug. She cried as we hugged, and I reached up and wiped a tear from her cheek. I tried to tell my dreams to my father again, but I don't think he really wanted to hear them. I dreamed of my eldest sister struggling with her life, with her child, with her husband. I shared these dreams with my father. He said not to say anything to anyone, especially not to my mother so she would not worry. I told him I dreamed of my middle sister and her struggles in her life, of her traveling to another country and having a child, and again, my father said to keep the dreams to myself. I told him of my dreams of my other sister, who wanted so much more than her school would let her do—how she wanted to get away from home where she had to do so much for my mother.

My father told me to stop dreaming and not share these thoughts or dreams with anyone. I told him I also dreamed my brother was struggling with his schoolwork and just wanted to be with animals on our great uncle's farm. My father's patience was running out. He said, *Stop. Keep it to yourself. Act your age. Be still.*

I was still only five, going on six.

Day 21

Read: Exodus 10–12

During the night Pharaoh summoned Moses and Aaron and said, "Up! Leave my people, you, and the Israelites! Go, worship the Lord as you have requested."

Exodus 12:31

From time to time, my father would leave me with our neighbor. She was younger than my mother with several children younger than me. She had traveled from another country in the war and spoke languages other than English: German, French, and Yiddish. Sometimes she would offer me the food she gave her children, which was very different from what we ate. It was simple and good. When her children slept, she would tell me stories of her journey from her home, of escaping from people who chased after her, who wished her harm, her death. She shared how she had hidden in a convent in a country called France with nuns who protected her.

She also told me stories which I came to know were in the big book my father used to read to us from. Her husband let me help him build a little room made of woven reeds behind their house. They would use it for a special religious festival they were going to celebrate. He would tell stories from the book, mixing them with the stories of both of them running from danger and the stories of people long, long ago.

I would not know for many years that the nuns who had reached out and saved our neighbor's life were the same nuns I would stay with when I was older and that the brother of one of the nuns was the father of my French pen pal, whom I would be friends with for the rest of my life. I would not know for some time that his father was on the receiving end of help during the Second World War from a friend I would make years later in another country.

No one is a stranger; they are just someone you don't know yet.

Day 22

Read: Exodus 13–15

*I will not bring on you any of the diseases I brought on the Egyptians,
for I am the Lord, who heals you.*

—Exodus 15:26

My mother took me with her to church during the week, and I was left to my own devices while she helped the ladies get the church clean and ready for Sunday. Sometimes they would get me to help them—polishing, dusting, or sweeping—but mainly they wanted me to stay out of their way. I learned that in church there were places to sit and read, or sit and draw, where I could just be myself. I was home. My godfather was sometimes there, too, and he would have me work with him in the garden around the church, weeding and caring for the surrounding grounds.

He would ask me to help him hold things that needed fixing, or painting, or getting to work properly, and sometimes he let me help him count the money that had been given on Sunday and put it in bags to take to the bank. At other times, my godfather and I would just sit in the memorial garden, and I would read while he smoked a pipe and shared his stories about the war. He spoke to me about how he was glad I was his godson, as he and my godmother had not been blessed with children of their own. He shared his stories and always reminded me that we did the best we could because everything we did was for God, so we should do the best we can.

Day 23

Read: Exodus 16–18

Then the Lord said to Moses, "I will rain down bread from heaven for you."
—Exodus 16:4

The women at church took it in turns to bake. When my mother had to visit the doctor, she would leave me with my godmother, and my godmother would let me help her bake. We would bake cookies and cakes to eat and share, and sometimes she let me bake the special bread for the church service. My godmother always told stories as she baked and would link them to something we were reading from the big book. She wanted me to understand how important it was that women did the things they did and how men could help them too.

One time, I asked her why we all couldn't gather after church and share some bread, break some bread together in the parish hall, so we all felt like family. I said I dreamed that this would be something that would bring us together at church and help us overcome some divisions and ease some loneliness of the older people at church.

My godmother thought I was an *old soul*, but that it was a good idea we should try. So, we baked enough bread for everyone to have a bite—just enough—and it brought people together. Some of the people who only saw and talked with someone on a Sunday felt loved by others in a way they hadn't felt before. My godmother said she would share this idea with the other women so they could all take turns baking the bread, and then, it wouldn't use up a family's flour ration for the month, as we still had rationing in England.

She wanted each of us to share what we could, and by sharing, build community.

Day 24

Read: Exodus 19–21

> *. . .Although the whole earth is mine, you will be for me a kingdom of priests and a holy nation.*
>
> —Exodus 19:5–6

My father still used to read to us from the big book, but I was often the only one sitting and listening as he read. My brother and sisters often had other things to do in the evenings, from homework to burying themselves in the latest novel. My mother seemed to be only physically present and struggled to be there spiritually.

My mother really struggled with some of the things it said. One evening she got really angry at the phrase "honoring your father and mother." Forgetting I was listening, she and my father talked about my oldest sister and my other sisters. They shared their concerns about how they might be failing my sisters if they didn't live their lives as they were supposed to. My father said he felt they could only do the best they could and should trust in God. My mother said something different. She had doubts in God, and my father spent time reassuring her of God's love for us and how we needed to simply trust God.

I listened as they talked this out, then I simply went over and hugged my mother—holding her, healing her, and letting her know by my hugging that I loved her and God loved her. My father closed the book and sat still.

Day 25

Read: Exodus 22–24

See, I am sending an angel ahead of you to guard you along the way and to bring you to the place I have prepared.

—Exodus 23:20

The priest didn't look like an angel. He came through our front doorway looking starved and so thin, malnourished from his time spent living among the very poor in South Africa. My father had known him from before the war, and the priest was visiting his aunt who was a member of our church. My parent's immediate response to seeing him was to feed him and offer him somewhere to rest. As they talked, I heard how the priest had been recalled by the church at the same time as the government of South Africa ordered him to leave because he spoke up for African people.

I knew this priest was unlike any priest I had ever met. He was rough and ready, and said challenging things loudly like, "Is it the function of a priest to remain silent in the face of injustice?" He talked long into the night at my parents' dinner table while I sat on my father's lap and listened. He talked of beauty in poverty, of hope in fear, of babies born in the streets with nowhere to lay their head, of people—black people—who were treated as less than a person by white people, and yet of the hope and faith and a belief that Christianity would bring them through into a new and fairer life.

His passion for the people and the country shone in every word he shared, and I listened and paid attention, soaking up every word. He left us early next morning. My father said he was traveling up north to the Community of the Resurrection at Muirfield, where he would become the Master of Novices. I do remember how he carried everything he possessed in a small case—smaller even than a carry-on—and I remember how God was truly in him.

Day 26

Read: Exodus 25–27

Then have them make a sanctuary for me, and I will dwell among them.
—Exodus 25:8

My mother sat me down on the floor in a side aisle of the church. She gave me some small books, paper, and pencils to keep me busy. She and my father joined the others who were already practicing the hymns for Sunday. My godmother came and sat near me while my godfather also sang in the choir. I sat and drew.

After practice was over, several of the men were talking about the absence of a steeple on the church. One of the men said it had always been designed to be built, but they couldn't afford it after the war, so they hadn't built it. Another man said it left the church looking unfinished. Everyone wanted it to be finished so it would stand for what we believed in. My godfather said it didn't need to be finished to be church, as *we* were the church.

I remember my father reaching down and picking up my drawing and quietly saying, "Maybe we don't need a spire. Look at what he's drawn."

I had drawn our church, and, on the tower, I had drawn not a spire but more of a pergola, or as one person said, *a pepper pot*. My father asked me what it was, and I said I had drawn a lighthouse, to show people the way to God. My godmother stood and said she thought it was not surprising that a child could see what adults couldn't.

My godfather stood and said to the group, "That's settled then." And so it was. The *pepper pot* would be added and brightly lit so that all around could see its light and find the way to us in the church, a place of safety and friendship.

Day 27

Read: Exodus 28–29

So, I will consecrate the tent of meeting and the altar and will consecrate Aaron and his sons to serve me as priests.

—Exodus 29:44

Sometime later, I was allowed to stay up late in the evening when something special was happening at church. The church was full of people, and smoke filled the air. My parents and brother were processing in with the choir, and my sisters sat with their friends, so I sat with my godmother in the congregation. She sat me in the aisle seat so I could see what was happening.

One person walked in front of everyone else, and he held something he was twirling around, and smoke billowed out of it. Two people followed him carrying candles, and a third carried a cross. Then the choir followed them, and another two people carried more candles, and another carried a big golden book. Then, several more people followed, wearing beautiful long robes and sashes, and at the end was a man wearing amazingly detailed robes with a pointed hat and a shepherd's crook, which I thought looked like my great uncle's crook he used on the farm.

As they walked in, the sounds of the choir and organ were amazing, and as it was night, the candles and lights around the church made it magical. I sat with my godmother, and my eyes grew bigger and bigger. Afterward at the back of the church, my parents came to get me from my godmother, and the bishop came back to greet her too. He reached out and put his hand on my head, thanking me for my dream, a dream which was becoming a reality—finishing the church with a light to show the people the way to God and church.

Day 28

Read: Exodus 30–32

> *. . . for in six days the Lord made the heavens and the earth,*
> *and on the seventh day he rested and was refreshed.*
>
> —Exodus 31:17

Sundays were usually quiet in our house. We walked to church in the morning. I was left with my godmother while my parents and brother sang in the choir. My sisters seemed to be in some sort of youth group and disappeared to the parish hall, meeting up with us after church. We normally stopped for the parish breakfast—a bread roll with butter and jam and a cup of tea that was quite watered down for me by my godmother. My parents would chat with other parents, and my brother would play with his friends.

I would sit and eat my roll with jam, draw on the paper tablecloth, and listen.

Walking home, I walked between my parents, holding their hands while they talked about things from church. They would sometimes swing me between them to make the walk pass more quickly. When we got home, my mother and sisters would get lunch ready, and usually they found some job for me to do, like helping set the table. Only two of my sisters were living at home since the eldest married and moved out.

In the afternoon, we often went for a walk around the neighborhood and to a park nearby that had animals and swings. Sometimes, a band played on a bandstand. Then home again for tea. We listened to the radio in the evening, or my father read with us, and we talked about what we were reading—what we liked about it, what we didn't. Sometimes he would share news of the priest who had visited and what he was doing to help people far away and that we had to think how we could help.

Things seemed to be getting back to normal. Life seemed to be safe again. In truth, it was just the lull before a storm.

Day 29

Read: Exodus 33–35

Six days you shall labor, but on the seventh day you shall rest; even during the plowing season and harvest you must rest.

—Exodus 34:21

Sundays were days we went to church, sometimes two or three times during the day, As I got older, I would spend more and more of my time in church on a Sunday. For me, the day of rest became a day of work, laboring for God, bringing people to God, sharing God with them, dreaming up new ways to bring and share God with others. But Sunday afternoons were family time.

I'm not sure when I realized that I had another problem, something else my parents would worry about. They were already worried about the rash I kept getting on my skin, my mark of Cain. Apparently, it had a name. The doctors called it *psoriasis*. I was taken to different doctors who each prescribed something different to deal with it. Then, one of them noticed my hands. My hands shook a lot. My parents had not noticed. It meant more visits to more doctors, who either said I would grow out of it or there was nothing to worry about or it was just nerves.

My father decided to give me things to do that required focus on my hands. As I liked houses, he got me a building kit called *Betta Bilda,* made by the English company Airfix—a cheaper version of Lego—with little white bricks and small squares of plastic that clicked together to make houses or whatever I could dream up. They were challenging to use as I had to work out how to build the best structural support to construct bigger objects. I built bigger and bigger and more complex buildings. Each week, I would use some of my pocket money to add another small box to grow my set.

Gradually, I learned to steady and manage my shaking hands.

Day 30

Read: Exodus 36–38

So, Bezalel, Oholiab and every skilled person to whom the Lord has given skill and ability to know how to carry out all the work of constructing the sanctuary are to do the work just as the Lord has commanded.

—Exodus 36:1

I would sit for hours, patiently putting model buildings together. It required patience, imagination, and a way of visualizing spaces in 3D, which I appeared to have. This task required my hands not shake. For hours at a time, I would sit and build buildings, oblivious to what was happening around me—the family discussions, the sibling arguments, the household changes. I would stay focused on building my buildings the very best that I could.

Gradually I moved from building houses to bigger buildings, larger buildings, and suddenly I found I was building churches or even monasteries. All the time, I focused on building the best building I could, the best building for God. I stayed focused on creating as beautiful a design as I could for God: churches that people could live in, move in, breathe in, and be alive in for God. People could gather in my churches to pray, to eat, to worship, or to just be.

And always in my head were the words of Moses talking with the Israelites and a children's nursery rhyme: *Here's the church; here's the steeple. Open the doors, and out come the people.* It would be many years before I felt the church *was* the people and God was building the church within us.

Day 31

Read: Exodus 39–40

The Israelites had done all the work just as the Lord had commanded Moses.
—Exodus 39:42

My father spent time looking at the model buildings I made. He would patiently listen as I described what I could see in the building: How the church flowed. Where the people would sit. Where the choir would be. Where the organ would be. Where the altar would be. I'm not sure he could see any of those things, but he listened to me as I shared my dream and vision for the church. I had the enthusiasm of a child looking at church through a child's eyes.

He looked at my models carefully and asked me questions about how they worked and what I could see. One day, he called my mother in from another room and shared my model with her, commenting on both my hands not shaking and my understanding of how *church* worked. He said he had a surprise for me next Sunday.

When Sunday came, he took me back to the robing room with him and found a small cassock and surplice and helped me into them. The cassock was still a bit long, and I had to be careful not to trip. Then he showed me a beautiful silver incense boat and told me I would carry this and walk next to the server who carried the censer or thurible. So, for the first time, I was part of the service, which went all right until I tripped on the cassock and spilled the incense all over the marble floor of the church. The congregation thought it amusing to watch the choir processing in behind me, sliding all over the marble floor and making a dance part of the service! They forgave me, though, and let me carry it again the next week—this time in a cassock my godmother had shortened and fitted on me. One that they all prayed I wouldn't trip on.

35

Day 32

Read: Leviticus 1–4

When anyone brings a grain offering to the Lord, their offering is to be of the finest flour. They are to pour olive oil on it, put incense on it.

—Leviticus 2:1

Summer turned to autumn, and I got a new task at church. One Sunday, I sat at the back of the church as everyone came in. Everyone brought packages of food and olive oil and other things from their own homes. My mother and godmother had been at church in the week, and the altar was covered with flowers and large sheaves of corn and bales of hay. As the service started, I was invited to come forward with several other children, towing our wagons and carts loaded with gifts. I had a red-painted wagon my godfather had made me for my birthday, and it was full.

We became an integral part of the thanksgiving service and stayed together up at the altar throughout the service, standing right with the priest at the altar. At the end of the service, we processed out in front of the choir and priest. Then my godmother, with several other children's mothers, guided us to the parish hall where we sorted and put everything into boxes. In the afternoon, my father took me to visit with a family who were still struggling with rationing, and we left them one of the boxes. I noticed my father giving them an envelope, too, with something to help them pay some bills.

Soon rationing would end, but for a while, we gathered food like this at church each month to help others in our parish who needed help. I asked my father if I could give them a gift from me, a book I had read and wanted to share. Next time we went, I gave them a Beatrix Potter book and the next time, a Winnie the Pooh book. I kept giving my books away, sharing them every month.

Day 33

Read: Leviticus 5–7

These, then, are the regulations for the burnt offering, the grain offering, the sin offering, the guilt offering, the ordination offering and the fellowship offering.

—Leviticus 7:37

My godmother would shepherd a small group of us out of the main church into a side room during the service so we could share in the Bible stories. Often, we just drew while she and anyone who was helping her read to us, but sometimes they would ask us to read the stories and then share what we thought about them.

I think at this age my favorite word was *why?* I seemed intent on uncovering the story behind the story and the reason why a story was in the big book. *Why did they have to burn the offerings? Why did only Aaron and the priests get to eat the offerings? Why didn't they share the food with others?*

Looking back, my godmother's patience with me asking so many questions was amazing. She was like a rabbi; she knew what the stories meant and what questions she could ask to encourage me to think about the words and find answers. I understood then that if the priests were spending all their time leading the congregation and caring for them during the week, too, they couldn't go out to work and earn money. So, the congregation had to feed them, clothe them, house them. And to give them an offering was the same as giving a gift to God so that God could guide the priests in what to do and how to care for us.

I still had a question she couldn't answer, which was, "How do they know for sure what God wants them to do?" I thought about that a lot.

Day 34

Read: Leviticus 8–10

So, Aaron and his sons did everything the Lord commanded through Moses.
—Leviticus 8:36

When I got home one Sunday, I was still struggling with the responses from my godmother. So, I asked my father about what we had shared in Sunday school with my godmother. Instead of my father explaining what it meant—or what he thought it might mean—he asked me what I thought it all meant. After thinking about it for a few minutes, I said I felt that it would be difficult being a priest unless God called you to serve as one. If you were called to serve God, the people needed to help you stay focused on what God wanted you to do and help you by feeding you, clothing you, and maybe even giving you somewhere to live.

But then I asked him, "How can you know if God called you?"

Again, my father—rather than tell me what he thought—asked me what I thought. I thought about it for a few more minutes and said that I guessed it was a bit like Moses when he argued with being asked to do something he didn't think he could do. God said with God's help Moses could do it, which is also why God told Moses that his brother Aaron would speak for him too. So, the priest is doing what Moses did, and my godmother and him (my father) were doing what Aaron did in teaching us all the decrees God gave through Moses.

My father just smiled and gave me a hug.

Day 35

Read: Leviticus 11–13

When anyone has a defiling skin disease, they must be brought to the priest.
—Leviticus 13:9

The following week when it was time to go home after the parish breakfast, my father found me crying in the side chapel of the church, the Lady Chapel. He asked me what was the matter and, between tears and sobs, I said that one of the other children had said I was *unclean* and should be sent away. This child said that I would be sent to live on my own, that I wasn't loved by God, and that my parents would have to send me away because that's what it said people had to do in our reading—that the priest would send me away.

My father held me, and between my sobs, he said not to worry about such a silly thing and that the other child had misunderstood the reading. He reassured me that he and my mother knew I had psoriasis, and because the other child didn't understand what psoriasis is, they were saying something hurtful. He would make sure that either he or my mother would speak with their family and make sure they understood what it was and that I wasn't unclean. Then he just hugged me.

Despite him hugging me, the child's words had cut deep. I felt a grain of truth in what they said. I tried all sorts of things from then on. I avoided wearing short sleeves or trousers, and instead, I wore long sleeves even in the summer, even at the swimming pool or the beach. It took me years and years before I could truly feel confident about my skin. I certainly wasn't confident on that day, but my father and I prayed about it together. Praying the Lord's Prayer made it seem better at the time.

Day 36

Read: Leviticus 14–15

The person to be cleansed must wash their clothes, shave off all their hair and bathe with water; then they will be ceremonially clean.

—Leviticus 14:8

At first, my mother was angry when we got home, and my father shared with her how hurtful someone had been at church. She took me upstairs and made me take a bath in the middle of the day. We normally only took a bath once a week then, so this was something unusual. Afterward, she sat me down in the kitchen and proceeded to cut all my hair short, so short it was just fuzz on my head. She and my father poured oil on my head and rubbed it into my scalp and my skin. I smelled like peanut butter!

I sat in the kitchen, wrapped in a towel, and just sat there. I wasn't crying. I wasn't sobbing. I just sat. My father explained to my brother and sisters what had happened, and I was surprised that they didn't make fun of me. My sisters actually hugged me! One of my sisters shared that I was lucky because I was a boy so I wouldn't have periods. She shared that there had been girls at school who had made fun of her when her periods started at school. I'm not sure I understood what she was talking about, but it didn't sound nice at all. I wasn't looking forward to school the next day, especially with my hair cut so short and smelling of peanut butter!

Tomorrow is always another day.

Day 37

Read: Leviticus 16–18

Then, before the Lord, you will be clean from all your sins.

—Leviticus 16:30

As soon as I took my school cap off, the snickering started. The teacher commented to stop the other kids being mean, which, of course, made it worse. After school, my mother took me on the underground to the big hospital she had stayed in. I was absolutely petrified as I associated it with her staying in hospital for months. We met with a doctor who immediately handed me off to a large nurse from Jamaica who took me off into another room. It had a shower cabinet in it and a place to get undressed. She kept reassuring me, but the more she reassured me, the less sure I was about anything.

Under my breath, I whispered the Lord's Prayer. Suddenly she noticed and said there was nothing to worry about as this wouldn't take long. I had to get undressed completely, which felt strange as I think only my mother and father had ever seen me naked, and then she sprayed me with a coconut and coal tar oil concoction. She handed me some goggles and told me to get in the shower. It wasn't a shower at all; it was a light cabinet with fluorescent tubes all the way around. I stood there while the light blasted me all over for what seemed like forever. Suddenly, she turned off the lights and let me out, telling me to get dressed.

My mother was back in the room with the doctor who shared with us that I would only have to do that once a year. It would help clear up the psoriasis and bring it under control. I would be clear of it and my skin would become like others.

At the time, it seemed like a cure.

Day 38

Read: Leviticus 19–21

The Lord said to Moses, "Speak to the entire assembly of Israel and say to them: Be holy because I, the Lord your God, am holy."

—Leviticus 19:1–2

The following Sunday after church, a group of women took my mother and me to one side after the service. My godmother seemed to be in charge of the group of women, and she asked me to sit on a chair in the center of a ring of the women. The women, including my mother and godmother, placed their hands on my head. Then my godmother led them in prayer. Just at that moment, the sun shone through a stained-glass window and touched my head too.

I prayed with them, and for them, and to God to help my body, my skin heal and not be so scary to other people. I prayed I would never do anything bad and would always work at being as good as I could. I prayed I would do anything my parents said, and I would observe all their rules—and God's rules too. Suddenly, they all stopped praying and went off to the Parish Hall, and my mother and godmother talked for a while. I just sat there quietly in the sunshine, with my eyes closed, thinking, praying, waiting. I felt a warmth wash over me. I opened my eyes, and I looked up at the stained-glass window, then looked down at my arms, my knees, and my elbows. I still had psoriasis.

Guess I needed to keep praying.

Day 39

Read: Leviticus 22–23

There are six days when you may work, but the seventh day is a day of sabbath rest, a day of sacred assembly.

—Leviticus 23:3

Every Saturday evening, my father would write a check, put it in an envelope, and take it to church to put on the offering plate that was taken up to the altar during the service. Every Monday morning, he would meet with my godfather, and together they would open all the envelopes, count the collection, and put it in a lockable bag. My father would drop it off at the bank's deposit drawer on his way to the underground station as he went to work. He explained to me that it was a religious rule that they didn't handle any money on Sundays. I asked him if that was why we always made sandwiches on a Saturday if we were planning to go out on a Sunday afternoon, and why we always had a thermos of tea to drink, so we never needed to buy anything if we went out on a trip. He said the less we worked or handled money on a Sunday the better, as that was our Sabbath.

Not long after that, our neighbors knocked on our door on a Saturday—which was their Sabbath—and asked if we could turn their gas on to heat their baby's milk as the gas had blown out and they were not allowed to start a fire on their Sabbath. My father did so, and our neighbor shared the story of keeping the fire burning with us from his Bible. I found it was in our Bible too. I asked my father why we didn't do that, too, and he said we remembered special times and events in other ways.

My father reminded me that we would be at my great-aunt and uncle's for Harvest Festival, and because they lived out in the country, we would get to see the true meaning of this festival in the church.

Day 40

Read: Leviticus 24–25

When you enter the land I am going to give you, the land itself must observe a sabbath to the Lord.

—Leviticus 25:2

My great-aunt's church was smaller than ours in London and a good walk away. It took us over thirty minutes to walk there. When we arrived, people were already gathering, having brought baskets of fruit, vegetables, eggs, cakes, cookies, bread, jams, and even marmalade. Someone even brought a whole box of different meats. The front of the church had been decorated with an amazing display of flowers, dried grasses, and wheatsheaves. Everybody carried their gifts forward and placed them by the altar. My great-aunt and I carried up our basket filled with jams, scones, and marmalade, placing it by the altar.

During the service ,the priest blessed all the gifts, and afterward, several people carried everything out to a van and loaded it up. It was all being taken to a nearby hospital that treated patients with spinal injuries and housed patients of every age from babies to pensioners, even veterans from the First World War. As it was becoming well-known, patients came from all over the world.

My great-aunt asked if I would like to go with them, so I was able to visit and see what an incredible place it was. I would visit again in future years as several friends had accidents and became patients there, sometimes for months at a time. On the way back, my great-aunt told me she had something special to show me the next day. It would be a surprise, and we had to get up early—before dawn.

Day 41

Read: Leviticus 26–27

When the field is released in the Jubilee, it will become holy, like a field devoted to the Lord; it will become priestly property.

—Leviticus 27:21

Before dawn, we got up, had breakfast by the fire in the kitchen, and my great-aunt told us a story of her friend who had fought in both the first and second wars. In the first war, he had lost some close friends and wanted to create something special for them, and that's what we would see today. When we left their house, my great-uncle guided us in the half-light along a path through some allotments and over some farmland, walking along the stubble edges of the fields through several gates and tracks, past ponds, and crossing the village green. My great-uncle pointed out a house where their friend lived and some other cottages their friend had built to provide holidays for war veterans from London.

Finally, we got to a gate that led into what looked like a forest. The gate was set high in a privet hedge, seeming to go on forever in both directions. As we went through the gate, the sun was just starting to rise in the east. We were standing at the beginning of a long line of beautiful trees laid out as the nave of a cathedral, facing east toward a chancel area bathed in sunlight on a dew pond. It was breathtaking. We stood still, listening to the birds and trees as they woke to a new morning. We spent time walking through the different parts of the cathedral, experiencing different trees in different parts of the planting. My great-aunt said their friend was gifting it to the National Trust so that everyone would always be able to come and enjoy it for free. I realized I had experienced not just a special place, but a thin space close to God, made holy by God's creation and man's gardening to please God.

Day 42

Read: Numbers 1–2

Take a census of the whole Israelite community by their clans and families, listing every man by name, one by one.

—Numbers 1:2

Another great-aunt and uncle came over to visit with us while we were staying with this great-aunt and uncle. They brought the youngest of my older sisters who had been staying with them and would travel back to London with us. My two great-aunts sat and talked with my mother over tea about cousins and relatives I had never heard of, yet whose names seemed familiar. Aunty Gladys opened her Bible, and inside was a tree of names. Not like the trees at the tree cathedral, and yet somehow, they were all related. My Great Aunty Gertie ran her finger over the names: Minnie, Bill, Fred, Agnes, Sid, Gertie, Gladys, and Alfred, and their parents, Ben and Frances. Great-great-grandfather Ben had died in the year I was born, and Great-great-grandmother Frances died before him, so I never knew them, or Great-uncle Fred, as he died the year I was born too. These relatives suddenly sprang to life in the words, thoughts, smiles, and tears of my great-aunts, my mother, and my father.

They shared stories of lives lived, of loves had, of journeys taken, of dreams unfulfilled. My brother and sister asked questions, prompting even more tales of adventures taken and travels experienced. My aunt pulled out an old album full of photographs taken on trips to church, to school, to the seaside, to the tree cathedral, and the zoo—their somber, frozen faces looking out unsmilingly at us. Suddenly, I felt the spirit of those who had gone before me, those I was still a part of—part of their legacy—and realized to them I was like a grain of sand, a mustard seed, waiting to be watered, fed, and allowed to grow into something more, all with God's help.

Day 43

Read: Numbers 3–4

All the men from thirty to fifty years of age who came to do the work of serving and carrying the tent of meeting numbered 8,580.

—Numbers 4:42–44

Suddenly there were the three brothers, Bill, Fred, and Sid, in their uniforms with my great-grandparents, having a last photo taken before they went off to serve God, King, and Country. I could feel their fear and pride intermingled together as they faced the unknown. I could see my great-aunts, Minnie, Gertie, and Gladys, and my grandmother Agnes, crying as their brothers left to go to fight in the war. My great-aunts Gertie and Gladys shook their heads as they whispered under their breath to my mother how nearly 60,000 British soldiers were injured on the first day alone, and nearly 20,000 died, and as it went on, the numbers crept up and up.

Every day, they waited for news of them until they came home, and they thanked God all three survived. But they were never the same. My great-aunts started gently crying as they remembered the stories their brothers shared. The nightmares they had. The pains and problems they faced for the rest of their lives. My mother reached out to both my great-aunts, stood between them, and placed her arms around their shoulders, sharing that her father, my grandfather, also suffered from his fighting in the war and with catching malaria, so he was never the same either.

So many lives lost and broken, so many families never the same, so many women never married, grieving the loves of their lives. *For God, King, and Country* rang out in my head as I listened to the stories being told. The number of lives lost, families broken, people changed forever were staggering numbers. My thoughts were bouncing around in my head, and as a child all I could think was, *Lord, in your mercy, hear our prayers.*

Day 44

Read: Numbers 5–6

The Lord bless you and keep you; the Lord make his face shine on you and be gracious to you; the Lord turn his face toward you and give you peace.

—Numbers 6:24–26

My father talked about how my grandfather had registered for the draft to serve in Durango, Colorado, in America in 1918. He was never called up to fight as that war ended. The war everyone called, *The war to end all wars*. He was glad his father had not had to fight in that war as my father felt conflicted about fighting in war at all. He registered as a conscientious objector in the Second World War, losing his job and being placed in a war support job in London's Docklands.

My mother picked up a photo from the table of two babies with my great-great grandparents and asked my great-aunts about it. They were twins, born in October, christened in November, and died in December—Beatrice and Alfred. Silently, my two great-aunts held the photo together. Aunty Gertie softly said she was born a year later, and Aunty Gladys four years after that. My mother gasped as she never knew about them; nobody had ever mentioned them to her, ever. My father took the photo, held it, and then from somewhere deep within him he softly sang:

The Lord bless you and keep you;
 the Lord make his face shine on you and be gracious to you;
 the Lord turn his face toward you,
 and give you peace.

Day 45

Read: Numbers 7

Then the leaders of Israel, the heads of families who were the tribal leaders in charge of those who were counted, made offerings.
—Numbers 7:2

My sister had spent time drawing and writing while she had stayed with our Great-aunt Gertie, and on this day, she was busy sharing pictures with my parents and my other aunt. She decided to give each of my aunts a picture she had made, and my Great-aunt Gladys immediately had to get some sticky tape and put hers up on her kitchen cabinets where she would see it every day. My brother had been drawing, too, and he also gave each great aunt a drawing, which again my Great-aunt Gladys put on her kitchen cabinets. My father herded us all out into the garden where he busily arranged us so he could take a picture of the moment, capture this moment of all of us together: a moment in time with Great-aunt Gertie and her husband Bill, Great-aunt Gladys and her husband Stuart, my mother and sister Hilary, my brother Nick, and me, and last, but not least, my father ran around into the photo as the mechanical timer clicked down on the front of the camera—the timer being a fancy, new gadget my father had recently found in an old camera shop in London.

I looked around. I didn't have anything to give my great-aunts. I didn't have any drawings. I didn't have any pictures. What did I have to give? Inside my head, I could hear a voice saying, *Just give them your love.* I went up to each of my great-aunts and reached out, put my arms around their necks, gave them a big hug, and told them I loved them. I hugged my mother too.

Day 46

Read: Numbers 8–10

So they set out from the mount of the Lord three days' journey with the ark of the covenant of the Lord going before them three days' journey, to seek out a resting place for them.

—Numbers 10:33

As we got into the car to drive home, there wasn't a dry eye *in the house.* My great-aunts hugged us and hugged us. I looked out of the back window of the car as we drove away, watching them get smaller and smaller, waving at us until we went round a bend out of sight. I peeked into the basket on my sister's lap which was full of goodies: eggs, bacon, sausages, cheese, cookies, and bread, especially fresh bread. The smell of fresh-baked bread filled the car as we drove back to London. My parents talked softly to each other in the front of the car all the way back as if we were not even in the car. My brother and sister dozed off, but I sat and listened as I looked out of the window at the hedgerows and lights of houses we passed.

They talked of many things about my great-aunts and their lives outside London, of how much my great-aunts liked having us visit as they had no children of their own and how my sister had really taken to my Great-aunt Gertie in particular. They talked about how much my brother liked spending time with Great-aunt Gladys and helping on their neighbor's farm. He really seemed at home around the animals and the farming life, which was a hint of what was to come for both my brother and sister. I sat quietly, waiting to hear what they thought I would like, but they didn't mention me as if I wasn't there. Finally, my father said he liked the way I hugged my great-aunts, how it hit the spot with both of them. I was just what they needed, a good hugger.

Day 47

Read: Numbers 11–13

They will share the burden of the people with you so that you will not have to carry it alone.

—Numbers 11:17

My father had been called to a national meeting of the church called a synod, and he was not looking forward to it. He talked with my mother and my godparents about it for several evenings in our home, then invited several other members from church to our home and talked with them too. Most of what I understood about what they were discussing—often very loudly—came from the experience my father and mother had of my eldest sister wanting to marry a divorcé against their wishes and the resulting decision by the courts against them, prompting my mother's sadness and illness.

It seemed so complicated to them and yet so simple to me. They spent several evenings poring over Bible verses, discussing them backwards and forwards without coming to any firm decision. They made notes and argued points, with no answer. My father seemed to be struggling with something that deeply troubled him. On the night before the synod, he was sitting in our front room with the big Bible open on his lap when I came into the room and found him.

I'm not sure I know why I did what I did, but I came to him and asked how God showed that He loved us. My father went into a long sharing of the key messages from the Bible about love and the four types of love found in the bible. He had been talking for a while, sharing with me, when he suddenly stopped, looked at me and said, "That is the answer. Love is the answer." With that, he closed the Bible and sat for a moment with his eyes closed. Calmly, he said, "Thank you, Lord, for showing me the way."

Day 48

Read: Numbers 14–15

The priest is to make atonement before the Lord for the one who erred by sinning unintentionally, and when atonement has been made, that person will be forgiven.

—Numbers 15:28

My father was going to a meeting of the synod to explain how his daughter broke several of the rules the church held dear. She did not know her action would lead others across the country to copy her. My father went alone to speak with them, without my mother. That was a long day. My mother kept us busy doing things that really didn't seem to need done. When he finally returned, my mother grabbed my father as he came through the front door and just held him silently. After what seemed like an age, and repeated requests from my brother and I to tell us what happened, he took us all into the front room where we sat as he described the synod, gathered in a large hall in Westminster. He said he kept it simple, speaking the words he had shared the night before.

He said that having looked around the room, he talked about love, referencing not only the Bible but also the writing and thinking of C. S. Lewis. There were four types of love found in scripture: 1) familial love between family members, 2) friendship between people, even between churches or cities, 3) a healthy passionate love between husbands and wives, and the fourth type being 4) God's love for us and ours for God. Repeatedly, we are reminded:

"Love the Lord your God with all your heart and with all your soul and with all your mind. This is the first and greatest commandment." And the second is like it: "Love your neighbor as yourself."

Then, with this in mind, he had recalled a text from his namesake, 1 Peter, 4:8:
Above all, love each other deeply, because love covers over a multitude of sins.
and with that, he sat down.

Day 49

Read: Numbers 16–17

Then Moses said to Aaron, "Take your censer and put incense in it, along with burning coals from the altar, and hurry to the assembly to make atonement for them."

—Numbers 16:46

Much was said about my father's presentation to the synod over the next few weeks. His words were even discussed on the radio as a change in culture and the church's reaction to those changes post-war. People at church asked him to take a leadership role as a warden at church and to lead a men's Bible study group.

I realized that when I had asked the right question, God had given my father the right answer. Not immediately. He still had to listen and pray for guidance, but God had the answer when he listened. I think that was when I started to realize something. While the Bible can create a lot of damage—and, in fact, as I grew older, I understood just how much damage it had done—I am amazed at how much good the Bible can do as well.

That good was what I wanted to share with others, the possibilities for all the good things it contained. Something else dawned on me, even at this early age. I had to listen quietly to focus on what Jesus said, not only to the stories the disciples shared through the New Testament, but to what Jesus said about readings from the Old Testament books. After all, Jesus only had the Old Testament books to read from.

Strangely, even as a child, I realized that reading them through Jesus' lens made the Old Testament books new again. At this point, I started to jot little phrases down, most of which I lost long ago, except in my memory. I also started to let the Bible transform me rather than box me in. I realized not only to think outside of the box, but I realized *there is no box*, and anything is possible.

Day 50

Read: Numbers 18–20

But the Lord said to Moses and Aaron, "Because you did not trust in me enough to honor me as holy in the sight of the Israelites, you will not bring this community into the land I give them."

—Numbers 20:12

The bishop came to visit our church again, and I was given the job of carrying a small silver bucket full of water, which he blessed and then put a small handheld sprinkler into as we walked past the congregation. He sprinkled holy water over everyone in church. I got soaked each time he changed direction—absolutely soaked—so much so my godmother pulled me aside near the altar and mopped me down with a towel. At the end of the service, we did it again as he left, and again I was soaked through. This time as we entered the robbing area, my godmother pulled the wet vestments off me, *tut-tutting* as she did so.

After the service, we had a big meal in the Parish Hall and the bishop announced that our priest of many years was leaving us, and a new priest would be coming to serve us. Our priest gave a long speech about how much he cared for us all, how he was glad to have been with us as we adjusted to life after the war, how glad he was to have baptized, married, and buried so many of us, and how sorry he was that he couldn't continue with us on our journey into the future. He knew—like Moses who guided the Israelites to their promised land—we were leaving the 1950s and preparing to enter a new age of the 1960s, with the end of rationing, new experiences, new jobs, new lives, and new hopes. He shared his hope that we had learned with him to trust in God to guide us as we went forward. There wasn't a dry eye in the house, as they say.

I wondered what our new priest might be like.

Day 51

Read: Numbers 21–22

But the people grew impatient on the way; they spoke against God and against Moses, and said, "Why have you brought us up out of Egypt to die in the wilderness?"

—Numbers 21:4–5

At first glance, the new priest was exactly what our church needed. He was married with several children, and we made them welcome in the way a church could at the end of the 1950s—with a potluck. My father became the new senior warden with new responsibilities at church, particularly helping the new priest and his family settle in. Over the next few months, we saw lots of changes in our church, from the way we worshipped to how we used our space. Lots of the older members of church complained about the changes, and lots of the younger members of church complained about the slowness of change.

I wondered how Jesus would have handled this, or Moses. We couldn't very well keep on breaking open rocks to make water flow or defeat our enemies in battle as a church in the late 1950s suburbs of London. More than anything, I remember there were a group of people at church who gathered to read scripture together, sit with the texts, and pray about them. My godparents were part of this, along with my parents, which meant I got dragged along, too, whether I wanted to attend or not. I would sit to one side and listen to them read out loud, hearing them breathing in and out while they sat meditating silently. Hearing them sharing their thoughts and understandings of the texts and—probably the most important for me—the relevance to their lives and the life of the church. There were a lot of complaints from some and reassurance from others, so that by the end of the evening, people could go home peacefully.

I remember a phrase my father spoke to one member at church that stood out to me then and it does now, *Be careful what you pray for; it might just happen.*

Day 52

Read: Numbers 23–25

Even if Balak gave me all the silver and gold in his palace, I could not do anything of my own accord, good or bad, to go beyond the command of the Lord.

—Numbers 24:13

Older members of the church kept winning. From my viewpoint on the edge of everything, this was obvious. I was viewed as a child whose opinion didn't count. Clearly the older members of the church didn't really want to change much: *It has been all right for us growing up* and *We've always done it this way* were phrases I heard again and again.

A family who had turned to the church for support after the husband had died, leaving a young widow with several children, was one of the first to move away. They moved out of London, and my mother encouraged me to stay in touch with one of her children by letter, which we did for a while. Another family moved away as a church nearer to them seemed to do more for children. Some of the older people either died or moved away to be nearer their children who lived elsewhere. Some of the older people started groups for youth, but they never seemed to be about what the youth wanted to do, and, as the youth couldn't take any responsibility for the groups, there was always someone older in charge.

I voiced to my father one day that if things continued as they were heading, the church might have to look for another way of encouraging people to spend time at church. I asked him if they had prayed about it. The look on his face was stunning as he realized that in all their planning, discussions, and workgroups, prayer was one thing none of them had done. It took a child to guide them back to prayer.

Day 53

Read: Numbers 26–27

> *"Take a census of the men twenty years old or more,"* as
> *the Lord commanded Moses.*
>
> —Numbers 26:2

My father stood at the end of the service and asked everyone to wait a moment. He asked our new priest to lead us in prayer for our church, its future, and God's purpose for our ministry. When the priest finished, he asked us all to join him in the Lord's prayer, and the sun came out through the stained glass. You could feel the spirit moving among the congregation. Over the parish breakfast, people were sharing stories as my father moved around the room checking names on a clipboard, making sure everybody's address and phone number were up to date, asking what they were interested in, why they were members of the church, how the church could serve them, and how they, in turn, could serve the church and God.

The following week, he stood up at the end of the service and shared with everybody the good news. People cared. People wanted to help their neighbors in the community in ways the church had not done before. People had identified others who needed help and were offering to help again. Everyone had felt the church was dying. Suddenly they were aware of it being reborn. New groups were formed, Bible studies were planned, and opportunities to help others would be found. My father encouraged a young man to join the vestry and help lead the changes, bringing him in front of everybody the next Sunday to confirm his role in the church. His wife planned to make a new banner for the church, a banner to show our new hope.

I realized what I was seeing was God being more a verb than a noun. God was working with us, so we weren't afraid of making mistakes or being right or wrong. We had re-found our faith.

Day 54

Read: Numbers 28–30

*In addition to what you vow and your freewill offerings, offer these to
the Lord at your appointed festivals: your burnt offerings, grain offerings,
drink offerings and fellowship offerings.*

—Numbers 29:39

The church took on a new life with younger and older people mixing
and sharing. It was not unusual to see groups of men working in the gardens
around the church or working on the buildings together. Older men showed
younger men how to do the tasks around the church, and younger men
showed older men new techniques or more modern tools they could use.
Groups of women were sharing with each other their favorite recipes and
how to cook them—the little tricks they used but didn't write down in their
recipes that made all the difference. Older women shared ways of making
clothes or how to save and reuse things. A men's group of all ages started
taking, fixing, and repairing broken toys to be given away at Christmas.

Suddenly the church was becoming a community. My godfather
encouraged people to commit to the weekly freewill offering, showing
how the church could plan better if it knew what support the members of
the church could commit to. A group of men and women got together to
visit in pairs with people who were homebound or just hadn't been seen at
church for a while, finding out how we as church could support them, help
them, and nourish them, both physically and spiritually. A weekly gathering
of women shared prayers for people in the parish and across the diocese,
and soon they were praying for the church across the city, the country, and
the world. I saw people praying and serving God in many amazing ways,
offering service and support as part of their offering to God.

Day 55

Read: Numbers 31–32

Moses and Eleazar the priest accepted the gold from the commanders of thousands and commanders of hundreds and brought it into the tent of meeting as a memorial for the Israelites before the Lord.

—Numbers 31:54

The lady who helped me learn to read left several gifts to the church. She left her library, which not only had some wonderful books, but also almost every book published for the previous twenty years while she had been a book reviewer. Our church library was never so well stocked. She also left a considerable sum of money to the church. Some she designated for new hymnals and prayer books, though the bulk of it she left for the vestry to do whatever they felt was needed. And then, there was her house. There was a lot of conversation about what could be done with that donation. They decided to have a parish-wide meeting to discuss it.

My father suggested we all needed to pray on it. That night I prayed and dreamed that her house, which was right by the church, became a place where several older women in the parish—who lived alone—could live together. I told my father and mother about that the next day, and my father smiled. The parish-wide meeting after church had lots of people suggesting how the donations could be spent: if the house was sold, it would give the church even more money to spend. My father waited until everyone who wanted to speak had spoken, then shared that he believed it would be wrong to sell the house and force her long-time companion out of her home. Rather, he asked them to consider making the house into a home for elder ladies in the parish to share. He suggested modernizing and updating the house accordingly. The house was large and could comfortably provide a home for at least four or five ladies who were active in the parish.

That is what they did.

Day 56

Read: Numbers 33–34

The Lord said to Moses, "Command the Israelites and say to them: 'When you enter Canaan, the land that will be allotted to you as an inheritance is to have these boundaries.'"

—Numbers 34:1–2

Five women in the parish were approached by the vestry and asked if they wanted to move into the house together, explaining how it would work. They came over to my parent's house and sat with my mother and godmother, excitedly talking about what it would mean for them. I listened as they shared their stories with each other over a nice cup of tea. Each of them had lost someone in the First World War, either husband, fiancé, boyfriend, or just a boy who might have been more. None of them had any close family. They all ended up renting rooms in others houses, or working as domestic help, living in with a family. The lady who was already living in the house was the most excited, as the men at church told her they would be fixing lots of things at the house and painting it throughout.

That is exactly what the men did, gathering in the evenings and weekends, transforming the house into a comfortable home for five ladies. They could live there as long as they lived or needed, and they did. The men of the church kept it in good shape, and the women of the church helped with curtains and finding all the other things a home needs to make it a great place to live. As they now lived right by the church, parishioners saw them almost every day. Gradually other members of the church got to know them better and came to know their lives and stories. The women said they felt like they had been wandering since the First World War, and forty years later, they were home at last. It was as if they had formed their own community, finding a place among us to call home.

Day 57

Read: Numbers 35–36

Zelophehad's daughters, Mahlah, Tirzah, Hoglah, Milkah and Noah, married their cousins on their father's side.

—Numbers 36:11

After settling the five women in the house, the vestry had to decide what to do with the remaining donation, which led to lots more late evenings for my father. They agreed on updating and finishing several things around the church and the parish hall, and then they still wanted to do something more. I had gone with my father to church one evening for him to go to yet another meeting, and while he sat with the vestry members discussing the donation, I sat and read in the library. I was amazed at the range of books we had been given. Several of them were too hard for me to read, though I did start to do so. I suddenly realized the vestry members had gone quiet and were looking at me sitting and reading.

My father suddenly suggested we should start a literacy program for other children in the parish who had not been given the opportunity to learn to read because we had several families in the parish who had children who struggled with learning and reading. The other members of the vestry agreed, and a safe place for children to learn and read with someone to assist was established as a memorial to the donor. The vestry went further, though, deciding to help at least one young woman a year go to college and to help them with the cost of books and housing in honor of the donor. My father shared with my mother their decision when we got home and how he thought of it while watching me enjoy the books at church—the books which our friend had shared with us.

That night I slept well, dreaming of forests and wardrobes and boats and bears and adventures with happy endings.

Day 58

Read: Deuteronomy 1–2

Choose some wise, understanding, and respected men from each of your tribes, and I will set them over you.

—Deuteronomy 1:13

My father was going to make a trip for work that would take him out of the country for a while. He talked with several people at church about who could stand in for him while he was away. In the end, he chose several younger men in the church, asking them to consider helping on the vestry and with the things that needed to be done to keep the church growing. My godfather continued as the treasurer and a safe pair of hands on the *tiller* of the vestry, which was good as he was skilled at being able to guide others in making decisions about the things needing to be done.

My father was being sent by his company to the Far East, and I asked him where that was, as it sounded a long way away and rather exotic. My father got out his big stamp album and showed me pages in it where he had stamps from Singapore, Malaya, and Japan. I asked him why the company was sending him, and he said that he knew the business well and also had something most of their other employees didn't have. He had been a conscientious objector in the war, and, particularly in Japan, the company was sensitive to the feelings of the Japanese as they helped them rebuild their businesses after the war. It helped that it was known that he was a man of faith, a scientist, and a good businessman. The contracts he negotiated in Malaya for his company would last fifty years, which seemed like forever, but in fact, passed by quickly. It gave the rubber planters and growers the stability to replant rubber trees and other crops to provide rubber and food for their country. The friendships he made in Japan lasted his lifetime.

Day 59

Read: Deuteronomy 3–4

See, I have taught you decrees and laws as the Lord my God commanded me, so that you may follow them in the land you are entering to take possession of it.

—Deuteronomy 4:5

Who can tell when some small change happens in your life that will become a habit. My father going away for a few weeks turned into months, then almost half a year. It was such an event. My father said to read the Bible every day, so I did. My brother and sisters did to start with, and my mother did too, but they all gradually had other things to do, places to be, friends to play with—more important things going on in their lives.

I didn't have other things to do except go to school, come home, go to church on Sundays, and spend lots of time on my own. Though we did have a black-and-white television, evenings were often spent reading or listening to the radio, or both. So, I read, first with the others, then gradually on my own. I had a *children's* Bible, too, which my father gave me before he left. It wasn't written for children specifically, but rather, had some beautiful paintings in it, reflecting stories from the text. It opened with camels resting at eventide, which immediately took me away into the desert, far from North London to a place of adventure and mystery.

I realized later it was a King James translation of the Bible, full of magnificent poetry in the language it used, with a whole section of maps at the back to help me understand the places, tribes, and journeys taken in the stories it shared. Sitting, listening to music on the radio, looking at the pictures and maps, and reading the stories in the Bible changed me, comforted me in my father's absence, and brought me closer to God. Even though I wasn't sure who God really was then and am not sure I even know today.

Day 60

Read: Deuteronomy 5–7

"Hear, O Israel: The Lord our God, the Lord is one. Love the Lord your God with all your heart and with all your soul and with all your strength."
—Deuteronomy 6:4–5

The stories came to life as I read and reread verses to understand them better. I saw that my father loved God. He told me so. I saw it in so many things he did. I think I must have decided to show my father when he got back from his trip that I had heard him and read the Bible every day to both grow closer to him, and to God. The simple faith of a child.

I understood there were a set of rules given to Moses to share with the Israelites, and through them, with us. These rules made sense for a people living as nomads in the desert but were harder for me to relate to living in a suburb of London.

They made sense to me as I talked about them when I sat at home, or when I was walking to school or church. What was harder for me to understand was how tying them to my head or writing them on the doorframe or gate of our house made any sense. Then, I saw that our Jewish neighbors had a small object attached to their doorframe, and I asked them about it. They shared with me that it contained a small piece of parchment with teeny, tiny writing on it, sharing the words of Deuteronomy 6:4–9. They called it a *mezuzah* to remind them that every time they enter or leave the home, they have a covenant with God. Additionally, anyone who walked by would know this was a Jewish home.

This made sense to me, though I didn't yet understand why my family didn't have a mezuzah on our front door as well. My mother said we didn't because we were not Jewish.

I asked her, "Wasn't Jesus Jewish?" All I remember was that she rolled her eyes multiple times!

Day 61

Read: Deuteronomy 8–10

He defends the cause of the fatherless and the widow, and loves the foreigner
residing among you, giving them food and clothing.
—Deuteronomy 10:18

Reading the Bible every day gave me lots of clues to who God was and why God mattered. However, the more I read, the more questions I had. I would ask questions of anyone who would listen. Often, I asked questions as an aside to another conversation so people didn't think I was weird, but I inquired often with my godparents—because after all they were my *god*parents—and I felt they might know the answers. My godmother had no children of her own and dedicated herself to working with the church. She served however she could. She took on lots of responsibilities across the church: in our church locally, across our diocese, and nationally, particularly organizing Mother's Union groups across the country.

Through those groups, she also organized relief efforts across the world for people who were immigrating to the UK after the Second World War. We had lots of new immigrants coming to the UK in the 1950s and 1960s, and she was extremely active in helping them settle and find their way. She often stressed to me that we had to help people who were orphans or widows, and if they were foreigners, we should welcome them and help them however we could. She often had people stay a few days—or weeks—with her until they had their own home to move into, a job, and were settled. She and my godfather did what they could, and their words were their bond. Always, she would say prayers with them and for them and encouraged me to always do the same.

Even though I was still little, I helped in whatever way I could. Sometimes it was enough to just sit with someone and read slowly in English with them, or listen to them read, as they learned to speak, read, and understand English.

Day 62

Read: Deuteronomy 11–13

It is the Lord your God you must follow, and him you must revere. Keep his commands and obey him; serve him and hold fast to him.

—Deuteronomy 13:4

Listening to the foreigners who immigrated to the UK, I heard stories of faraway places and lots of different religions with their ways of worshipping. Some of them, though they came and worshipped with us at our church, shared the different ways they carried out services in the country they left behind. One family had travelled from the Far East, from islands near where my father was traveling, and they used coconut milk and breadfruit to celebrate communion—something I had not stopped to think about before.

I asked our Jewish neighbors what bread and wine Jesus might have shared at the Passover supper, and it didn't sound like any of the bread we ate in London in the 1950s. The wine sounded familiar as our church received its wine from the Mediterranean island of Cyprus, which I was told was quite near the Middle East of Jesus' life. I knew there was a difference between our neighbors and us, but they did seem to have lots of information about the things I was reading about in the Bible, so I listened to them.

My mother would listen, too, and if someone knocked on our door, she would listen as they talked. We often had people with Bible tracts turning up at our house, normally traveling in pairs, telling us that they could save us. My mother patiently listened to them and then shared about our church. She invited them to come to our church, but I don't remember any of them ever doing so. She would explain to me we should always listen to another person talking about their beliefs, but we should always remember our faith and beliefs and share them too.

Day 63

Read: Deuteronomy 14–16

Three times a year all your men must appear before the Lord your God at the place he will choose: at the Festival of Unleavened Bread, the Festival of Weeks, and the Festival of Tabernacles.

—Deuteronomy 16:16–17

I asked our neighbors about the three festivals, and they shared where I could find these stories in the Bible. In our church, we only celebrated Easter, Harvest Festival, and Christmas. I suddenly saw the parallels in our stories. However, our faith went further in that each week, when we had communion, we remembered the last supper, death, and resurrection of Jesus. I also knew this story took place when the Jews were remembering the festival of unleavened bread, their Passover. All of this seemed to be a lot for me to take in and understand, but I kept asking questions, and for the most part, I got answers.

I asked my godmother what the gift was we brought to church each week. She shared that she and my godfather tithed to the church but also brought themselves and their hearts to church each week to share with others. She explained that by bringing herself to church and sharing her love with others, she could find ways to help others and open their hearts and minds to God too. Each Sunday, she would give me a small coin to put in the offertory plate that went up to the altar but also reminded me to ask people at church how they were, how their week had gone, if they any family news, and to generally give of myself and listen to their replies to see if there was a way I could help them. I often spent my Sundays wondering how I, a child, could help them, but I found little ways to do so, mainly by reaching out and asking them about their lives—and listening.

Day 64

Read: Deuteronomy 17–20

I will raise up for them a prophet like you from among their fellow Israelites, and I will put my words in his mouth. He will tell them everything I command him.

—Deuteronomy 18:18

We had a new deacon visit our church. He was to be the new deacon at our neighboring church and would also be spending time with us. He had come to London because of the priest who visited my parents a few years earlier. He had come from South Africa to complete his theological study at King's College. Even though I was only a child, he didn't seem to be much taller than me.

He and his wife and children were nice. They got to live in the curate's apartment behind the church, and while there, they gave birth to a daughter, which caused great excitement among the congregation. My mother sorted out lots of baby clothes with other ladies at church, and we had a gathering in which the women shared the clothes and all the things they would need.

Even with that excitement, I was not ready to hear him preach. One Sunday, he took the pulpit. He had a quiet, calm voice. In fact, I had to strain a little to hear him. What he said mesmerized me as a child. He talked about God in a way I had not heard before. He said we all had a personal relationship with God. Suddenly, he said something which made us all gasp. "Everyone you see, and everyone you meet in your day-to-day life, everyone, you need to find God in that person, and love them."

People around me shifted in their pews, knowing what he said was true, but also knowing how hard that was to live by. He went on to say that if our priest in South Africa had not seen God in his mother and him, he would not have shown her the respect he had. The deacon might never have become a priest. I realized I had been holding my breath and breathed.

Day 65

Read: Deuteronomy 21–23

If you enter your neighbor's vineyard, you may eat all the grapes you want, but do not put any in your basket.

—Deuteronomy 23:24

I was listening to his quiet words of wisdom—breathing in, breathing out, listening. The priest's stories and his application of the Gospel to day-to-day things, like walking in the street or through someone's field or garden, brought the Gospel to life. The whole church was hushed as he spoke, so that even though he spoke quietly, everyone could hear every word he shared. I realized my godmother was crying as she listened. I looked around me and up at my mother sitting in the choir and realized many of the choir were crying or dabbing their eyes.

His words were truly prophetic and reached us in a way I had not experienced before. Afterward in the parish hall, I remember his wonderful laugh and huge smile. He also paid attention to all the children from church and asked them questions and listened to them when they spoke as attentively as he listened to the adults gathered around him. He was with us for about a year or so and preached at several of the churches around us, though he officially served at our neighboring church, St Alban's. That church would one day become the sole parish church in the area, incorporating my church and another one as a single community.

His words, his message, were truly prophetic as he spoke out about the way people were being treated in his home country and the work that was needed to bring about change. I didn't understand it all then as a child. I am glad I lived to see the change happen as a man. He also taught me to *breath in* and experience God within me, and to *breathe out* and experience sharing God around me.

Day 66

Read: Deuteronomy 24–27

When people have a dispute, they are to take it to court and the judges will decide the case, acquitting the innocent and condemning the guilty.

—Deuteronomy 25:1

When he preached, I could see people listening. When he shared that the law might not be fair to all people, we listened. The priest had many stories of how, even though they had right on their side, the judges and courts in South Africa were not fair to people like him—people of color, people who were poor. He knew we had heard some of this from Father Trevor Huddleston when he was with us, and of his story in his book, *Naught for Your Comfort* (Collins Fantana, 1956). He shared the story how Father Huddleston had been asked by a magistrate in court, "Is it the function of a priest to defy the government?"

Father Huddleston replied, "Is it the function of a priest to remain silent in the face of injustice?"

He said they all knew the government would bar him from South Africa as it wasn't ready to hear that. He spoke of how they turned to scripture for guidance, yet some of that guidance only spoke to white people, not black people. He asked us: *Is that fair? Is this what God wants? What do the scriptures really tell us? Who wrote the scriptures, and why?*

I think this was the first time I had heard people challenging what was written in the Bible—challenging the hundreds of laws in the Old Testament scriptures. This church in North London became a place where eyes and ears and hearts were opened, something I would never forget. For that—and many other things—I thank that priest, Desmond Tutu, for coming into my life when I was just a child. I could not know then that his influence would bring me to a life in Ferguson, Missouri, many years later where I can live and seek God in everyone I meet.

Day 67

Read: Deuteronomy 28–29

If you fully obey the Lord your God and carefully follow all his commands I give you today, the Lord your God will set you high above all the nations on earth. All these blessings will come on you and accompany you if you obey the Lord your God.

—Deuteronomy 28:1–2

When Desmond Tutu spoke, it was as if a veil was pulled back from the words I had read with my father or listened to at church. He was offering hope from the same scripture he had criticized, showing if people loved and obeyed God, then God would bless them. He shared how important that truth was to all the people he knew back in South Africa as their whole lives were built on hope, hope for a future in which they would receive respect and understanding from the people who ruled over them.

He preached in great sweeping stories, sharing tales from life in South Africa and how there were others who could see what was happening and what change was needed. He shared that it was Father Huddleston who had shared the simple recognition that *all* men are made in the likeness of God and that, in consequence, each person is of infinite and eternal value. Thus, the state exists to protect the person but is always of inferior value to the person.

Father Tutu shared with us that the South African government was like Jerusalem. By not opening their eyes, they were sadly blind and deaf to the prophets. However, he hoped and prayed for change, and as we would learn years later, change *can* happen. I was only five years old when I first heard Father Huddleston speak and preach and not much older when I first heard Father Tutu speak and preach. Yet, as a child, I stored up their stories and teachings, not realizing how deeply their words were ingrained in my soul and that by listening, I was making a new covenant with God. And I didn't even know it.

Day 68

Read: Deuteronomy 30–31

No, the word is very near you; it is in your mouth and in your heart so you may obey it.

—Deuteronomy 30:14

Realizing the words had a far greater meaning was the proverbial thunderbolt. Reading the words again over the years just made them more and more real. Sifting through them as I was in seminary and looking at the translations from Hebrew, Greek, or Latin, was not what an eleven-year-old expected to do in his life, but sift and study I would. I realized the words were not *up there* somewhere, rather *down in the ditch* with us. Not in another part of the world, or across a sea, or in a jungle, or on a snowy mountain top, but rather in my mouth, in my heart. This realization was huge.

I still wonder about it to this day as I struggle living out my life in a way that meets the standards and challenges set by the words of these two prophets who had passed through my life so early. Like most ten- or eleven-year-olds, though, I quickly moved on like a butterfly to deal with the day-to-day struggles facing a boy switching schools, dealing with family, and exploring further afield than just his home, church, and family. I didn't know it, but I was already reaching people in a way that would be demonstrated to me as I dealt with death up front and in my life for the first time.

I delivered newspapers every day to homes near where I lived in North London, greeting some of the people every day, particularly an older lady who was always up and out at her front steps every day waiting for her newspaper. Until one morning, she wasn't. I peeked through the letterbox opening in her front door and could see her laying on the ground. I went to a neighbor and shared this with them, and they called the police who came and broke down the door. She was dead.

Day 69

Read: Deuteronomy 32–34

Blessed are you, Israel! Who is like you, a people saved by the Lord? He is your shield and helper and your glorious sword. Your enemies will cower before you, and you will tread on their heights.

—Deuteronomy 33:29

It was the first time someone I loved as a friend died. The neighbors called the shop I delivered papers for, and the shop owner called my parents. However, I went on delivering the rest of my news round. My father found me a few streets away, delivering the papers and softly crying, but I finished my task that day. I didn't want to disappoint anyone by not delivering their newspaper. My father walked beside me the last few roads, not talking, or hugging, or crying—just being and walking in my shoes with me. I remember this lesson all these years later as a chaplain in hospitals, homes, and churches.

The next day I discovered I had already been reaching people without knowing it. Apparently, as I delivered papers in the morning, I whistled as I walked. Sometimes just songs, but sometimes a whole symphony or musical show. After my older friend died, I did not whistle as I walked the rest of the newspaper delivery round. People called the shop to ask if I was okay, and the newsagent shared with them that I had experienced the death of the older customer. It clearly affected the others, too, as the next day, people were coming out to see me as I delivered their papers to *check* on me and to thank me for what I had done the day before. Many of them said they hoped to hear me whistling again as it was a nice way to start their day—it sounded so happy, like a bird singing in the morning.

Day 70

Read: Joshua 1–4

The priests who carried the ark of the covenant of the Lord stopped in the middle of the Jordan and stood on dry ground, while all Israel passed by until the whole nation had completed the crossing on dry ground.

—Joshua 3:17

I would spend summers riding my bicycle around the neighborhood, especially on Hampstead Heath Extension. I would ride and play games on the open field areas and build forts and fight battles. My summer holidays would have made for a good story in a C.S. Lewis book or two. A small drainage ditch laid between the various field areas where people played sports, and it ended in an area that became a bog. The ditch was surrounded by quite a few trees and was really overgrown. Sitting by it, I decided to become a human beaver. I collected up lots of fallen tree branches and built up a mud bank, blocking off the ditch from draining and creating a small pond.

Each day, I would go back and build it higher. I noticed that more and more birds were coming to drink from the pond. One morning, there were a pair of ducks and footprints from some other animals who had visited in the night. A friend of mine helped me at first, but then he went off to play at other things. On the way, he shared with a groundskeeper what I was doing. Suddenly, a groundskeeper appeared while I was just sitting by the pond watching the ducks and listening to the birds. He told me I couldn't do what I was doing and proceeded to break the dam, letting the water flow out of the pond all at once, on down the drainage ditch into a culvert, and away to who knows where. The ducks walked around for a minute or two, looked at me, and then flew away. The birds went silent.

I sat by the muddy, empty pond and cried until I realized it was getting dark and sadly went home.

Day 71

Read: Joshua 5–8

*Afterward, Joshua read all the words of the law, the blessings and the curses,
just as it is written in the Book of the Law.*

—Joshua 8:34

My father got a letter from the people who looked after Hampstead Heath, asking him to make sure I didn't block the drainage ditches again. No punishment, just a request not to do it again. My father did not know I had done it in the first place, so he sat and asked me why. I went down a rabbit hole about St. Francis and caring for God's creatures, and I just blubbered my heart out.

My father patiently spent time sharing with me that what was written in the Bible, and the stories in the Bible, should not be taken literally, and something like caring for animals on the Heath must be done within the boundaries of the organization that cared for the space. He said if I wanted to join one of the organizations who volunteered, I could do so, and then I would see what they already did for the animals and birds—and how I could help.

Before that evening was over, though, he sat and prayed with me, and we read several stories from the Bible together. He explained how, even when the stories seemed incredible, they had meaning beneath them and meaning to us in our current lives. He talked about how the walls of Jericho were brought down by the sound of trumpets and shared that overcoming difficulties that seemed insurmountable was always possible with God's help and prayer. He said if I wanted to help the animals and birds, I needed to pray about it and ask for guidance on how I could help and trust that God would guide me.

I'm not sure I fully believed him then, but I believe him now, as I have experienced people overcoming enormous challenges in their lives with God's help.

Day 72

Read: Joshua 9–11

So Joshua took the entire land, just as the Lord had directed Moses, and he gave it as an inheritance to Israel according to their tribal divisions. Then the land had rest from war.

—Joshua 11:23

Going from my house to Hampstead Heath Extension would take me past the crematorium and gardens where my grandfather's ashes were. Often, I would slip in to say a quick prayer to a person I had never known, yet felt drawn to. It was always cool and dark, compared to the alabaster whiteness of the urn holding my grandfather's ashes. Then I would cut through a little lane, Wild Hatch, lined with small arts and crafts houses—cottages for artists and workers that had been built on the edge of London as part of a new suburb, Hampstead Garden Suburb.

The last house had added a huge aviary on the side of the house that was always full of birds. I would stop as I went past, listen, and then talk with the birds there. The woman who owned the house was friendly, and we chatted about the birds—mainly finches and canaries—which she said would not do well in the wild. I shared with her what I had done on the Heath, and the increase in bird life I had seen happen. She told me she wrote books about birds and would investigate it for me to see if there was a way we could help improve the bird, and other animal life, on Hampstead Heath.

A few weeks later, she contacted my parents to say the grounds people said I could volunteer to help them build some new ponds further up on the Heath where they needed to improve the drainage. I spent the remainder of that summer happily digging in the mud, helping create three new ponds that would help the wildlife on the Heath. I felt I had done something to give back, to make a difference—a small legacy, three small ponds—and I found out who my neighbors were.

Day 73

Read: Joshua 12–15

The western boundary is the coastline of the Mediterranean Sea.
—Joshua 15:12

We talked about my volunteering over supper in the evenings. My father would listen as I excitedly shared what we had completed that day—raising a dam higher here, deepening a stream there, planting new bushes to give cover or helping plant young saplings. I would listen to the groundsman explain why we were planting what we were planting. He would explain what birds might like it to nest in, or if it attracted squirrels or other animals. One day, we planted some aspen, and he explained how they would spread underground through their root system as if it was all one tree.

The groundsman was a quiet person who was incredibly patient with me. I also noticed, which I shared with my father, that he prayed a lot. Each time he planted something, pruned a plant, or dug a hole, he would say a prayer under his breath, saying he was *just doing God's work.* He said we were blessed to have been given this land to share with others, and he felt our job was to steward it the best we could. He shared what we were doing was helping everyone who lived near the Heath have a beautiful place to come and visit, whether to go for a walk, play a sport, paint a picture, or read a book. To him, the Heath was a gift from God, and our job was to be God's hands to take care of it for others who would come after us. The trees we planted then would be seen by people in fifty years. He hoped they would like the trees and bushes we planted. At the end of the day, we could stand and look at our work flowing to the boundary of the Heath and know it blessed everyone as far as the eye could see.

Day 74

Read: Joshua 16–18

As the men started on their way to map out the land, Joshua instructed them,
"Go and make a survey of the land and write a description of it."
—Joshua 18:8

Working through the summer alongside the groundsman was challenging and exciting, as I got to see how this space could be used by different people for different things. He asked me to map out where the stream ran across the Heath extension and then to survey areas that could be used for sports or other purposes. I spent several days measuring areas, drawing them up on sheets of paper for him. I showed how we could fit in several cricket and soccer pitches and highlighted an area that might be good for a children's playground.

By surveying where the stream ran naturally, we could see how to drain certain areas to make them more usable for sports fields. We could place them nearer to the boundary roads where people could have easy access. We spent quite a lot of time just working out where they would go. As we worked, I noticed he was considering which way the sun shone on the areas, which areas were more exposed to wind, and where footpaths gave easy access. When we had finished all our planning, he said he would take it to a committee and ask for the funds needed to make it happen.

Then he surprised me by saying we better say a prayer to get God's help, and we stopped what we were doing and prayed. To me, his praying for God's guidance was powerful. I shared with both my parents over supper that night that it also seemed perfectly natural, matter of fact, and normal just to say a prayer, not from a book of prayer, but from the heart. I would remember that.

Day 75

Read: Joshua 19–21

*So the Lord gave Israel all the land he had sworn to give their ancestors, and
they took possession of it and settled there.*

—Joshua 21:43

I marveled at what we achieved. Each of the sports had its own field
and was near to the boundary road so it was accessible. Each of the paths
crossed from one boundary to another. Most people came to the Heath by
walking, riding bicycles, or catching a bus. So, each path started near a bus
stop so people could be dropped at the bus stops when they visited. The
stream, which had caused my trouble initially, wasn't altered in its flow. It
simply flowed. Trees were planted. Paths were finished. Lights were placed
along the paths, kept low to shine light only on the paths. It was becoming
a special place. The ponds filled up. Fish were introduced. Birds started to
come back. Where no one had seemed to care about the land, it was clear
that someone did now. People started to notice and told others too.

My parents came and looked at what we had done, what I had been
doing with my summer. And it was good. They met and talked with the
groundsman, who shared how hard I had worked. He was proud of what
we had achieved and how it would be a lasting legacy. He said it would
show others how to care for and be good stewards of the land and all that
lived on it. He and my father talked for quite a while. My mother thought
he reminded her of Brother Lawrence, whom she had shared about with
me before, in that he continuously prayed in everything he did. His work
was his prayer.

Day 76

Read: Joshua 22–24

On that day Joshua made a covenant for the people, and there at Shechem he reaffirmed for them decrees and laws.

—Joshua 24:25

The last weeks of summer flew by as we worked on tidying up all the work we had done—making sure the sports fields were clearly marked. Making sure the pathways were clearly signed and lit. We documented which birds and animals we knew had made nests or burrows on the Heath. We took photos to use on signs posted at the boundaries so people could look for and recognize the different species. My bird friend added a description of each so people would learn more about them too.

The seasons were changing. I was very aware that I would be back in school soon as summer was ending. One time was closing and another beginning. When I looked back on that summer, I saw how God had worked to teach me what was meant by being a steward of the land. To care for animals. To care for the planet. It was a lesson I would carry with me the rest of my life. As my father and I sat and read from the Bible together, he asked me if I understood better how what was shared with us in the Bible guided us. We had to listen to what it said and not take it literally, rather, we needed to allow it to open our minds. I understood what he said and would think about this the rest of my life.

Day 77

Read: Judges 1–2

After that whole generation had been gathered to their ancestors, another generation grew up who knew neither the Lord nor what he had done for Israel.

—Judges 2:10

After spending an entire summer volunteering to prepare a space to be used by others, working as hard as he could to make it a special place—interesting and caring—it came as a shock to this young boy to find that the people who started to use the sports fields and walk around the ponds did not treat it the way he thought they would.

I went back to visit at the end of my first week back at school to find the groundsman repairing one of the signs. He was quite philosophical about it and shared that it was the third time that week that he had to fix the signs. Someone had also spray painted over some of the information about the wild birds, making fun of the work we had done. He said that it was just people who didn't understand what we were trying to do, and they clearly did not want to care for the land like we did. He did remind me that at one point I had been like them, too, and it was only as I came to understand that we were stewards of the land that I had invested so much time and energy to improve it.

I was angry initially and then realized it was another lesson for me to understand what God's purpose for me was, and that I needed to understand what I needed to do to help. First though, the groundsman and I prayed for the people who had damaged the signs and prayed they would not do it again. I went home extremely sad that day after realizing that people could do this. I shared what had happened with my parents, and we added those people to our prayers that evening.

Day 78

Read: Judges 3–5

So may all your enemies perish, Lord! But may all who love you be like the sun when it rises in its strength.

—Judges 5:31

My godmother came at this problem from another point of view. Yes, she thought I should pray about what to do; however, she was a very practical person and suggested I think about what else could I do that could help the groundsman and keep the Heath in better shape. She made me sit down and think about what practical solutions to the problems might be options. Wow, a light bulb went off! I could pray and come up with a solution too.

She suggested I also talk with her husband, my godfather, about this problem as he was a keen gardener. So, I looked for him and found him working in the church's garden. He was delighted to have me help him. Listening to my experience, he suggested that I might like to share with others what I had been doing through the summer and why it was so important. My godfather asked me to write down my thoughts and then suggested I share them with the groundsman and see what he thought as well.

Later that day, I found the groundsman and shared with him the draft of what I had written about caring for the Heath, building the dams and the ponds, encouraging new bird and wildlife, and, at the same time, respecting others who might just want to play sports on the sports fields. He liked it and suggested I send it as a letter to the local paper. He liked that all these ideas had come from praying with him, my parents, and my godparents. I went home and shared with my parents what I was going to do, and they helped me correct my spelling before I mailed my letter. That night I slept well and dreamed of the birds and animals on the Heath, and all the people playing sports and games happily alongside them.

Day 79

Read: Judges 6–7

"Pardon me, my lord," Gideon replied, "but if the Lord is with us, why has all this happened to us?"

—Judges 6:13

Over those days in conversations with the groundsman, my parents, and godparents, I came to realize several things. We inherit the planet from those who have gone before us. They also teach us how to care for it, ourselves, and others. They show us how to be in the right relationship with everything on earth, and we get to choose our path on this journey. From our first breath to our last, we can choose to make the world better, and we can do so intentionally.

That summer, I intentionally helped by damming streams, creating ponds, draining bogs, creating sports fields, making signs, and sharing knowledge of birds and animals. Now I had to look deeper and learn how to maintain and share that legacy with others—how to create a domino effect, inspiring others to contribute as they felt they could, so they would take ownership also.

My letter to the local paper shared the joy I experienced, how nourished I was by the place called the Heath and the elements—sun, rain, wind, and soil—which, in turn nourished the land itself. What a joy it was to experience the plants and trees, the birds and animals, and the people enjoying the sports fields! I realized by intentionally living our lives, we can make our neighborhood a better place not just for today, but for future generations too.

I acknowledged I was only a child seeing the world through a child's eyes, but then I had to wait and see.

Day 80

Read: Judges 8–9

Have you acted honorably and in good faith by making Abimelek king? Have you been fair to Jerub-Baal and his family?

—Judges 9:16

Other people wrote to the local paper expressing different views. I quickly realized my dreams were not necessarily others' dreams. Different views on how to care for the Heath became known. Some wanted it left alone completely. Some wanted it to be built over to house people. Others thought it should be sold to the highest bidder. Voices were raised on how to share the Heath, how it could be kept for the greater good. It was hotly debated by people. I could only watch from the sidelines.

At that time, my father had a friend come and stay for a visit. He was a Benedictine monk who lived in Buckfast Abbey in Devon, in the Southwest of England. He would come up every summer for a week or two to visit London, go to museums, see plays, and refresh his spirit, before returning to the Abbey to teach in their school throughout the year. He would also donate time performing daily services, allowing a priest to have a week off from their church duties in the city. On his first week with us, he invited me to go with him to the morning service, after which we went to visit a museum together, The Natural History Museum in South Kensington. As we walked around the museum, he asked me who I thought had made the museum possible.

After a few false guesses by me, he said, "People like you." People who cared about animals, birds, fish, spiders, dinosaurs, and even bugs we could barely see. People who cared about God's world and leaving something for others to see.

As we walked around, I noticed he prayed at each of the displays, thanking God for the person or persons who had made the display possible. I prayed too.

Day 81

Read: Judges 10–12

I have not wronged you, but you are doing me wrong by waging war against me. Let the Lord, the Judge, decide the dispute this day between the Israelites and the Ammonites.

—Judges 11:27

Several other voices were raised about the Heath, and gradually people who cared for the natural state of the Heath seemed to be winning over. By this time, local TV, radio, and regional media started to take an interest. Several members of parliament who lived nearby started to talk about it on the media too. The debate raged back and forth for weeks. I had to learn patience to avoid being sucked into the arguments.

My parents spent a deal of time, especially in the evenings, just talking with me about what was happening, encouraging me to pray for it to all work out well in the end. In the meantime, people were using the Heath for sports and to walk and play. My friend wrote about the birds and published a book on the birds of the Heath—how to recognize them and how to ensure they continued to come and visit. My friend, the groundsman, got full-time help with his work to maintain the Heath, and people seemed to care. My parents and I went for walks on the Heath, and we stopped by the ponds and prayed, giving thanks for all we had done in our lives and all we still had to do. My father shared verses from the Bible and the Psalms to emphasize how nature was core to a belief in God. He shared with us that we are God's eyes and ears and hands, here to do God's work, and that is what we had done for the Heath.

I was just a child, and I saw things through a child's eyes and heart, but I stored it all away.

Day 82

Read: Judges 13–15

Then Manoah prayed to the Lord: "Pardon your servant, Lord. I beg you to let the man of God you sent to us come again to teach us how to bring up the boy who is to be born."

—Judges 13:8

My father shared many things with me that fall after I was back in school. He wanted me to share my experiences from the summer in a way that was hard for me to hear at first. He wanted me to be both proud of what I had helped others achieve with protecting the Heath, yet at the same time he wanted me to be humble about my role in it. He read various parts of the Bible to me, including this story from Samson to show me what he meant. He also shared that the prayer from Manoah was one he had prayed himself before each of us children had been born. He stressed it had helped him and my mother through some difficult times and choices with each of us.

He told me to consider that who I was in relationship with was important—whether it was someone I worked with, like the groundsman, or just interacted with, like the woman bird writer. When I was older, it might be someone I would fall in love with. Getting involved with someone means becoming part of their community, their family, and their neighborhood. I learned a lot from our conversations and was surprised how often he would illustrate our day-to-day life by referring to examples from the Bible that made me stop and think.

However, I was also in this new school, a difficult transition for me, so I had a lot to pray about. My father went with me for the first few days as I learned to navigate walking to the underground, finding my platform, getting on the correct train, getting off at the correct station, and walking from there to the school—a journey I would take every school day for the next seven years.

Day 83

Read: Judges 16–18

Then Micah installed the Levite, and the young man became his priest and lived in his house. And Micah said, "Now I know that the Lord will be good to me, since this Levite has become my priest."

—Judges 17:12–13

My father and I spent several evenings and weekends taking photos of the Heath. Taking photos together was something that brought us closer together. He had given me my first camera, a proper camera, with knobs and switches, not just a box camera or a basic picture camera, for a Christmas present a couple of years before. He taught me how to frame shots and showed me how to develop the film and print out photos at home too.

I discovered I could take photos of the plants and flowers and put them through the process in the darkroom at home and change how they looked in the photos. Gradually, I put together a whole set of photos summing up what we had been doing on the Heath—pictures of plants, animals, birds, and people playing and simply enjoying being in nature. We sent a set of photos to the local paper to illustrate what we meant about the beauty of the Heath and its importance to the community.

I felt I was still doing *something*, even though it didn't seem to be having an effect. My father would say we were doing what God guided us to do, and even when they used some of the photos without saying who took them, he quickly helped me not be upset, but thankful to do God's work. Gradually, people were seeing the purpose in what we had spent the summer doing: how beautiful nature was, and how it was all around us, and how it needed protecting.

When nobody seemed to be taking care of it, anyone could really do anything they wanted, and other people's feelings could be ignored. Gradually, though, people accepted that for the common good and the long-term care of the Heath, they needed some rules and regulations to protect it, almost to protect it from itself.

Day 84

Read: Judges 19–21

In those days Israel had no king; everyone did as they saw fit.

—Judges 21:25

I followed up with the groundsman about it, and he shared that it was what he had been praying for. Then he surprised me by sharing a new challenge he had been given. Another part of the Heath, which had previously been a private garden of a big house adjoining the Heath, had been donated and was being added to his work. He was just starting to plan what it would look like and how best for it to reflect a special place. This new part of the Heath was going to be just a garden. A place to walk, sit, and pray. A quiet place with a pergola and a pond with fish.

Because of the work we had done that summer, the parks people had decided to trust him with it. I met him there a few days later with my parents, and we were stunned at how beautiful it was. It was a formal, walled garden that had clearly been built many years before. Attached to it was a large house on the edge of the Heath that had not been well cared for and had really become completely overgrown, like a secret garden.

Over the next few months, I was able to visit with him often, watching the progress as it slowly changed into an amazing garden, surrounded by the wildness of The Heath. I liked visiting there and noticed my mother did too. She had a lot on her mind as my grandfather was not well, and it comforted her to be able to just sit and pray in the garden. It is there to this day, bringing joy to people as a place to walk, sit and pray—a place of peace, known as The Hill.

Day 85

Read: Ruth 1–4

*But Ruth replied, "Don't urge me to leave you or to turn back from you.
Where you go, I will go, and where you stay, I will stay. Your people will be
my people and your God my God."*

—Ruth 1:16

I held my grandfather's hand while my mother and grandmother whispered together outside the hospital room. He was breathing peacefully with his eyes closed. The hushed whispers grew agitated and concerned, while he was only peaceful. He opened his eyes briefly, looked at me, recognized me, and smiled.

"Hello boy. Tell Nan I love her," he said, squeezing my hand.

And then he was gone. I just sat with him, holding his hand. His breathing stopped. My mother and grandmother came back into the room and stopped. My grandmother pushed by me and grabbed his hand, crying out. My mother called out for the nurse. I was pushed to one side. They were both crying now. I was not. Days, or maybe weeks later, my parents helped my grandmother move from her apartment in Kings Cross to our home in North London. We moved bedroom furniture around, and my brother and I moved into a room together, and my sister moved into a smaller bedroom, leaving a big bedroom for my grandmother to make into a bed-sitting room, with some of her favorite pieces of furniture and mementoes of a life lived with my grandfather.

My mother and her mother—an interesting dynamic. Two people who had lived different lives yet would always be tied together by an invisible thread. Their roles were reversed, and the child would care for the parent, and would for the rest of their lives. We would also get to know the person from whom our lives had come.

I discovered I had a part to play in her life that I never suspected. She would sit and read her Bible every day and asked me to read with her. This was how I discovered my grandmother could barely read, and I found out she had never been to school.

Day 86

Read: 1 Samuel 1–3

Pardon me, my lord. As surely as you live, I am the woman who stood here beside you praying to the Lord. I prayed for this child, and the Lord has granted me what I asked of him. So now I give him to the Lord. For his whole life he will be given over to the Lord.

—I Samuel 1:26–28

After my grandmother moved in, I became aware that in the afternoon she would sit and read her Bible. At least that is what I thought she did. I would get home from school and go up and chat with her about my day and what we had done at school. I realized quite quickly that she seemed to read the same pages again and again, so that was when I asked her if I could read with her.

Soon after that, she shared with me that she had never been to school. My grandmother was born in 1894 in the parish of Old St. Pancras Church and was the fourth child of a large and very poor family. I asked lots of questions about where she grew up as I had only known about the Somers Town area from what I had read in books by Charles Dickens. So, in the afternoons, we would sit and eat McVitie's Digestive cookies and read the Bible together—a little more each day, picking up where we left it the day before.

She talked about her life growing up. It was extremely different from what I had experienced. When she was just seven years old, she had been sold into service as a between-stairs maid, known as a *Tweeny*. She would describe how she slept in a cupboard under the stairs in the basement kitchen of a big house. She went up and down stairs all day, carrying whatever was needed, from chamber pots to fresh towels. She said she liked her place in the basement under the stairs as the kitchen was always warm in winter and cool in summer. She got to visit her family on Sundays when they all went to church, but she always had to be back at her employer's before dark.

Day 87

Read: 1 Samuel 4–8

But when they said, "Give us a king to lead us," this displeased Samuel; so, he prayed to the Lord. And the Lord told him: "Listen to all that the people are saying to you; it is not you they have rejected, but they have rejected me as their king. As they have done from the day, I brought them up out of Egypt until this day, forsaking me and serving other gods, so they are doing to you. Now listen to them; but warn them solemnly and let them know what the king who will reign over them will claim as his rights."

—I Samuel 8:6–9

My grandmother identified with the people in the stories of the Bible—their struggles, their difficulties, and particularly how ordinary they were, while being expected to do things by a God who always seemed close by. To my grandmother, God was someone you could sit and have a conversation with—even argue with, strike a deal with, or even chat with about your day.

God wasn't a distant person sitting up in the clouds, out of touch with what was happening on the street, and the street was what my grandmother knew. She shared with me that the same people she saw in church on Sunday were falling out of the pubs drunk on Monday. And the men who walked their families to church on Sunday were visiting prostitutes by Thursday. Her descriptions seemed to be right out of Dickens' stories, yet had such a grain of truth about them that the rawness of what she shared made the tales come alive.

She wasn't paid anything by her employer, because her parents had indentured her at seven. Any payment went straight to her parents. When she turned thirteen, nobody had told her about women's periods, and she thought she was dying. Her employer's response to her concerns was to get rid of her. She proudly told me that after only a week, she got a better job as a servant for a family a few miles away in Tottenham, but this time they paid her, not her parents, so she worked for them for several years. She still had some Sundays off to visit with her parents or her siblings, who had moved to the Kentish Town area, near Hampstead Heath.

She didn't go to school, though, and struggled with reading and writing. But, as she said, she could pray!

Day 88

Read: 1 Samuel 9–12

Saul answered, "But am I not a Benjamite, from the smallest tribe of Israel, and is not my clan the least of all the clans of the tribe of Benjamin? Why do you say such a thing to me?"

—I Samuel 9:21

My grandmother told me stories about working for the new family. She enjoyed it. It opened her eyes to a larger world than her cupboard under the stairs. She had also started going to a church near her parents on Sundays before spending time with them—St. Jude's on the Grays Inn Road. She went there one Sunday and knew she was called to spend some time just sitting with God—whoever God was—chatting about her week, her challenges, her successes, her hopes, and her dreams.

One Sunday, a woman approached her after the service and asked her about herself and what she did. When she shared that she worked for a family, the woman asked her if she would like to work for another family nearer her parents. This family was from another country, and the father worked at an embassy in London. When my grandmother shared this with my great-grandmother, she was thrilled. Having given birth to my grandmother, my great-grandmother had six more children. Two of them, twins, died after a few months, and she was struggling to raise the remaining four. More than anything, though, she missed my grandmother. Also, with a war brewing with Germany, she would like her daughter nearer to home.

That Sunday, she went back to St Jude's and thanked God for helping her and answering her prayers. She started with the new family nearer her parents as war broke out between England and Germany. Her brothers and their friends all were called to serve and went off gleefully to war. She said they were like boys on an outing to summer camp, with no idea what lay ahead.

Day 89

Read: 1 Samuel 13–14

All the days of Saul there was bitter war with the Philistines, and whenever Saul saw a mighty or brave man, he took him into his service.

—I Samuel 14:52

My grandmother's brother Bill was the first to go off to serve. He also came back first, but he came back a different person. Neither were her brothers Fred or Sid. My grandmother went with her mother and her sisters on Sunday, and the church was full of women, all wearing black, praying together for their men fighting in the war. She would look around her and see lips moving with silent prayers. Most of the women could not read and said prayers in their own words, from their hearts, while the priest stood at the altar with his back to them, mumbling away up front in a cloud of smoke.

I started to understand the Bible really meant far more to her than I could imagine. As we sat in her bedsitting room, Grandma—or Nan as we all called her—sat in her very straight back chair with wooden arms, a chair she had saved up to buy herself, a chair she used until she died. I would sit on the floor, waiting for her to ask me to read from where I had left off the day before, and I would continue for a while. When she stopped me, it was to talk about some story prompted from her memory. It was as if the Bible passages triggered deep memories she needed to share out loud, so someone else would always know the stories. Through her, I began to understand the Bible was not just a collection of God stories.

Much later, at Eden Seminary, I heard theologian Marcus Borg say, "The Bible is a human product: it tells us how our religious ancestors saw things, not how God sees things" (Borg 2014), and I knew my grandmother was right all along.

Day 90

Read: 1 Samuel 15–17

> *All those gathered here will know that it is not by sword or spear that*
> *the Lord saves; for the battle is the Lord's, and he will give all of you into our hands.*
>
> —I Samuel 17:47

My grandmother would often weep as I read, and I wondered why. Then she shared how many young men she had seen going away to war with her brothers, and how few returned. Additionally, those who returned were never the same.

One day, she suddenly quoted these words:
If I should die, think only this of me:
That there's some corner of a foreign field
That is forever England.
(Brooke 1915)

This is from a poem by Rupert Brooke, called "The Soldier." Many people learned it by heart after the First World War. She had seen so many young men walk away and never come back. Lots of them came up from the country, straight from the farms, through the stations at Kings Cross, St. Pancras, and Euston, before going off to war.

"They were so young," she would say again and again.

She first met my grandfather with a bunch of guys, up from the country and going off to war. She met him with her brothers as they drank in the pub, but they would not leave her alone with him, protecting her from getting involved with someone who might not come back. She prayed he would.

My grandmother sat with her eyes closed and remembered, gently weeping. Several days of reading would go this way as she shared that she couldn't write to him as she didn't know how to write, and she didn't want anyone else to write what she felt—so she didn't write, only prayed. Each time stories came back in the papers, she listened when people read them out to all who would listen, but there was never any news.

When the soldiers started to come back—broken, battered, and crushed—they all wept. It didn't matter whether they had won or lost; the men were broken.

Day 91

Read: 1 Samuel 18–20

After David had finished talking with Saul, Jonathan became one in spirit with David, and he loved him as himself.

—I Samuel 18:1

My grandmother shared that when they came back from the war, her brothers and my grandfather seemed to be close friends and spent a lot of time together, mainly in the pub. She still worked for the embassy family, now as an upstairs maid, and my grandfather got a job as a valet in the house next door. My grandmother continued to go to church on Sundays at St. Jude's and prayed for her brothers to heal. She started to include my grandfather in her prayers also.

The war was finally over. They had lots to celebrate. Her older brother Fred got married, and they went to a different church for the wedding, St. James in Hampstead. That was the first time she spent time with my grandfather, at the celebration. Suddenly, my grandmother went very quiet, and we sat in silence for a while.

"My brothers thought he was a great guy," she said. "They loved him like a brother. You know, I prayed for him while he was away in the war. God kept him safe for me. God brought him back for me." She paused a long while, then said in a whisper, "Three months later, it was our turn to get married."

She didn't say much more, for a while. It was like she had to explain something but couldn't say it out loud. "My dad didn't come to the wedding. My brothers did. My mother did. But my dad didn't come."

She sat silently, looking down at her Bible, not saying anything, just touching the pages we had been reading.

Day 92

Read: 1 Samuel 21–24

*As the old saying goes, "From evildoers come evil deeds," so my hand
will not touch you.*

—I Samuel 24:13

My grandmother listened to what I was reading and suddenly interrupted
me. "I got pregnant with your mother at my brother Fred's wedding. Your
grandad did the right thing, though, when I told him. After my brothers
chatted with him, he said he wanted to get married all along. His family
didn't come to the wedding, though. Only my mother and brothers came,
and we didn't have a big party or anything."

She sat silently looking down at the page in the Bible we had just read.
"He did the right thing," she said again.

I was surprised at what she shared, yet felt honored that she would share
this with me, her grandson. We sat in silence for a while that day. It was the
first time I felt like I had shared something with a person in a confessional
moment. Somehow, I knew it was not to be talked about with others in my
family until much later, if at all. I think it was one of the first times I realized
it was important just to sit with someone as they processed their thoughts
in their own mind—sharing what they wanted to when they were ready.

Years later, when sitting with patients in hospital or by their bedside,
I realized that often the person just wanted to know someone was in the
room with them. Not judging them. Not talking with them. Just sitting
and waiting to hear whatever they wanted to share. I do believe there are
moments when God is present in a conversation, in a silence, in an action,
and this moment with my grandmother was such a moment, a moment
to treasure.

Day 93

Read: 1 Samuel 25–27

*Abigail acted quickly. She took two hundred loaves of bread, two skins
of wine, five dressed sheep, five seahs of roasted grain, a hundred cakes
of raisins and two hundred cakes of pressed figs and loaded them on
donkeys. Then she told her servants, "Go on ahead; I'll follow you." But she
did not tell her husband Nabal.*

—I Samuel 25:18–19

When we started reading about the story of Abigail, my grandmother
opened up about how difficult it was in the 1920s for my grandfather. He
was truly broken by his experiences in the Great War. He had served in
Gallipoli, and not only did he have a piece of shrapnel in his body—which
doctors decided was safer to leave alone than try and remove it—he also
had contracted malaria.

Shortly after they got married, he lost his job as a valet because he
kept suffering relapses of malaria. It took him a while, but he got a job as
a night watchman. After my mother was born, my grandmother had to go
back to work, cleaning houses and doing laundry, which she could do in
the day, while my grandfather watched my mother. My grandmother said
she had to be very careful. She had to hide some of her money as otherwise
my grandfather would take it and spend it drinking.

She stopped talking and just sat for a while. "He was a good man, your
grandfather. He just hurt a lot. That made him drink a lot. I needed to
spend my money on food for us. For the baby, for your mother, for clothes,
and rent. I always put a bit aside for insurance and to give to the church."

Her brothers would drop off things from their jobs they had selling
fruit and vegetables in a market, and delivering milk, which my grandfather
tried doing for a while also. He couldn't manage walking up and down lots
of stairs, though, and as all the tenements around Kings Cross were all five
or six stories high, he went back to being a night watchman. It sounded so
hard. For a while she said, they didn't want to have any more children as
they just couldn't afford to.

Day 94

Read: 1 Samuel 28–31

The share of the man who stayed with the supplies is to be the same as that of him who went down to the battle. All will share alike.

—I Samuel 30:24

My grandmother's brothers all got married and had no children. She said they tried, but none of the three of them seemed successful. So, six years after she had my mother, my uncle was born, and six years after that, my aunt was born. She talked about all this in a matter-of-fact way and shared that her brothers and sisters-in-law all doted on her children and loved spending time with them. Her sisters had no children either, so they loved having them visit.

The reading made her think about how she shared her children with her brothers and sisters. She felt blessed to have three children, so she shared them, and later, her children did the same with their grandchildren. My aunt was even sent out of town to stay with one of them to avoid the bombing in London, or *The Blitz,* as it was known. Over the years, we would all spend time with our great-aunts as they moved out of London into the countryside before the Second World War. My grandmother said that sharing was important as some have plenty and some do not, and we all ought to share with each other.

I had not thought about sharing children before, as I thought more about sharing things. Her words helped me realize it wasn't sharing in a socialist way; it was sharing of oneself in a Christian way.

Or, as my grandmother would say, "If it was okay for David, it is okay for me."

Years later, I also shared my children with their aunt and uncle who were childless, and it was great to see them grow from that friendship.

Day 95

Read: 2 Samuel 1–3

Saul and Jonathan, in life they were loved and admired, and in death they were not parted. They were swifter than eagles, they were stronger than lions.
—2 Samuel 1:23

Sitting with our open Bible, my grandmother would talk about her parents, their move out of London before the war, and her two younger sisters who went with them. Both sisters married and lived outside London, which gave us all places to visit for holidays. She talked of her brother Fred who had died unexpectedly just after her father, and then she talked of my grandfather's death. Although he had struggled for forty years since World War One, he had been a good husband and father.

In talking about him, she was already painting a picture of him that was different from the grandfather I knew. His mother died while he was away fighting in Gallipoli. His father had not told him until he returned from the war. He struggled with that as well as with his injuries from the war. She talked about her father and mother, her brothers and sisters, but barely mentioned my grandfather's family.

My grandfather could do no wrong in her eyes. She said he was swifter than eagles and stronger than lions, all words which I know now she found in the Bible. She used these words to grieve him and create a legacy for him, allowing her to grieve the myth of the man and create new memories of him to carry for the rest of her days. When she talked of him, she only shared good stories, rarely the difficult or hard days they shared.

It was my first real experience of not speaking ill of the dead, and yet, later as a chaplain, I often heard stories of the departed that seemed light years away from the reality I knew. It is how God helps us heal, though, and that's okay.

Day 96

Read: 2 Samuel 4–7

Then King David went in and sat before the Lord, and he said: "Who am I, Sovereign Lord, and what is my family, that you have brought me this far?"

—2 Samuel 7:18

There comes a day, a moment, when things change. Her days of sharing about the family seemed to have ended. It was as if she buried deep down the memories that were painful. She did share that the way we lived was different from how she had grown up, repeating the story of living in the cupboard under the stairs in the basement of the big house on Portland Place. She repeated stories of washing and cleaning and carrying for others, and repeated stories of her friends who lived around her in Kings Cross—many of them single mothers who survived on their wits and using their bodies to earn enough to feed themselves and their children. Her stories were always full of details about what the women wore, and always with a tenderness as she shared her young hopes for better days.

She talked of one man who had children by several women and even compared him to David. He appeared to be the man who was in everybody's business. Apparently, he had to do that because he had so many children to support that he had to work harder than any other man in the neighborhood. He was charismatic to her, and she could see no wrong in him—he accepted his responsibilities and raised good children. Several of these children went to school with my mother in the neighborhood, and my grandmother was proud of that. She saw getting my mother into school as one of her greatest achievements. She was determined to see my mother do better than she had. She was creating her legacy.

Instead of going into service when she was seven, my mother was able to start at Hugh Myddleton School when she was five, not long before her brother was born.

Day 97

Read: 2 Samuel 8–12

Then David sent messengers to get her. She came to him, and he slept with her. Then she went back home. The woman conceived and sent word to David, saying, "I am pregnant."

—2 Samuel 11:4–5

My grandmother wrestled with this passage and struggled with even talking about it. When I found her sitting, reading it slowly with her finger tracing the words, she was shaking and angry. "He had all the power, all the wealth, and she had no choice but to go to him."

My grandmother was angry. We sat with it for a while, then she shared with me about so many men she had met in her life who acted like this. Men who thought the rules didn't apply to them. Men who felt they could take any woman they wanted. Men who didn't look at the consequences of what they did. Even if David did right by her in the end, he did so much wrong first. She just kept saying it wasn't *right*. Again, and again. The fact that the baby died didn't change anything for her. *Where is God in this?* she kept saying.

I guess I was old for my age, with something inside me that allowed my grandmother to talk with me about matters way beyond my years. She called me an *old soul* and saw something in me that others couldn't see. With her, I could let go of my fears about what I saw, heard, felt, or thought. Instead, I felt grounded and present to her and could respond intuitively to what I felt called to share with her. Somehow what I felt, what I could share with her, was *just right* in the moment, even when I couldn't know where I was drawing it from. I drew on this inner self more each day, and sometimes I was okay, and other days, I was not.

The story of David began to make more sense to me each day.

Day 98

Read: 2 Samuel 13–15

As surely as the Lord lives, and as my lord the king lives, wherever my lord the king may be, whether it means life or death, there will your servant be.
—2 Samuel 15:21

How do you know if you are following someone who is good, or serving someone who is good? My grandmother and I talked about this question a lot. She told stories of people she worked for over her lifetime—some were good employers, some not. Throughout it all, she was always loyal to them unless they lost her respect. Respect was important to her, and she struggled to explain what she meant by the word until she quoted this passage from Samuel. If she respected the people she worked for, then she would work hard and long hours for them. She compared Ittai's story to the story of Ruth and her mother-in-law. Ruth said she would stay with Naomi and support her as long as she lived.

At this time, I had a Saturday job helping in a shop and repairing bicycles. I realized the bicycles needed to be repaired and returned to their owners quicker than they had been with just the owner fixing them during the week. His partner did not seem to fix any of them. So, I started dropping by on my way home from school and fixing bicycles to help get the repairs completed. I noticed he was a bit overwhelmed with his shop, and his partner, who was also his friend, did not seem to pull his weight. So, I started finding ways to help him by just keeping the shop stocked up and tidier, improving how it looked from outside, making it look nicer to people walking in.

After a while ,he said he needed to give me something for my extra help and gave me a bicycle. Not a new one, but one that had been traded in. Still, it was in great condition, and I was grateful for the gift.

Day 99

Read: 2 Samuel 16–18

Joab said, "I'm not going to wait like this for you." So, he took three javelins in his hand and plunged them into Absalom's heart while Absalom was still alive in the oak tree.

—2 Samuel 18:14

My friend's partner seemed to be taking cash out of the till in the shop. My father suggested I wait and see if it was a *once-only* thing or if he was taking money out all the time. My grandmother asked me if the owner worked hard in his shop, and I said he did. She said I had to share what I'd seen with the owner. So, I consciously prayed about it. The following weekend, I shared with the owner what I had seen, and that I'd prayed about what to do before sharing this with him. He became very quiet and said he would talk to his friend about it.

The next time I went into the shop he told me they had talked about it. He and his friend had agreed he would be the sole owner going forward. He was clearly sad about this as he had known his friend for a long time; they started the shop together. He was quiet for several weeks, sharing with me that he felt betrayed by his friend who had been well paid from the shop, but just found it easy to take cash from the till. He asked me if I could come in after school for a while to help until he could find someone else to help full-time, and I did.

However, the joy I had felt working there had changed. The owner seemed to be sad a lot of the time, even though the shop seemed to be doing better. After he got someone else to come and work for him—someone who could help in the shop and repair bicycles—I stopped working for him during the week after school. I switched my Saturday job, too, going to work at our local supermarket.

Day 100

Read: 2 Samuel 19–21

David brought the bones of Saul and his son Jonathan from there, and the bones of those who had been killed and exposed were gathered up.
—2 Samuel 21:13

My grandmother wanted me to go and visit the cemetery where my grandfather had been buried. We walked to the underground station and took two trains to get to the station we needed. Then we took a bus. It was raining softly—typical cemetery weather. When I was older, I lived only two roads from there and could visit on my own more frequently. It was an old cemetery, and the church at its heart was closed. We didn't need to look around as my grandmother knew exactly where to go and sit by my grandfather's grave. She asked me to say a prayer with her for him.

"Just talk with him," she said. It seemed slightly strange to be sitting there with her and him, but I prayed for him. I included memories of him taking me to see my first soccer game at the Arsenal and riding on his shoulders for the whole ninety minutes. Of going to the pub and sipping *Tizer the Appetizer*, a red-colored, citrus-flavored fizzy drink, and playing games of checkers and cards. I realized my prayer had become almost a litany of my life relationship with him, and all the time, my grandmother kept squeezing my hand and crying softly, like the rain.

Squeezing my hand even more, my grandmother suggested we have tea at a nearby Lyons Corner House, which had changed to be a *Wimpy Bar*, an English hamburger chain. Even with all the changes, the young woman serving turned out to be a granddaughter of a friend of my grandmother. It's a small world after all.

"I like how you prayed," my grandmother said. "Just talk with God like you did today, and you'll be alright."

Words to live by.

Day 101

Read: 2 Samuel 22–24

*He brought me out into a spacious place; he rescued me because he
delighted in me.*

—2 Samuel 22:20

Sitting and having tea with my grandmother was an experience not
to forget. The fact that our waitress was the granddaughter of an old
friend of hers from her Kings Cross days just seemed to make it *righter*.
It was if the world wanted to share something with me. Before we ate our
tea—which looked amazing with cake and scones and sandwiches—my
grandmother surprised me by asking me to say grace. I thanked God for
the gift of the day, for my grandfather, for the memories, for the life he
had with my grandmother, for my mother and her brother and sister, for
my grandmother's brothers and sisters, and all my cousins and, and, and
for this wonderful tea set before us.

My grandmother smiled at my attempt to include everyone and everything
under the sun in my prayer, and said, "Don't forget your grandfather's
family, his parents, and my parents, and all those who have gone before."

I rarely heard her ever mention his family or their parents or grandparents,
and it left me thinking about them and their lives. It would be years before
I was able to find and discover the families going back in time through a
website, which wouldn't be invented for thirty to forty years after we sat
and had tea together that day.

On the way home, I wondered what my grandfather would have thought
of me, which made me wonder what God thought of me. My grandmother
thought he would be proud of how I was turning out. How caring I had
become. I said I might still mess up sometimes.

She said, "That's all right, boy. We all mess up sometimes. Just say
you're sorry, mean it, and God will forgive you, and you can move on."

Good advice from my grandmother to store away for another day.

Day 102

Read: 1 Kings 1–2

So be strong, act like a man, and observe what the Lord your God requires: Walk in obedience to him, and keep his decrees and commands, his laws, and regulations, as written in the Law of Moses.

—1 Kings 2:3

I had transitioned from helping out with the choir at church to helping more with serving and at different services during the week in addition to Sunday. On Sunday, we had three services: an early spoken service at 8:00, the full service with the choir at 10:00, and evensong at 6:00 in the evening. Sometimes, with work that needed doing around the church, I seemed to spend the entire weekend at church. Both my parents and godparents were extremely active and committed to the church.

In fact, my godfather helped build it as he was a skilled woodworker and gardener. He actually worked every day at a desk job for a large insurance company in a dry office that felt like something out of Charles Dickens—as I discovered when I visited him one day at his office for lunch.

He showed me around and then said, "Let's go and have lunch."

We walked from his office down a few side streets to the River Thames where we sat and ate sandwiches my godmother had made for us—breaking bread together, quietly sitting by the river, watching the clouds roll by. It was a strange and wonderful moment, especially when we sat down, and he said grace after opening the package of sandwiches. He praised my godmother for making the food with love and care, and he thanked God for everything. He shared that my godmother would have said a prayer over the sandwiches as she made them, so he always said *thank you* in a prayer when he opened them.

Breaking bread with someone became a moment in time for me on many occasions and often the Spirit moved me. The sharing was real, and Jesus's presence was among us.

Day 103

Read: 1 Kings 3–5

So, give your servant a discerning heart to govern your people and to distinguish between right and wrong. For who is able to govern this great people of yours?

—1 Kings 3:9

I was blessed to have several older people who mentored me as a child. My parents both guided me by their examples of how they lived their lives, and I saw both the good and the bad. My godparents, unable to have children of their own, reached out and offered support and help whenever they could. The women at church seemed to think they could ensure that I acted properly and understood what they needed me to do as service to and around the church. I had teachers who experienced the Second World War, and some who had even experienced the First World War; their shared experiences taught me how actions speak louder than words.

People I worked with—at the news agents, or the bicycle repair shop or the supermarket, or the park, or the crematorium—all shared their wisdom and knowledge with me. The other members of the church or even the customers on my newspaper route always had a word or two of wisdom to share about the day's news or about things happening in the world.

Through all those years, I was like a sponge: listening, asking questions, talking with them, sharing my thoughts and beliefs, and honing my understanding of what this world was all about. I was truly learning, far beyond what I was taught in school, by listening to and reading with so many people who wanted to share their wisdom with me. All this did not necessarily give me all the answers, but it did give me lots of questions, positive thoughts, feelings about life, and a better understanding of God.

Day 104

Read: 1 Kings 6–7

I will fulfill through you the promise I gave to David your father.

—1 Kings 6:12

I realized all my experiences were molding me into *being* something. I wasn't sure what yet, but I was changing. Every day, I was asking God to help me discern between right and wrong in all sorts of daily matters—asking God to help me be nice to people I interacted with every day. All the people in my life were sharing their wisdom and guidance with me in order for me to provide help, support, love, and understanding to others, fulfilling whatever purpose God had for me.

The hardest thing I had to learn was obedience, which remains the hardest to this day. Knowing how to be obedient to what God wanted was something I kept questioning. I could follow the rules at church and school but was always looking for ways to think outside the box and challenge what the rules were. If we followed the rules, then God would keep an eye out for us. I understood that, but sometimes I wondered, a bit like Adam and Eve, *what if?*

For many years, my parents had encouraged me to draw buildings, imaginary buildings, and to build models of the buildings. Anyone paying attention might discern I wanted to be an architect. However, I realized something. The physical structure of the church—building it, taking care of it, honoring it, respecting it, worshipping in it—was not enough. Worshipping and being obedient to God was what God wanted. Not the building. We could be anywhere as *church* when we gathered for worship, and the building really didn't matter.

I quickly discovered that not everyone agreed with me.

Day 105

Read: 1 Kings 8–9

Israel will then become a byword and an object of ridicule among all peoples.
—1 Kings 9:7

It was about this time that an assistant priest at our church got into trouble. He was married with children, and somehow, he got involved with a widow. My parents were talking about it over dinner. They felt he had turned away from God, and the consequences he faced were as a result of that. What I found interesting was that they were forgiving of him personally but still said he had to accept the consequences, which meant he had to leave our church, and his wife and children had to leave too.

I said I didn't think that was fair. Why did they have to punish his wife for something he had done? My parents talked a lot about shame and how his wife felt. They believed they needed to help him get a new start somewhere else, but he might not be a priest anymore. I felt they were exiling him from everyone who professed to love him and could support him in healing his actions.

This was when I first saw the other side of church and how it responded when it felt someone had turned away from the its teachings. I saw a lot of pontificating and not a lot of love for people. My father shared that he didn't feel any different about the priest, his wife, or the widow, but they needed to accept the consequences of their actions. Trust had been broken. It was as if the church was set in stone, and the stone was unresponsive to the people.

I struggled with this, and any questions I asked were shut down. People did not want to talk about it; they wanted it to go away and for people to *move on.*

Day 106

Read: 1 Kings 10–11

*The Lord became angry with Solomon because his heart had turned away
from the Lord, the God of Israel, who had appeared to him twice.*

—1 Kings 11:9

My father shared his thoughts with me on all this and shared far more
with me than I probably needed as a teenager. He wanted me to understand.
The priest had been warned about getting too close to the widow. She needed
pastoral care to help her through a difficult time; however, he needed to avoid
becoming emotionally involved or having her misunderstand his role in her
healing. Part of what happened was the priest blurring the lines between
pastoral care and taking advantage of her vulnerability with his position of
authority. He also stopped seeing her as a parishioner and, instead, saw her
as a potential sexual partner.

The woman turned to the church after becoming a young widow and
was more committed to finding a new sexual partner than finding healing
for herself. This focus had upset people at church who would have been
committed to helping her grow as a person and heal from her bereavement,
but were not going to help her find a new sexual partner. The discussions
in the church followed this pattern, too, and I noticed something else.
There were splits appearing among the church members. Some people
stopped coming, and others stopped helping. This didn't affect the church
immediately; however, as time passed, numbers dwindled, and the viability
of the church building was brought up for consideration. I don't think the
church members realized then, but this event would lead to them losing
the church to another denomination.

To me, it showed the importance of remaining faithful to God and
following the guidance on boundaries in relationships, which I remembered
years later as a chaplain and used to guide myself.

Day 107

Read: 1 Kings 12–14

He asked them, "What is your advice? How should we answer these people who say to me, 'Lighten the yoke your father put on us?'"
—1 Kings 12:9

Our diocese had a new bishop who came to visit us. Yet again, we had all the pageantry of the visit and the service with incense, bells, and full choir. Afterward, the Bishop met with the gathered congregation in the church and shared with us the diocese was considering our future. Many of the older members spoke out about keeping the church going as it was. Then some of the younger members spoke out about the discord over the loss of the assistant priest and the unforgiving nature of so many of the members of the church.

My parents and godparents were particularly quiet at first until the bishop pointedly asked for their advice. All four of them shared their concerns for the church, its diminishing size, its sense of lost direction, its sense of loss personally, and feeling unsure of where it might be in the future. My parents shared how most of their own children no longer came to church and no longer felt its relevance in their lives.

The bishop asked each person to speak and eventually even turned to me. I shared how I felt the saga of the priest had unraveled the church, how I was surprised at the lack of forgiveness or love shown by members, how they seemed to preach one thing and live another. As I finished, I said I believed we had to examine ourselves and accept our own responsibility for what happened. *How could we have helped both people to a different outcome?*

The bishop paused for a while, then resumed sharing how he felt we needed to discern the changes for us, merging with another parish, and seeking out another denomination to replace us in the use of the church building. There were a lot of tears that night.

Day 108

Read: 1 Kings 15–17

"Look, your son is alive!" Then the woman said to Elijah, "Now I know that you are a man of God and that the word of the Lord from your mouth is the truth."

—1 Kings 17:23–24

Prayer is an interesting thing. Following the bishop's visit, our church seemed to have endless meetings. In fact, it seemed that my father and godfather went to meetings almost every evening, and my mother and godmother were in meetings every day. An approach was made to a Greek Orthodox community, and they started coming and holding services on Sunday after our services were over. They also used incense and bells, so the feel of the church did not change, and we felt we were helping another community have a place to gather. At the same time, members of the church met with the two other parishes nearby and talked about the possibilities of merger.

Gradually the Greek Church brought various icons and statues to the church, and it felt more like their church than ours. The church gathered one Sunday, and after the service finished, the members of the vestry stood at the front of the church and announced they would take a parish wide vote on merging with two other churches—with us all relocating to St. Alban's, which would become the parish church for the whole area. (The third church that joined us at this time passed their church on to a Jewish group, and it became a new synagogue.)

As we settled in together, there was a new energy. People talked of mission and how we could better support our community It had been a long time since I had heard anyone talk of mission within our community. Prayers and trust in our community resulted in a miraculous outcome and strengthened my faith and the faith of all those who witnessed it. When the bishop returned, he was welcomed and seen as someone who had the vision to see how we could both survive and grow in a new way.

Day 109

Read: 1 Kings 18–20

And after the fire came a gentle whisper. When Elijah heard it, he pulled his cloak over his face and went out and stood at the mouth of the cave.

—1 Kings 19:12–13

Many times, I wondered if I had heard clearly what God wanted me to do with my life. I was struggling with school and had taken up swimming and running long distances. Not running fast or winning any races, but just swimming and running long distances. I kept to myself, very much the loner. People at school chose not to understand me or relate to me; rather, they wrote me off as a loner. I had a few friends, but we were all similar.

Through this time, I was discerning if I should try and go to university or not. *Should I study something else other than architecture? Was that what I was called to do?* I stayed with my sister's godfather, a monk in Devon, and my time there was nice, but I didn't hear anything to guide me.

I went and stayed with my godparents who had retired to the south coast, and my time with them was nice, but I didn't hear anything. I went and walked in the local park, The Hill, and my time there was nice, but I didn't hear anything. I know now I was hoping to hear something from God.

I sat with my grandmother, reading the Bible together. We read for a whole afternoon, then sat with the quietness of having been reading. With the light fading, my grandmother asked me, "What do you really want?"

At that moment, God spoke to me, and I knew I still wanted to go to university and study to become an architect. God would guide me in many ways in my life, but this was the first step on a new ladder in my life. God was walking with me. Lots would tempt me, but I would persevere.

Day 110

Read: 1 Kings 21–22

Say to him, "This is what the Lord says: Have you not murdered a man and seized his property?"

—1 Kings 21:19

This was a time in my life when many things tempted me away from the path I thought I was called to follow. A friend asked me to help him with his mobile discotheque, which meant late nights on Saturdays and no desire to go to church on Sunday morning. Yet most Sundays, I found myself going through the motions at church, which was strangely comforting.

My parents were dealing with other issues from my sisters and brother, so I could just slip through the cracks if I didn't make any waves. So, I learned not to make waves. One of my sisters brought her two children to live with us while she and her husband went on a three-to- four-month course. My niece was a toddler, and my nephew was a baby. My mother was struggling with her arthritis and could barely cope during the day.

So, despite my being in the middle of exams at school, the baby—my nephew—was put in my room at night. I would get up during the night, change and feed him. I found it comforting to sit and rock him for hours at night. It was good practice for later in my own life when I would have twin sons, then a son and a daughter, then jobs in which I worked through the night, whether in broadcasting or as a hospital chaplain. My sister and her husband could not see how ill our mother was, how much caring for an infant tired her and wore her out—how much it affected all of us.

I felt she was taking advantage of my mother and me, and I voiced this opinion, which wasn't received well. But we survived the four months, and then the quietness of the house was strange and empty.

Day 111

Read: 2 Kings 1–3

Elijah said, "yet if you see me when I am taken from you, it will be yours, otherwise, it will not."

—2 Kings 2:10

My father came and sat with me for a while. He shared with me that even if I felt taken advantage of or hurt by my sister's lack of consideration, my sister had needed our help and we, as a family, gave it to her. He helped me see things in a different and a more loving way—not so much about me but more about others. He talked much more about our lives and how blessed we had been to have had our siblings with us growing up. As he had grown up alone, in Australia, far from his father or sister, he missed that. He laughed and said he would have liked to have had the chance to fight with his sister like I could.

His words, sharing something from his life, helped me realize the truth in what he said. I began to channel my feelings into painting and writing poetry, both of which were ridiculed by my sisters and brother, but my father liked my art and encouraged me to continue as he saw it bring me to a calmer place, a quieter place, closer to God. However, I found reasons to be out of the house more, joining some local groups, and starting to date, which was a whole other thing. My brother and sisters had all left home by now, so there was just my parents and my grandmother at home now. Dating was a new thing for me and led me into another set of challenges and visions. But before that, something else changed.

Day 112

Read: 2 Kings 4–5

Naaman's servants went to him and said, "My father, if the prophet had told you to do some great thing, would you not have done it? How much more, then, when he tells you, 'Wash and be cleansed!'"

—2 Kings 5:13

How many times do we think we know better than God? That God's ways are not always what we expect or want? If we trust in God's wisdom, and we follow God's lead, everything will be okay. These words, spoken by an unnamed servant, have sat with me for nearly sixty years. Again and again, I have expected some action to take place, and yet God has other plans. So much so that my mother would say to me, "Stephen, if you want to make God laugh, tell God your plans."

I made God laugh a lot over the next sixty years. I think I also made God cry and worry. I have had psoriasis since I was nine years old. In fact, the doctor who first saw me shared with my parents that I was born with psoriasis inside me, but I was nine when they first diagnosed it. The doctor saw a link between my psoriasis and my stomach upsets, and he thought I might have Crohn's too.

It was the first time I would hear the name of that illness that haunted me the rest of my life. I had lots of different treatments, but ultimately, I had to accept that I had it and just get on with my life. I switched to swimming every week so I could confront people with my psoriasis. I took classes in life-saving and distance swimming, and my headmaster encouraged me to do it as he felt it helped me in multiple ways. In the summer, the swimming and sunshine helped my skin too. In the end, I had to trust the process and trust God.

When I did, it was okay. When I didn't, things happened. You would think I'd learn!

Day 113

Read: 2 Kings 6–8

> *Then he assigned an official to her case and said to him, "Give back everything that belonged to her, including all the income from her land from the day she left the country until now."*
>
> —2 Kings 8:6

My eldest sister came to visit my parents. She was having trouble in her marriage, and she was having a tough time. My sister married when I was only five years old and had a daughter who was diagnosed with epilepsy and was given the incorrect medicine that hurt her further, resulting in a lifetime of illness. My sister's second child, a boy, died a few months after being born from SIDS. Her third child was a healthy boy; however, her fourth child, another boy, died in childbirth. Through the early years of her marriage, her husband's job meant he had to travel a great deal. It was tough on both of them, but because of the brokenness that occurred when she got married, she didn't want to share most of this with my parents.

As he traveled more, her husband became unfaithful to her and then became abusive when he was home. I remember sitting with my niece and nephew, reading and playing with them, while my sister sat in the other room crying with my parents. I didn't know what postpartum depression was then, but I clearly know what it is now. My sister, who had a beautiful soul, seemed to be broken; her light had gone out. My parents sat with her for several hours. That day my sister went home with her children, but my parents talked and cried about her visit for days afterward. My sister's decision to marry had hurt my parents at the time, and now, several years later, they took no pleasure in knowing that their judgement was correct. Rather, as my father said, it was time to pull together and help however they could. Their examples in how to handle life, how to offer help, how to simply listen, stayed with me.

Day 114

Read: 2 Kings 9–11

He remained hidden with his nurse at the temple of the Lord for six years while Athaliah ruled the land.

—2 Kings 11:3

My parents' home was the place my sisters and brother came back to visit for Christmas, Easter, and holidays. My grandmother being there also meant her other two children, my uncle and aunt, would come with their families to visit, too, to spend time with her and us. It seemed we were constantly having someone or other visit to share their problems, worries, difficulties, and challenges, and my parents would sit, listen, and offer help. Each of these visitors had great dreams and hopes that they shared with my parents. Each of them had dreams dashed, needing the love of parents to help pick themselves up and start over again.

For several years, they were the lynchpin in the family, and I was left to get on with my own life, make my own mistakes, and fly *under the radar* in the family. My parents always seemed to be talking about others, rarely about me. I wasn't the problem. I just was. So, my life went off the rails quietly and alone. My relationship with my girlfriend became the place where she and I could both escape from our parents. Her parents were unhappy and fought all the time. Because her father was a celebrity, any unpleasantness was hidden, buried down deep, not to be discussed or talked about. Me? Just because. My friends and her friends got on okay, so we became a small band of friends who hung out together. But the depth of our friendship was hidden from both our parents.

Suddenly, she would not answer the phone, and her mother said she didn't want to speak to me. She seemed to vanish from the face of the earth, completely hidden from me, and from her friends too.

Day 115

Read: 2 Kings 12–14

The man of God was angry with him and said, "You should have struck the ground five or six times; then you would have defeated Aram and completely destroyed it. But now you will defeat it only three times."

—2 Kings 13:19

Two weeks passed before her father agreed to see me and explain. He was very matter of fact. His daughter, my girlfriend, had been in hospital. He had decided to arrange an operation for her. A fetus had been terminated. He had taken care of it. I was in shock as he told me. The thoughts running through my head were so many, so confused, so hurtful. I'm not sure if I heard everything he said. He talked about how she wanted to hurt her parents and had done this deliberately to hurt them. Everything he said was all about them, all about him, and nothing about her at all.

When he stopped speaking, I asked how she was and when could I see her. He was stunned I wanted to see her, but after a pause, he agreed I could see her if, and only if, she wanted to see me. He said he did not want my family to know, and I couldn't tell anyone as it would reflect badly on him if it was made public. He had his image to consider. He said he would let me know if and when she might see me. I didn't know what to do with all this. I went to church and prayed for several hours quietly to myself in the lady chapel, then went to my favorite spot, The Hill, and sat by the pond for the rest of the day.

When I got home, my parents were talking about the problems of one of my siblings. I didn't tell them anything then, and it would be years before I told one of them. I felt broken and alone. I didn't know what to do next, yet I still knew God was with me and would guide me.

Day 116

Read: 2 Kings 15–17

Do not worship other gods. Do not forget the covenant I have made with you, and do not worship other gods. Rather, worship the Lord your God; it is he who will deliver you from the hand of all your enemies.

—2 Kings 17:38–39

Where do you turn when you are alone with no one to talk to? I turned to prayer. I still delivered newspapers in the mornings, though instead of whistling joyously, I quietly delivered the papers and talked, argued, and screamed inside my head with God. If anyone asked if I was okay, I would say *yes* and walk on. In the afternoons, I still sat with my grandmother. I still went to church. I went through the motions of living and kept putting one foot in front of the other. I met with my girlfriend. She told me she had wanted to hurt her parents, and it was complicated. When she realized what she had done, she couldn't tell me. Her parents just took over and arranged everything. She said her parents were surprised we still wanted to see each other. They thought, particularly her mother, that she would just end it with me. I didn't say anything until she finished, then simply said that I was there for her and wanted to still have a relationship with her.

So, we carried on seeing each other, more carefully and with an air of sadness. I held what had happened to myself and didn't share it with anyone, though she did share it with two of her close friends. After a few more years dating, we decided to get married. It seemed to be the right thing to do. It surprised her parents, and, in some ways, surprised us also. As she was not baptized, we had a civil marriage, and neither my mother nor godmother could be there as they were both in different hospitals at the time. My father was great, though, making it as special a day for us as he could.

It struck me years later that a huge sadness hung over the day.

Day 117

Read: 2 Kings 18–19

For out of Jerusalem will come a remnant, and out of Mount Zion a band of survivors. The zeal of the Lord Almighty will accomplish this.

—2 Kings 19: 31

Our first year of marriage was not easy, with criticisms from her parents about everything we did. But we persevered and got by with me studying at university and working part-time, and her working in an office. The second year we retrenched and moved to my parents' for a while to save some money for a deposit on somewhere to live. In the third-year, cracks appeared. We even had a short separation, then reunited and decided to go ahead and start a family. We had twin boys. I felt things were good, and our lives were on track with our children, our own home, and my good job with the BBC.

I did realize we were not going to church, though. How many times had I read about how easy it had been for the Israelites to lose their way? When we are living our lives, dealing with the daily things of life, things creep up on us. First, we are too tired to go to church as it is our only day off. Then we think that it doesn't really matter, and before we know it, we are barely picking up a Bible or a prayer book. That is, until something wakes us up.

In my case, I was sitting at the BBC on a night shift, and a colleague said, "You look tired, why don't you leave early? I'll finish your shift."

I was able to leave early. My high school friend's car was parked outside our house when I got home. He had been there the evening before, and for some reason, instead of stopping and going in, I drove round the block and passing our local church, I stopped, went in, sat, and prayed. When I got back to the house at the time I was expected, his car was gone.

Day 118

Read: 2 Kings 20–22

Go and inquire of the Lord for me and for the people and for all Judah about what is written in this book that has been found.

—2 Kings 22:13

It took a while before we talked. She was distant and guarded about what had happened, but we gradually talked it all out. This was the second time during our marriage that she had slept with someone else, one of my friends. I asked her why, and she couldn't say, except she liked them more than me. So, we decided to separate, which led to our separation and divorce.

My twin boys could not understand what was happening. That broke my heart. When my family found out we had separated, my eldest sister came up to my work to ask me if there was anything any of my family could do to help us not get divorced. When I shared almost everything with her, she cried and said she understood, as her own marriage had been loveless and abusive too.

I still didn't share with her about my wife's abortion before we married. I hadn't shared that with anyone. I found a place to stay, nearer to work, a basement apartment that I shared with a roommate who understood to leave me alone. The person who owned the apartment lived upstairs but also left me alone. It became a safe space.

I threw myself into my work at the BBC, working all the shifts they would let me work, often back-to-back and overnight. In fact, I worked for three months without a working day off until someone in management realized and insisted I take a break. But it was on a night shift, sitting in the cafeteria on a break, that I opened my Bible and started reading again, and I kept reading every day, picking it up where I put it down, setting a practice that I continue to this day.

Day 119

Read: 2 Kings 23–25

But the commander left behind some of the poorest people of the land to work in the vineyards and fields.

—2 Kings 25:12

In the 1970s, my ex-wife married my best friend, and she and her husband bought me out of my share of the house. We came to an agreement in which they didn't pay me anything for my share, but I stopped paying for any support for the twin boys. Although this seemed like the best solution at the time, it was not. It separated me more and more from my sons. Then they decided to move out of London for her husband's work and moved nearly two hours away.

For several years, I drove two hours each way on a Friday night to pick them up to have them stay with me for a weekend, and two hours each way back on a Sunday night to have them back for school on Monday. Then it became every other weekend, then once every three weeks, then once a month. She would not tell me anything they were doing in school, and as the school did not know anything about me, it took several years to convince them to keep me informed about my sons or anything they did at school.

I felt that they had left me *behind* in exile rather than going into exile. I stayed behind in exile in London. My emptiness was filled by new friends who felt sorry for me, and several of them became lovers. The situation wasn't really fair to them as I was in no state to be involved with anyone. I barely liked myself at that time. Slowly, with the help of friends, continuing to read the Bible every day, becoming involved with a church again, and finding a community, I was able to heal, but it took a while for me to journal regularly again as I worked out my thoughts and gained some clarity in my life.

Day 120

Read: 1 Chronicles 1–2

These were the sons of Israel: Reuben, Simeon, Levi, Judah, Issachar, Zebulun, Dan, Joseph, Benjamin, Naphtali, Gad and Asher.

—1 Chronicles 2:1–2

It seems simple to say who you are and who your father is, then trace your ancestors. The Bible does this a lot as the people of Israel justified their relationship, their unique relationship, with God. Even though they only list the names of sons and don't list the names of daughters, they do list the names of mothers as they are cited to establish property ownership. This sense of lineage was important in their culture, which I found more and more in the Bible.

I did notice how much forgiveness played out between God and the people and the people and God. To forgive somebody is to somehow say, *You've done something really hurtful, and I really ought to never be in any relationship with you again. Though there is part of me that is always going to be broken, I refuse to let it stay a barrier between us. so I still want to be in relationship with you.*

I remember summoning up my courage and saying this to my ex-wife and my high school friend. I also remember that they didn't accept they had done anything wrong or hurtful to me. I swallowed my pride in sharing those words and was met with a deafening silence. I hoped my forgiving of them helped them; I know it allowed me to move forward and stop beating myself up over my failure. Years later, I found it mattered to my ex-wife that I had said that. It allowed her to reach out to me when her husband died, and I could listen to her then and remember better times with them both.

My life was lonely though, and I was surprised at the different turns in life that happened as I found where my family came from and heard stories I had never known.

Day 121

Read: 1 Chronicles 3–5

*All these were the sons of David, besides his sons by his concubines. And
Tamar was their sister.*

—1 Chronicles 3:9

When you read through the list of names in the Chronicles, you can
easily glaze over. The names do not appear to mean anything. When I first
really read them, I was sitting alone in the middle of the night, in a corner
of a BBC studio, broadcasting to another country somewhere around the
world, and they left me glazed over and numb.

Then, I suddenly realized what they truly meant to me. This simple
list of names shared with me that this book I was reading was a human
product, telling me how our ancestors, all our ancestors, saw things. Was
it influenced by God? Absolutely. However, I realized in that moment
that the truth was that everything was influenced by God. I also saw that
at times we rather poorly attempt to speak as we believe God would speak
to us. We put words in God's mouth. Even when we knew we could not
possibly know how God spoke.

These words reminded me in those dark nights, even though I was alone
in my life, I was never going to be alone again. Others had gone before me,
made decisions before me, lived lives before me. If they had not, I couldn't
be there, in that moment. I wrote the words, "When the world is dark, cold
and grey, and dawn is a long way away, then the thought of you brings the
sun in the middle of the night."

In the middle of that night, I realized I would never be alone. I could
always speak with God. I could listen to God. I could argue with God. I
could love God. I could just chat with God, be quiet, and listen so that I
could begin to love myself again.

Day 122

Read: 1 Chronicles 6

These were the locations of their settlements allotted as their territory.
—1 Chronicles 6:54

I started to rebuild my life one step at a time—sometimes slipping back, catching myself, and stepping back on track. I know I failed a lot, much like the addict who slides back into addiction. It really wasn't easy, but in the back of my mind was my mother saying, *Stephen, if it was easy, God wouldn't have asked you to do it!*

I was feeling pretty sorry for myself as Christmas approached. I had volunteered to work extra shifts to cover for others with families so they could be home. For various reasons, I wasn't going to see my sons as they would be with their mother and her parents. I couldn't travel up to Scotland to see my parents, so I would be alone in London. My local pub in London had become a home away from home, but on Christmas Day, even the pubs close. The couple who ran the pub asked me what I was doing for Christmas, and I shared that because of working late on Christmas Eve, I wasn't able to spend it with my family, so they invited me to be with them in the pub where a few would be gathering.

When I walked in on Christmas Day afternoon, I was surprised to see not only several locals, but a few people I had not met before. They were thrilled I had come, and one of them immediately said, "After all, you are family." I laughed, but they said, "No, really, we're related through your grandmother's family."

Suddenly, I found I had a whole new extended family I never knew I had, who lived near me, worked the fruit and vegetable market in Camden Town right by me, and would continue to be my friends for a long time to come. They were *salt of the earth* people, just like my grandmother.

Day 123

Read: 1 Chronicles 7–8

Benjamin was the father of Bela his firstborn, Ashbel the second son, Aharah the third, Nohah the fourth and Rapha the fifth.

—1 Chronicles 8:1–2

Good *down to earth* people are hard to find. I sat surrounded by at least a dozen people who patiently explained to me how through my grandmother and great-grandmother's families, we were related through marriage. Sometimes, we were connected by common law marriage, where they—to put it in their own words—"didn't bother with that legal or church stuff." But they were related to me. One couple had been *together* for over fifty years since they were in high school. Both left school at sixteen: one because she was pregnant, the other to get a job and support her. They now had five children, and he ran a market stall which supported them well.

When I thought I was a stranger, alone in the world, I found I had a family who accepted me as I was. They laughed a lot. Cursed a lot. Smoked and drank beer a lot. It felt like the below-deck party from the *Titanic* movie. Good people having fun. I thought I knew who my family was, but that Christmas evening, I came to really know who my family was. It was the man who ran a market stall selling fruit and vegetables. It was his wife, who cleaned houses and knitted and sewed all year to make her children Christmas presents to wear—hats, gloves, dresses, even a homemade pair of blue jeans.

Somebody gave me a package to open. Inside, I found a really long knitted scarf, just like Dr Who! I simply said *Thank you.* I wasn't sure who gave it to me, but I thanked everybody for everything. In the process, I found myself thanking God for bringing me to this point in my life.

Lesson learned: God is looking out for us, and we never know who our family is or where our paths with them will cross.

Day 124

Read: 1 Chronicles 9–11

All Israel was listed in the genealogies recorded in the book of the kings of Israel and Judah.

—1 Chronicles 9:1

On the day after Christmas, I wrote to my grandmother, sharing with her the fun time I had the day before and the names of the people I found myself related to. It seemed strange to write down the names of people I only knew from the pub and yet felt close to because of their warmth and unconditional acceptance. To them, I was the stranger they welcomed, and fed, and gave comfort and succor. I was the one made welcome in their *home*.

I was working that day after Christmas at the BBC, and all day, I noticed things I hadn't seen before. People I hadn't sat with before in the cafeteria. People who were far from their homes and families, strangers in a foreign land. At that time, we broadcast in about forty languages on the BBC World Service. On that day after Christmas, Boxing Day in England, I think I heard every one of those forty languages being spoken as they shared stories, news items, and joy with the world. Not all of them were broadcasting to countries where Christianity was the primary religion, yet the message was translated and welcomed wherever it was shared.

In between broadcasting sessions, we gathered in the cafeteria to simply be together, sharing each other's company in a way I'd not experienced before. I listened to stories from all over the world that day, realizing how close we truly were to each other in our lives and beliefs. Many of the language service members were missing their home countries, which they left for their own safety and the safety of their families. This season of Christmas made their separation from family back home all the harder. A lot of comfort food was eaten that day.

Day 125

Read: 1 Chronicles 12–14

*Let us bring the ark of our God back to us, for we did not
inquire of it during the reign of Saul.*

—1 Chronicles 13:3

One of the things that happens when we sit and listen to people from another country talk is we find out the differences and similarities between our lives. We also share what different phrases mean in different languages. On that night shift, one of the people from Southern India asked when I had seen the writing on the wall, and who had written it. After going backward and forward a few times, I realized he meant about my marriage and divorce.

His words were a form of shorthand for something that had been obvious to many around me and oblivious to me until someone else pointed it out. It had taken me a while to realize that my marriage, which I viewed as sacramental, wasn't sacred anymore and maybe, for my wife, it had never been. Listening to my colleague from another country talk about it, I could see all the signs were there, and yet, I chose to ignore them.

I didn't want to be seen as a failure in my marriage when my sisters had stuck with their difficult marriages. Then, I realized that *till death do us part* can also mean until the death of the relationship. That day and night shift, listening and chatting between our broadcasts to countries all over the world, I gained greater clarity in what God wanted me to hear, and it took a person from thousands of miles away, from another culture and language, to help me hear God's message. It was as if I had to reach far and wide to hear. I had much more to learn if I was open to listening. I needed to keep my heart open, which was harder to do than I thought.

Day 126

Read: 1 Chronicles 15–17

Give thanks to the Lord, for he is good; his love endures forever.

—1 Chronicles 16:34

I think it was on that double day and night shift that I first heard a voice within me, urging me to truly glorify God, do it compassionately, and bring an awareness of God's presence to every person in the world. What still hadn't become clear in my head was *how*. Trusting God would *show me or guide me* was not exactly what I wanted to hear.

Yet I had to wait, listen, and wait some more. I thought if I just tried harder, and maybe smarter, I would *get it* and find a way to do whatever it was God wanted me to do. Yet, like David in the book of Chronicles, I wanted to do it my way. Again, it was another colleague from a country far away who shared the words I hadn't wanted to hear but needed to: *Let go and let God!*

I needed to let go, humble myself, and let God guide me. There were so many things tempting me down so many paths. So many people whispering in my ear. So many opportunities being laid before me. I was unsure, and hesitation led me down some wrong paths. I feel now that it was often out of my stubbornness that I shut out God's voice and didn't fully listen to the Spirit that had been shared with me.

Later in life, I would hear the words of confession, not for the first time, nor for the last, asking for forgiveness *for things done and left undone*. Those words reached out to me, reminding me of that double day and night shift and the words of strangers who saw me better than I could see myself—strangers who saw within me a calling that took years to find, hear, understand, and accept.

Day 127

Read: 1 Chronicles 18–21

Lord my God, let your hand fall on me and my family, but do not let this plague remain on your people.

—1 Chronicles 21:17

Could I really hear God's voice? I turned what was a voice in my head into chatter. It fought with all the other voices, sounds, and distractions in my life. I often thought I was doing what I was supposed to be doing, yet, in my heart, I knew some of the things I was doing were wrong. I needed to simplify my life; I was running from one thing to another—turning from one relationship to another. I needed to go to fewer places each day. I needed to share my time with less people. I needed to do less. I needed to have less mess in my life, declutter and strip away stuff, and empty myself, so I could make space for what was next.

This need became particularly important with personal relationships. I turned from one person to another, constantly accepting more than friendship but shutting down if it became too intimate or close. Being deeply hurt gave me no excuse to hurt others emotionally by being unavailable to them. Yet the pain and the inability to trust another person was front and center in my life.

Where was God in all this? I should have asked: Where was I? It was me who went missing, not God. I realize now that God was there all the time. Like David, I wasn't open to hearing God or truly finding God in my life at that time. It was too inconvenient. I didn't want to stop living the way I was, yet part of me was so empty, it hurt. When I stopped to sit and read the Bible or pray or journal about my life, I couldn't feel anything. So, I just carried on, going through the motions—accepting the physical side of love, yet denying the emotional side completely.

Day 128

Read: 1 Chronicles 22–24

The duty of the Levites was to help Aaron's descendants in the service of the temple of the Lord.

—1 Chronicles 23:28

I tried. I really tried. I got involved with a local church again. I threw myself into doing things for the church, serving in whatever way I could. However, I felt I was being dishonest because I was running from one relationship to another. Running constantly. Experiencing something new, somebody new. But, the relationships were the same, empty of feeling. I realized that in none of those relationships would I find the spiritual root I was searching for—the relationship to fill the aching void deep in my soul.

Several times I thought I'd found *the* relationship, yet each time it shattered and vanished before my eyes. So, I continued to stay busy, worked long hours, explored new work possibilities, stayed detached. At the same time, I was doing anything to help others, from covering their work to helping them move home. Always available. That's what I became. The person who could always be counted on to help. Always there, but never truly present.

The church became my refuge, my place to be present, if at all. I was able to apply my ability at planning and organizing to making church services happen and happen smoothly, without mistakes. Doing this work allowed me to empty myself before God in a different way by serving something greater than my own needs. The downside of this was that I could do this almost on automatic, which was good—and bad. Still, I did not hear what God was saying to me. I thought I did. I still wasn't listening, really listening, and understanding. Not then.

Day 129

Read: 1 Chronicles 25–27

All these men were under the supervision of their father for the music of the temple of the Lord, with cymbals, lyres, and harps, for the ministry at the house of God.

—1 Chronicles 25:6

There was something about the sounds of an acapella group chanting music, chanting prayers, echoing in the stillness of a church. I became involved with recording and broadcasting music from a church in Westminster.

For a while, I thought I was changing. Yet, as I got involved with someone and shared my feelings, I found they didn't feel the same way. Worse, I was completely off the mark. How could I be so wrong and misjudge the situation? My loneliness, in some ways, echoed David's— who, surrounded by thousands, was always alone in his heart. He, too, kept himself busy— planning, organizing, building.

I took on a BBC position organizing live actuality clips people could hear around the world, things being said by people across the UK. I seemed to have a knack for spotting the one sentence or phrase that could sum up the moment. The clips could come from a celebrity or a politician, a man in the street, or just a passerby. Somehow, I could capture the moment in a few recorded words, which I could share with all the foreign language services. In turn, they could share them in their stories broadcast around the world.

The beauty of this position to me was its anonymity. I worked away for hours on my own in a small windowless room with feeds of sound from all over the country running through the space—switching from one to another, capturing the moment. It was a time when I could *lick my wounds* and heal myself. Or in the very British way, I could stuff it down and not deal with it, much as David often did. Like him, I turned to writing poetry and words to songs. They were often more like laments, though gradually, they became stronger and more like songs of praise.

Day 130

Read: 1 Chronicles 28–29

Everything comes from you, and we have given you only what comes from your hand. We are foreigners and strangers in your sight, as were all our ancestors.

—1 Chronicles 29:14–15

It was quite amazing working for the BBC World Service. No matter where a worker had grown up, they were suddenly part of a new tribe—a tribe of people set on sharing the truth about things in the world with as many as would listen. The people who worked alongside me came from countries all over the world. Former diplomats, scientists, prime ministers, princes, and kings were all translating stories into their original languages. It was an incredible place to experience, much like a *Tower of Babel* after it had been split into a multitude of languages.

People were in the building day and night, and as the sun moved around the world, so did our transmissions. We opened with programs to Japan and China in the early hours and moved across the Far East countries, crossing to India, Pakistan, and Persia, with programs heard in Tibet and Mongolia. Transmissions in various Russian and Slavic languages would follow, then Eastern European with Turkish and Greek, then a plethora of African languages, and the transmissions to western European countries followed. Then suddenly, we would be transmitting to South America, Canada, and the United States.

The next day, we started all over again . Like a hungry animal with an insatiable appetite, the feeds kept going and going, and I kept giving and giving. I worked shifts and times when I didn't know what time or day it was when I went outside to go home. Through it all, I was sure what I was doing, though draining me of everything I could give, was what I was meant to do. I would sit on a bench outside before going home to think for a moment about my shift, and pray, thanking God for helping me through my tasks and guiding me in my work.

Day 131

Read: 2 Chronicles 1–5

Then the temple of the Lord was filled with the cloud, and the priests could not perform their service because of the cloud, for the glory of the Lord filled the temple of God.

—2 Chronicles 5:13–14

While sitting one morning on a bench a few blocks from work in a small public garden area overlooking the river Thames, it hit me. I found myself unexplainably crying, sobbing even. The effects of several years of working and giving my all washed over me. I felt full, yet empty. At the same moment, when I looked around me, everything was normal. Traffic noise rumbled in the background as cars, buses, and trucks motored along. Boats were moving on the river. People were coming out of the underground station and walking off to their offices. A newsagent was handing out newspapers by the entrance to the station and occasionally calling out the news headlines. Birds were hovering around me, swooping down to look for scraps or crumbs that may have been dropped days before. My head was full.

As I sat there, I found myself talking to someone. Not myself, and yet it felt like it was someone inside of me. I was looking for answers, yet the voice was telling me to stop, *just stop.* So I did, and after a while, I found myself looking around and seeing everything as if in slow motion. People seemed to speed up as it grew quieter. My head gradually cleared of all the busyness buzzing around in it. Everything around me seemed sharper, brighter, clearer. A bird flew down and settled on the arm of the bench and sat with its head to one side looking at me, caring for me. I felt like I had felt so many years before sitting in my pram on my parents' front porch as a child: safe with God.

Day 132

Read: 2 Chronicles 6–8

But the Lord said to my father David, "You did well to have it in your heart to build a temple for my Name. Nevertheless, you are not the one to build the temple, but your son, your own flesh and blood, he is the one who will build the temple for my Name."

—2 Chronicles 6:9

At what point do we really hear the words others speak? Clearly lots of words were and have buzzed through my head. Sitting there that day much like my grandmother would, Bible in my lap, quietly watching life go by, I realized that it was in my heart, in my mind, that I could find the answers I searched for. Later, I would realize it was not a physical building to worship in that I searched for. The temple I searched for was the temple within myself.

I suddenly understood what David and Solomon were sharing with us. It was in David's heart to build a temple, yet God guided David to allow his own flesh and blood to build a temple. Sitting there that morning, so many thoughts ran through my mind. I knew there were things I did that were not good, and somehow in this reading, Solomon recognized that we screw up sometimes. He shared a prayer with us to help us understand how we could seek forgiveness. If we truly sought forgiveness, then God would forgive, and we could forgive ourselves too. If we chose to mess up and did not seek forgiveness, then we would be like a heap of rubble, and disaster would happen to us.

This all seemed very judgmental to me, and I began to realize even more why the interpretation of scripture is so critical. How easy it was to take a passage and misapply it! It made me realize I needed to stop, think, pray, and explore how to understand these texts better. A long journey lay ahead.

Day 133

Read: 2 Chronicles 9–12

But Rehoboam rejected the advice the elders gave him and consulted the young men who had grown up with him and were serving him.

—2 Chronicles 10:8

My father had studied for the ministry at one point, then found marriage, family, and working were where his heart lay. Yet he continued with lay ministry throughout his life, serving in various ways. After he retired, he was ordained under Canon 9 to serve in the Borders of Scotland to bring communion service to several Border churches. As I thought about this, I realized I could maybe follow his guidance.

Yet, I wasn't him. I had a stubbornness in me that led me down different paths, sometimes at an almost completely opposite direction to what he might have chosen. I made excuses about not attending church regularly, often because I had been out with people the night before with fun-loving friends who wanted to party. I found many of these friends saw me as crazy if I even attempted to talk about the Bible or God. They only wanted to talk about music and celebrities. The group was mainly younger people who had joined the BBC after I did and came from backgrounds different than mine.

I was rudderless again and didn't see how this matched with the stories I read in scripture. It was as if a veil had been pulled over them, so I couldn't understand. I seemed to be on a pendulum as my life swung from one side to another. Somehow, through all those days and nights, I was able to continue to find the space and time to read my Bible, often in a quiet place or brief moment of time. I still always picked it up and continued reading from where I had stopped. This method kept me moving forward when other systems of following a lectionary (a prescribed set of readings arranged by date) might have been too hard to sustain.

Day 134

Read: 2 Chronicles 13–17

He repaired the altar of the Lord that was in front of the portico of the Lord's temple.

—2 Chronicles 15:8

I took my twin sons to visit my parents in Scotland and gave a lift to a friend who wanted a lift to the Edinburgh Festival. My mother knew I had been involved with several different people in London and thought that my friend and I were involved, so was surprised when I explained that we were actually just friends. I left my twin sons with their grandparents while I took my friend on up to the Festival in Edinburgh, dropping her off with some other friends there.

On the way back, I drove back down the coast to the walled town of Berwick on Tweed. It was still dark, and I sat by the river Tweed for a few minutes before deciding that instead of driving back along the river to my parents' home, I would drive on down the coast a short distance further. Something pulled me onward to the Island of Lindisfarne on the coast. The tide was just going out, and I was able to cross the causeway over to Holy Island. This was the first time I had been there totally on my own. I had visited with my parents before and taken my twin sons there but had never been alone. I crossed the causeway with the ruins of the abbey in front of me. I stopped, parked, and left my car. I was alone with the wind blowing across the ruined abbey, with the sound of the sea and sounds of calling birds. Running through my head were the sounds of the worship here, of the destruction of this place, the lives lost. I sat alone on a ruined stone wall, feeling the pain. I waited and prayed. As the sun rose from the east over the ruined abbey, I could feel my soul sing out.

Day 135

Read: 2 Chronicles 18–20

You rule over all the kingdoms of the nations. Power and might are in your hand, and no one can withstand you.

—2 Chronicles 20:6

A small bird alighted on the wall just along from me. It hopped toward me and stopped a short way off, head turned to one side. We sat like that for what seemed like an age. Then, it turned and flew off toward the sunrise. I looked around at the ruins, feeling the faith that had built it, the power of the place, and the sadness of its ending. The blessing of the abbey rang through my body, and all I could hear were prayers in the wind.

A lone person walked along a path at the edge of the ruins, reading from a prayer book, continuing the tradition of centuries. Suddenly, I felt a peace roll over me—a peace that passes all understanding. I still find it hard to explain, but I felt this peace deep within me.

I returned back across the causeway, following the river Tweed back to my parents' home, where everyone was still sleeping. I sat in the kitchen, a large room warmed by an Aga stove, and after a while, my father came down, and we sat in the kitchen sipping tea. I shared with him my side journey to Holy Island, and he listened, then said he was glad I still explored my faith and hadn't lost touch with it. I didn't realize that to him and my mother I'd seemed to lose my faith and was a *lost soul*. With my divorce and a job with the BBC, which was so far removed from their experience, it shouldn't have surprised me, but it did. I shared with him that I always searched, and would continue to search, and felt I had many temptations placed in my path to test me.

He reached out, placed his hand on mine, and we sat quietly as the house stirred.

Day 136

Read: 2 Chronicles 21–24

Although the Lord sent prophets to the people to bring them back to him, and though they testified against them, they would not listen.

—2 Chronicles 24:19

As we sat in their kitchen, I clarified for both my parents that I was not in a serious relationship with anyone. My mother was clearly upset, cautioning me about how I was living my life and the consequences of turning away from my faith. She continued for a while about the impact of how I was perceived by others. She wanted me to set a better example, especially to my twin sons.

Suddenly my mother got up and left the room to see if the twins were awake, leaving me with my father. He asked if I was still going to church and setting aside time to pray every day. I shared I was going to church, but I wasn't as regular as I used to be and felt a bit lost, which was why I had stopped at Holy Island on my way back from Edinburgh. Something was missing in my life, and I felt it. Stopping for a few moments on Holy Island really spoke to me, I said. It was as if I could hear God's voice in the wind and the waves and the birds—and the silence. I didn't know what it meant, but I heard it.

After a pause, my father said maybe I needed to go on retreat, maybe to my sister's godfather at the monastery in Devon, but I should focus first on the visit with my sons and helping them have a good time with their grandparents, as we never knew how long we had. It was the first time I had ever heard him talk of his own life in this way, and I wondered if he was unwell, but he didn't show anything. My focus for the next few days was totally on my sons and my parents, helping each enjoy their time together.

Day 137

Read: 2 Chronicles 25–27

Jotham grew powerful because he walked steadfastly before the Lord his God.
—2 Chronicles 27:6

My sons disappeared after lunch, and my parents and I couldn't find them at first. Then, we heard voices coming from my grandmother's room. There they all were. My grandmother was sitting in her favorite upright chair, my twin sons sitting at her feet, eating cookies while listening to her reading very, very slowly from her Bible. I mentally time-warped back to when it was me sitting at her feet in London and realizing how she could not really read as she had been in service from the age of seven.

Here she was reading, albeit very slowly, to my twin four-year-old sons. They sat still, eating their cookies, hanging on every word she said. I realized in that moment that I hadn't been reading every day like she was and needed to get back to that daily habit. I took seeing my grandmother reading with my sons as a sign that this was a way of guiding me back to God. We went for several other outings while staying with my parents, back to Holy Island, down to Bamburgh Castle, across to the ruins of Coldingham Priory, up the river to the ruins of Melrose Abbey, and across to Abbotsford. At each place, we ate picnics my mother had prepared, and my sons could run around among the ruins or gardens while my parents and grandmother could sit, watch, and reminisce about their lives.

Each place prompted me to listen. Listen to the spirits of those who had gone before. Listen to the long-gone voices of those who had built places to worship. Listen to the prayers of those who had walked in faith before. Listen to the memories of my parents and grandmother. Listen to the questions from my sons as they searched for answers in their young lives.

Day 138

Read: 2 Chronicles 28–31

Come to his sanctuary, which he has consecrated forever.

—2 Chronicles 30:8

My mother asked me if I could help her clean and prepare the church for Sunday. So, I made it into an adventure for my sons, sharing the history of their little church of St Mary's in Coldstream. Initially, it was just a room in a shop, then a little tin roof chapel, and finally a stone church. As we approached the church, I showed them the foundation stone laid in 1913 and shared with them that if we looked south from the church across the River Tweed we could see where they fought the Battle of Flodden Field between the English and the Scots. I told them the following week we would see a big parade of horses and riders come through the town past my parents' house as they commemorated this battle, riding from Coldstream down to Flodden Field where they would hold a service.

Even though they were really young, my sons seemed to be thrilled to know this history, which made walking up to the church more fun and interesting to them. While my mother and I set the altar, I sent the boys to find windows with birds and pictures in them, and they scampered around until they found the dove window and other stained-glass windows. While my mother and I set the altar, all we could hear were the two boys running around laughing, which my mother reminded me was exactly what I did so many years before. As we worked together, prayed together over the altar linens, prayed together over the chalice and burse, I realized I was still steeped in the traditions of the church, which constantly brought me back to God. As we worked together, I felt something wash over me and knew it was the presence of God watching over us.

Day 139

Read: 2 Chronicles 32–34

*The king stood by his pillar and renewed the covenant in the presence
of the Lord to follow the Lord and keep his commands, statutes and
decrees with all his heart and all his soul, and to obey the words of the
covenant written in this book.*

—2 Chronicles 34:31

Sitting with my grandmother on our last day of our visit to my parents, I realized how much I missed sitting with her for a few hours each day and reading the Bible together. It felt very comfortable and brought back many memories of our habit in London. I realized how far I had moved out of my comfort zone by living on my own, and also how much I had—and hadn't—managed to keep faith with. Reading the Bible every day had not been the top of my agenda as I had gotten *too busy* to do that.

I had challenged the limits of my comfort zone and had grown as a person, yet I lost some of the person I was in the process. The balance I was seeking was sitting with my grandmother, reading and thinking about the words we shared from the Bible. I had expanded my *comfort zone* to include new ideas, new activities, new goals, and new experiences, yet I had not found a way, until then, to balance those changes with the faith traditions of my upbringing. I saw that reading each day, just a little, could help me develop the tools I needed to cope with the changes and challenges I was facing. Listening to the words written so long ago, listening to the ups and downs in the lives of biblical characters and how they dealt with those challenges could help me meet the challenges I faced too.

I wondered: How I would fare going forward if I kept the covenants in the way Josiah said he would with all the elders of Judah and Jerusalem? That afternoon, before getting ready for our drive back to London, I felt I had taken two steps forward. I just hoped and prayed I would not take three steps back.

Day 140

Read: 2 Chronicles 35–36

Any of his people among you may go up and may the Lord their God be with them.

—2 Chronicles 36:23

Before we left my parents, we spent the morning in church, gathering afterward for coffee hour with other members of the parish. I soon realized how my mother needed to *show off* her grandchildren to other church members. I think it was a bit confusing for my sons; however, they dutifully greeted people and were bribed with chocolate-covered cookies. I also got to meet people my parents had talked or written about, as if I knew them as intimately as they did.

My father introduced me to former Prime Minister Lord Home, who was a neighbor and friend, who would play a crucial part in my own life and decisions later on. On that day, we just shared concerns about the weather and driving back to London, ordinary exchanges between people of faith.

My sons fell asleep as I drove the six hours back south, leaving me with my thoughts about the visit and the readings shared with my grandmother: How easy would it be for me to slip back into the habits I had before? What might it mean if I let go of the experience I had and went back to the ways I would be pressured to return to in London?

As I drove, my mind raced over all the things that could distract me away from just being in relationship with God and reading the Bible every day. After I dropped off my sons with their mother, the traffic grew busier on the drive back into London, and my mind focused on what faced me at work and in my life: How would I stay engaged in reading the Bible every day? How would I make the time? How would I build on this past week's experiences?

Day 141

Read: Ezra 1–3

And all the people gave a great shout of praise to the Lord, because the foundation of the house of the Lord was laid.

—Ezra 3:11

I started going to a new church on Albany Street, at least new to me. This was near my home in London, and I had driven by it many times without going in. I had always liked the Greek style on the outside and its interesting location, bridging between a public housing estate and a row of crown properties as if it was sitting on the fence between two worlds. I soon discovered it was a church in a period of transformation from what was once the core of the community to something else. It had a school attached to it, which, for many years, seemed to have had very little interaction with the church.

I started attending on Sundays, and then slowly interacted with some of its members as I saw them in the neighborhood. I could almost hear my parents' sigh of relief, or jump for joy, as I shared that I was back in church on Sundays. I think my mother was crying, though my father was just happy. A few weeks after I started there, I found out that they were going through an interregnum, an even bigger transition than I suspected. The senior and junior wardens of the church shared with me the diocese wanted to close them and merge them with a nearby church whose services and way of worshiping were very different. I hadn't been there for more than a few weeks when they were asking me to step up and take on some responsibility in the church so that the senior warden could concentrate on contesting the closure.

I asked for time to consider what they were sharing with me. In my heart, I wanted time to talk with my father about this.

Day 142

Read: Ezra 4–7

Because the hand of the Lord my God was on me, I took courage and gathered leaders from Israel to go up with me.

—Ezra 7:28

When I shared with my father what I understood of the issue at the church, my father reminded me of the words of the prayer by Thomas Merton:

> My Lord God, I have no idea where I am going. I do not see the road ahead of me. I cannot know for certain where it will end. Nor do I really know myself, and the fact that I think that I am following your will does not mean that I am actually doing so. But I believe that the desire to please you does in fact please you. And I hope I have that desire in all that I am doing. I hope that I will never do anything apart from that desire. And I know that if I do this you will lead me by the right road, though I may know nothing about it. Therefore, I will trust you always, though I may seem to be lost and in the shadow of death. I will not fear, for you are ever with me, and you will never leave me to face my perils alone (Merton 1956).

I spent the next few years listening to parishioners as the case between our church and the diocese rolled onward. Over a period of time and discussion, we moved the people to recognize that we would close and merge; however, we could be instrumental in deciding how our building would be used after we left. My father reminded me the church I had grown up in had transitioned to a Greek Orthodox church and suggested I reach out to them to find if they had need. When I shared this with others at church, I was asked to find out if there was any interest from the Greek Orthodox community.

Day 143

Read: Ezra 8–10

So, we fasted and petitioned our God about this, and he answered our prayer.

—Ezra 8:23

Christ Church, Albany Street had a long history. It was built in the Greek style with a beautiful arch and apse over the altar and handmade windows by Dante Rosetti and Willian Morris. Christina Rosetti worshipped there when she wrote the famous poem that became the Christmas carol, "In the Bleak Midwinter." The Blues and Royals household regiments had a long history with the church, and the first Duke of Wellington had given the organ to the church. So much history, so few people.

As we sat in a circle in the parish room, the thirty remaining members shared their stories: their births, their marriages, their children, their deaths. I listened and felt the gut-wrenching pain this remnant of a parish shared with each other as they faced the reality of letting go of the place they loved. We arranged a service to close the church and a service to welcome the new congregation of Greek Orthodox Christians who would be taking over the building. We all signed the papers from the diocese, and it was done.

Yet, God works in mysterious ways. The Greek Orthodox Christians, whose church had originated in Antioch in Syria, invited all the members of the parish back to celebrate their decision to make the church their Cathedral of St. George for the whole of the United Kingdom. What was once a sad and dying church became a thriving and joyous community, busy and lively every day and active across the community. Somehow God had led us to a positive decision, answering the needs of the church in many ways we could not have imagined.

I shared this with my parents, whose comment was: *right people, at the right time, open to listening and believing God has a reason, even when we can't see it at first.*

Day 144

Read: Nehemiah 1–3

Even if your exiled people are at the farthest horizon, I will gather them from there and bring them to the place I have chosen as a dwelling for my Name.
—Nehemiah 1:9

Bringing two churches together is not easy. Traditions are deeply ingrained, and there were a lot of hurt feelings at first. Some people simply stopped coming to church. Others came but complained about everything. Something else was going on within the diocese at the time that most people were not even aware of. The bishop of the diocese felt that ordaining women to ministry was not scripturally correct, so that even though many of us felt it was the way to go, the priest in our parish did not think so and supported his bishop.

Lots of arguments and discussions were held and not just at church. Parishioners had heated arguments in local shops, and in the local pubs and coffee shops as well. Several of us wanted to merge the two congregations and grow by shifting to a more modern view of *church*. It all came to a head when the archbishop asked the diocesan bishop to resign, and a new bishop was chosen.

The former bishop went public and told everybody that, even though married himself, he would embrace the Roman Catholic church and invited his clergy to join him. Many of the priests across the diocese decided they agreed with him, and almost half the priests left the Anglican Church and applied to join the Roman Catholic Church. Interestingly, the lay leaders of the church stayed focused on opening the doors and finding priests to bring communion to the church, rather than the bishop's attempt to take the churches over to Rome.

It appeared that in rebuilding the church, merging churches together, and finding new clergy, the church was not only going to survive, but grow and reach out in ways it had never been able to before.

Day 145

Read: Nehemiah 4–6

Nothing like what you are saying is happening; you are just making it up out of your head.

—Nehemiah 6:8

The priest who had overseen the closing of our church was furious with our lay leaders because we had been successful in finding the Greek Orthodox Church to take over the building on a long lease. This meant the church building was not sold for redevelopment—with the money going to the diocese or to the merged church. He spread rumors about what we wanted to do in the merged church, particularly, that we wanted to change the church dramatically.

When we became aware of what he was saying to the others, we decided to have a parish-wide meeting about it. Almost every member of the church was there, including the priest. Several of the older parishioners were angry because they believed what the priest was saying, so I suggested we start the meeting with a prayer.

As soon as we prayed together, the mood of the room changed. It's hard to be mad with someone after praying with them. Within a few minutes, it became clear that the priest had been spreading rumors about us, and the senior warden informed him that we would be asking the bishop to remove him as our priest. He left the meeting. We struggled for a while but found priests to bring us communion, and with guidance from the new bishop, we became more united, stronger, and more focused on what we knew to be our mission in that location. We also stayed in touch with the Greek Orthodox church, and they came to Easter and Christmas services as our guests, and we visited them for their Christmas and Easter services as their guests.

Day 146

Read: Nehemiah 7

Now the city was large and spacious, but there were few people in it, and the houses had not yet been rebuilt.

—Nehemiah 7:4

Even with merging the two churches together, it was still almost 80 percent empty on Sunday. The church was a large church, and an empty church most of the time. We decided to have a second parish-wide meeting, but this time, we had food. Everybody was asked to bring something for the potluck—a third was asked to bring main dishes, a third side dishes, and a third dessert. There was probably enough food to feed everybody for a month!

After everyone started eating, the senior warden stood up and asked people if they were enjoying our newly merged parish? The feedback around the room was very positive. He looked across the room at me and asked if I would come forward and share some ideas. For the next few minutes, I shared ideas with them. First, we could go out in pairs to knock on doors and let people know we were here and what time we met. Second, we could start lay-led Bible study three times a week: once for men, once for women, and once for children—when the mothers could meet and have a break from watching their kids for a while.

I shared that these were only the first ideas, and I was sure more would come along as we grew in numbers. One person immediately suggested displaying art by local artists around the church, another suggested starting a scout group, another restarting the choir. Suddenly, the space was full of life as ideas flowed, and people stepped up to help and make a difference. The senior warden and I both felt that when the new priest came to the church, we would have lots to share with them and new life in the church.

Day 147

Read: Nehemiah 8–9

*All the people came together as one in the square before the Water Gate. They
told Ezra the teacher of the Law to bring out the Book of the Law of
Moses, which the Lord had commanded for Israel.*

—Nehemiah 8:1

An interesting thing happened. Two churches that had both been
struggling to stay alive came together—even though they didn't want to—
and found new life. A church that had sat empty most of the time, suddenly
had something going on every day— sometimes two or three times a day
and into the evening. Not only that, but the church was also lay-inspired
with people stepping up to the plate and taking ownership of their church.

The three Bible studies took off and expanded to include a men's group
at midday because quite a few men worked in the area and wanted to meet
in the middle of the day. Because these men were not local to the church,
they came back and visited on Sundays with their families, which again,
grew the church.

A group of women formed a group that focused on childcare and
also a teens group. Remarkably, where there had been division, there was
now unity. An after-school group started to meet to help new immigrants
advance their English skills by reading, and the local artists, who initially
were only going to display their own work, started teaching small groups
so that others could draw and paint, make pots, and sculpt.

It really was as if the church had been in exile and returned to a newer
and better life. Potluck suppers and potluck breakfasts, especially after
services on Sunday, became a common thing to do. Neighbors, who had
crossed the road and passed each other in the street a few months before,
were now becoming the best of friends. The number of people attending
church grew, and they came from both sides of the street that had formally
divided them. They crossed the divide, and diversity was incredible.

Day 148

Read: Nehemiah 10–11

We also assume responsibility for bringing to the house of the Lord each year the first fruits of our crops and of every fruit tree.

—Nehemiah 10:35

The potluck suppers took on a life of their own. Because many people who lived in the public housing area came from countries far away, they had totally different ideas about what to eat. The range of foods and meals became incredible. People from other parts of London started coming to the potlucks, and the church realized it had a new ministry in feeding the homeless and those who couldn't afford hot meals. One group of men started serving an early breakfast for some of the homeless and read from the daily office to them while they ate. One person commented that it was like being at a monastery in which one of the brothers would read while the other brothers ate in silence.

As the body of people in the church grew in both numbers and diversity, worship changed too. One service always followed the traditional way; however, there were services at different times that suited different people. Especially popular was a more contemplative service held on Sunday evenings, following the traditional format of Compline (which means *completion*), a night prayer led by a small acapella choir with the church in candlelight.

The year after these changes, the altar and the chancel at the Harvest Festival groaned from the enormous amount of food brought by people in the neighborhood. Members of church came together, boxed it up, and then spent several days distributing it to seniors living alone. These church members were able to ask the seniors about their needs as they began to build new relationships between them and the church. The whole community changed in a very short time as people brought their gifts to God through the church.

Day 149

Read: Nehemiah 12–13

When evening shadows fell on the gates of Jerusalem before the Sabbath, I ordered the doors to be shut and not opened until the Sabbath was over. I stationed some of my own men at the gates so that no load could be brought in on the Sabbath day.

—Nehemiah 13:19

I went out of town for a few months for my work with the BBC, so I had not been at church for a while. When I finally had the opportunity to attend again, I was surprised to find several tables set up in the parish hall, selling items that had nothing to do with church—and selling them on Sunday, both before and after church. The sellers weren't fundraising for the church as far as I could see, so I asked the senior warden about them.

He shared that the church had a summer fair, and several vendors attended who had nothing to do with the church, but people seemed to like buying things from them: scented candles, scarves, jewelry, and some paintings of the neighborhood. I asked him if he felt this practice was in alignment with the mission and goals of the church. We discussed it, and he agreed it probably wasn't. I asked if the vendors gave anything to the church or toward the church's ministries, and he said they didn't.

He brought it to the next parish council meeting, and they decided to not have vendors in the church buildings on Sundays. Instead, they would host a Saturday *market* open to all local craft people. After the discussion, several members said they felt it restored the proper balance of Sundays being reserved for worship and better ensured balance with the local community. In fact, hosting the market on Saturdays grew the number of vendors, which not only helped support the church but also increased the involvement of the local community.

Day 150

Read: Esther 1–5

But Mordecai found out about the plot and told Queen Esther, who in turn reported it to the king, giving credit to Mordecai.

—Esther 2:22

My grandmother asked my mother to phone me. She wanted me to reach out to her son-in-law, my uncle, who was a police officer in London. I was to ask him whom we needed to speak to in order to help some old friends of hers. When I asked who needed help, it turned out that her friends were all women who worked the streets around King Cross. They were women, or daughters of women, she had first befriended after World War I when so many of them had been left without their husbands after the war. Many of these women had little choice in how they supported their families, and my grandmother had always done whatever she could to help them.

I reached out to my uncle. At first, he was surprised when I shared my grandmother's call with him. However, he reached out to his superiors and did what he could. He called me back to say there had been an "edict from on high" to "clean-up" the area, and maybe they were being a bit enthusiastic in arresting the women in the area. I suggested he tell them it would be more effective if they arrested the men who controlled the women, or altered the roads so the men who were *curb crawling* could no longer do so.

Before he could do so, the women organized themselves for the first time and occupied a church in King's Cross—the church where my parents married and my grandmother had worshipped. Suddenly, it was on the national news. My mother called and asked me to pray for the women, that they would be safe. She reminded me that my grandmother shared that poverty was at the root of this.

Day 151

Read: Esther 6–10

Then Queen Esther answered, "If I have found favor with you, Your Majesty, and if it pleases you, grant me my life, this is my petition. And spare my people, this is my request."

—Esther 7:3

How do we change society? It was clear to me that these women were struggling to live their lives in the current economy and were using whatever they could to survive. The national coverage showed how they were being hurt and mistreated by the police, the local council, and the media in general. By standing by them, the church showed the world how to be living true to the words of scripture.

My grandmother had a hard life, as I have shared. However, things had changed. Child labor laws and social services had improved over the years, so that children were not being sold into service at seven-years-old anymore in England. The media coverage exposed a side of life that needed to change, and members of parliament started asking questions about how women could be helped in this situation.

It seemed for a while that things would change, and some things did, yet it's clear to me that even though the church stood up and spoke out, not enough has been done to change the mindset about this, even all these years later. If we truly believe that God would sit down with prostitutes and tax collectors, then so should we. We should be open to helping and working with them however we can.

Years later, I saw this playing out in the church when we helped establish houses and homes for women's protection so they could rebuild their lives. I think back to this time when my grandmother called me and spoke truth to power. It reminds me that we can start fresh in this moment. We don't need to wait for a new day to start anew.

Day 152

Read: Job 1–4

Naked I came from my mother's womb, and naked I will depart.
The Lord gave and the Lord has taken away; may the name of
the Lord be praised.

—Job 1:21

Each time I read the book of Job, it always stops me in my tracks. I went back and looked at the journals from several different years in which I recorded how there were days when—as a child—I couldn't understand what was going on in our house. There were voices raised, doors banging, deep silences, sounds of crying, and I would drift into my own little world, creating my imaginary stories. The world of bigger people seemed to be loud and dramatic with sudden flashes of temperament.

Most of this concerning interaction was between my mother and my sisters. It was calmer after my sisters left home to marry or find their own flats or apartments. My brother and I experienced a short time when things were quieter and calmer, though sometimes we were interrupted by visits from my sisters with spouses, children, or boyfriends in tow. Then my grandmother moved in with us, and there was a time of adjustment in our lives as my mother and her mother sorted out their dynamic of living together again.

In all this, my father was the voice of reason. He was the calming influence who settled disputes. He brought the two sides of any argument into focus and mediated. He brought people back to the table after they had stormed away. And through it all, he prayed. Every day, he would read the Bible. He found time to center himself, to bring his thoughts and prayers to God. Every day, I heard him praise and thank God, even on difficult days. His voice and actions were the calm before, during, and after the storms. He was the voice in my life who always praised God, no matter what.

Day 153

Read: Job 5–7

When I lie down, I think, "How long before I get up?" The night drags on, and I toss and turn until dawn. My body is clothed with worms and scabs, my skin is broken and festering.

—Job 7:4–5

As a child, I laid in bed, scratching and picking at my skin. Every night I scratched and picked so that in the morning, I found spots of blood on my sheets. I snuck into the bathroom to wet a washcloth and sponge the blood stains out of my sheets. Then, I made my bed to hide the dampness. I hid this from everyone for a while, until my mother asked me what I thought I was doing. She asked it in a threatening way, which led me to deny everything at first—until I shared with her that my skin always itched at night, so I scratched myself and made myself bleed.

A visit with the doctor followed, and then more visits, and more doctors, and more tests, and more visits, and more tests. Then a doctor said I needed to get all my hair cut off again, so he could put a mixture of coal tar and peanut oil on my scalp. So, I visited the barber's where I had a crewcut, which at the height of the Beatles era was not a good look at an all-boys school! It also didn't help that the coal tar and peanut oil mixture really stank.

The boys at school were not kind, so avoiding boys at breaks or lunchtime almost became a sport. As I attempted to escape their attention, I found places to hide around the school at recess to avoid bullying, but often, I was caught. Throughout it all, my father stoically kept praying with me every evening. When he discovered how the boys at school were treating me, he spoke with the headmaster. He talked about caring for each other in an all-school assembly, which made the situation worse.

Day 154

Read: Job 8–10

Although I am blameless, I have no concern for myself; I despise my own life. It is all the same; that is why I say, "He destroys both the blameless and the wicked."

—Job 9:21–22

School became harder and harder to deal with. Every day, I would get ready for school and wonder if I could find a way not to go. I complained of feeling sick or having a stomachache, but my parents would still get me to school somehow. Several times, my father rode with me on the underground to the station near school and watched me as I walked away, telephoning the school from the payphone at the station to say I was walking up to school and to let him know at his work when I arrived.

There were days when I didn't, and on one occasion, the headmaster found me sitting in a local park, wondering if I could sit there all day until it was time to go home, so that my parents would not know I skipped school. The headmaster walked me up to school, but, instead of any punishment, he took me to his office, gave me a cup of tea and a cookie, and talked with me about school and his life on board ships in the war. Life could be difficult at times, he said, but we had to persevere through it all.

At the midmorning break, I joined my class, saying nothing to anyone, keeping my head down. The summer break saved my life. School was out, and I didn't have to see any of the other boys from school. I went to stay with my great-aunt and uncle in the country, and I helped on their neighbor's farm. I got sunburned! My skin peeled, and like magic, the skin healed over. The scabbing and itching went away. I slept well for the first time in a long time. To say I thanked God would be an understatement!

Day 155

Read: Job 11–13

I have become a laughingstock to my friends, though I called on God and he answered, a mere laughingstock, though righteous and blameless!
—Job 12:4

As the summer ended, back came my psoriasis. Even though I could name it, a few boys in school continued to bait and taunt me about my skin. With my father's words and prayers in mind, and armed with factual information about psoriasis, I thought I could fend off their taunts. Gradually, most of them stopped baiting me and presumably went on to other things, but one or two just wouldn't let go, baiting me day in and day out. It didn't help when I shared the facts. They just didn't believe me or accept the truth.

Almost daily, they said things to me between classes about how I must have done something wrong to get psoriasis. One of them kept calling it leprosy, rather than psoriasis, as that sounded more religious to him. He used Bible phrases about shunning me because of my skin, saying I shouldn't even be allowed out, let alone be present at school. All I could do was continue to say I was seeking help from my doctors to heal my skin, it wasn't contagious, and for them to leave me alone, which of course they didn't.

This truly was a miserable time with no end in sight. However, it was good preparation for dealing with what life would throw at me later. I couldn't appreciate that then, but with hindsight, I know it toughened me up and led me to put my trust more in God than anything else. I would still sit with my father in the evening and ask him why I had to get this skin infection. My father tried to help me by leading me into prayer, asking God's help in handling the challenges life throws at us

Day 156

Read: Job 14–16

People open their mouths to jeer at me; they strike my cheek in scorn and unite together against me.

—Job 16:10

My tormentors continued to throw words at me on a daily, sometimes hourly, basis. It seemed like the torment would never end. No matter what I did, they wouldn't stop. Plus, they threw a new topic at me. I was the youngest boy in our year, and I was a singer. Singing at church and in the choir at school was something that gave me pleasure, and it was as if this boy couldn't stand that I might receive any praise for singing. He teased that it was weird my voice hadn't broken, when every other boy in our year no longer sang soprano.

Not only that, one of my teachers was from Australia and was befriended by my parents, as my father had gone to boarding school there. They wanted to make sure she felt at home in England, so she would come over for dinner and go with my parents to concerts and plays. In class, she would sometimes refer to me by my first name, which noticeably contrasted with the school habit of calling boys by their surnames. This particular boy latched on to this and started name calling me her *pet* whenever he could, combining his hurtful words with other taunts.

I felt truly alone through this period. I thought I was supposed to ride it out and turn the other cheek. The problem was that each time I turned the other cheek, I felt he hit that one even harder. It reached the point where every day, every break, every time a teacher wasn't watching, he did something to taunt me. Every night, I prayed for help from God, and for a while, every night, I cried myself to sleep.

Day 157

Read: Job 17–20

Then Job replied: "How long will you torment me and crush me with words?"

—Job 19:1–2

Every morning, I faced another day at school, knowing the bully would be there. Every day, I went to school, hoping for a different outcome. Every day, it was the same—every day, day in and day out for most of a year. It's surprising I studied at all or achieved anything academically that year. I tried to be in different classes as much as possible, but that didn't work out. In our classrooms, we sat alphabetically, so he always sat right behind me. I truly was *looking over my shoulder* all the time.

I talked with another student about it, and they felt I must be exaggerating. Though after watching for a while, they saw what was happening, but then they thought it must be my fault somehow. The more I prayed about it, the more I felt unheard by God. In fact, some days I felt that nobody was listening to me, nobody was in my corner, not even God. No matter what I prayed, all I received was silence and a total lack of support from my friends. What I wanted was someone to bring justice and hopefully, some help.

I searched my thoughts to find what I'd done to deserve this constant and never-ending torture. The more I worried, the worse my psoriasis became and the more I was aware of how bad it looked. I had visible blotches and scabs on my face, all over my scalp, and all over my body. Changing for gym or sports at school was sheer hell, providing another opportunity for him to torment and make fun of me.

I felt totally abandoned.

Day 158

Read: Job 21–23

When I think about this, I am terrified; trembling seizes my body. Why do the wicked live on, growing old and increasing in power?
—Job 21:6–7

Nothing seemed to happen to my bully. He could taunt me, push me, make fun of me, and nothing happened to him. He constantly escalated what he did as well. One day, I would find my school desk—with all my textbooks in it—glued shut. Or, when we handed in homework, mine would go missing, and the teachers would ask me where it was—even though I'd handed it forward in class. Somehow, it vanished as one of the boys collected the papers.

On and on it went, day in and day out, never ceasing. No matter how hard I thought about it, no matter what I could imagine or rack my brains about, I could not find anything I had done to upset this boy. He just did not like me. He saw me as weaker than him and simply enjoyed making fun of me and bullying me constantly. I wondered: *If I asked him what it was I'd done and apologized, would he stop?* I hoped that someone, somewhere, might step in and help me out, maybe judge whether his grievance was genuine. Then, I could say I was sorry, and we could move on.

I prayed every night that God might hear me and help me understand what I needed to do to stop the boy from bullying me. At school, I wouldn't go near the bathrooms in breaks for fear of him attacking me. Rather, I would hide myself in, and spend time in, the library and pray I wouldn't need to go to the bathroom until I got home in the evening. There was a complete lack of justice in my broken world, and I had no idea how to fix it.

Day 159

Read: Job 24–28

*If even the moon is not bright and the stars are not pure in his eyes,
how much less a mortal, who is but a maggot, a human being, who is
only a worm!*

—Job 25:5–6

To say that I questioned myself is an understatement. I thought about what my few friends said, and, in the evenings and at night, I worried about it. In my head, I went over and over everything that happened during the day. Everything that was said. Every punch that was thrown at me. Every taunt. Every name I was called. These taunts ate me up.

I laid there, trying to calm my mind down and get to sleep. I forced myself to pray over and over again. I always started with the Lord's prayer, then acknowledged God had power over all this. I knew instinctively I had to *let go and let God*, and I knew in my heart that somehow God could intervene in this torture. I also knew deep in my heart that I was innocent. I struggled with seeing or finding any wisdom in all this pain. In the middle of the night, I felt that no mere mortal could solve this.

I knew I had to keep persevering and searching for a solution, and I ran over every option in my mind. I woke up again, and again, sweating and crying out in my sleep. Knowing true wisdom can only be found in God did not make this time easy. I felt I could only love God and honor him if I gained understanding of what I needed to do. More than anything, I knew that if God could create the winds, the storms, the rain, and everything else, then he could create wisdom for me to understand. In the middle of one lonely, sleepless night, I realized that shunning evil *is* understanding.

Day 160

Read: Job 29–31

Yet when I hoped for good, evil came; when I looked for light, then came darkness.

—Job 30:26

That year started out well. After I sang solos in the school fall concert, people complemented me about my voice. Maybe this boy was jealous of all the positive attention I got? What a contrast as the year went on! I grew depressed, eventually to the point of despair. Even though there was only one boy constantly on my case, several others would join in when it suited them. I felt like an outcast, and I was definitely the target for their sport.

There were days where I felt really abandoned by not only everyone at school, but by God. I had never felt so alone and isolated before. I had not lied, or cheated, or mistreated anyone, and I had been generous whenever anyone asked me for help. As I reflect back on it as an adult, I know I didn't do anything wrong, but I really wanted to stop being constantly beaten up, verbally and physically. It was hard to go every day, knowing the abuse would be going on all day. When would it end?

I prayed every day to find the answer or for God to show me what to do. The silence I felt from God was shattering, though, and even reading through the Bible with my father didn't lead me to the answer. The few friends I still had were being baited and threatened, too, and my tormentor constantly found new ways to hurt me. He told the few friends I had if they didn't stop talking with me, they would get the same treatment. They challenged him over this, so he threatened to have us all *Sent to Coventry*, a shunning by the whole school.

Day 161

Read: Job 32–34

For God does speak, now one way, now another, though no one perceives it.
                                                                —Job 33:14

I didn't think he would go through with it. One day, I arrived at school and found a mock trial would be held during lunch break—a mock trial charging me with being a teacher's pet. The goal was to get everybody in my year to *shun* me and not talk with me. At lunch, I went and hung out in the library, but several of his friends came, found me, and forced me to come to our classroom, where they had set up for a *mock trial.* They had a group of boys sitting like a jury and one student sitting like a judge. One of my few friends was sitting, waiting for me at a desk, and my nemesis was sitting with two of his friends at another desk.

Almost immediately, he started shouting out as if he was a prosecutor on a TV law series. He went on and on about how I was guilty of being a teacher's pet. I sat there silently, looking straight ahead, ignoring everything being said, not reacting to anything. Then I noticed the *jury* passing slips of paper to the *judge.* Before I knew it, I was found guilty and was *Sent to Coventry* immediately. No one was to speak with me, or to me, for two weeks!

Suddenly, it was over. I did not say anything. I sat there while people left the room to go to lunch. I sat there until lunch was over. I sat there while the boys came back into the classroom for the afternoon lessons. I sat there silently through the afternoon until lessons were over. I sat there while everybody left to go home. I sat there until the cleaning lady came into the classroom. Then I got up and went home.

Day 162

Read: Job 35–37

God's voice thunders in marvelous ways; he does great things beyond our understanding.

—Job 37:5

I was quiet when I got home from school. My parents didn't notice. They were dealing with the latest crisis between my middle sister and her husband, and that was their focus. I was able to slip away to my room after supper. I got up early and ate breakfast on my own after my paper round and left for school early. I went into the empty classroom, sat at my desk, and pulled out my books for the first lesson. After about an hour, the other boys in my class started to arrive. I didn't speak to them. I looked only at my books and didn't look at any of them.

The teacher came in and the lesson got underway. And then, it was midmorning break, and I stayed at my desk. Then another lesson, then lunch, and I stayed at my desk. Then another lesson, and then the end of the day. And I went home. I got there early the next day and sat at my desk while the other boys arrived. I stayed focused on my books, not speaking or looking at any of them. My nemesis couldn't resist commenting and throwing out some name-calling, which I ignored. And I went home. I arrived early the next day and prepared for the lesson. I kept looking down. In the evening, I went home. I went early again the next day. The doors of the school were just being unlocked by the custodian, who was surprised to see me. I went to my classroom, sat at my desk, and prepared my books for class. But my nemesis couldn't resist pushing again, a little bit more. I prayed all the time for God's voice to guide me, but all I heard was silence.

Day 163

Read: Job 38–39

Where were you when I laid the earth's foundation? Tell me if you understand who marked off its dimensions?

—Job 38:4–5

This went on for over a week, and every day and night, I wrestled with my situation. One night, my father was out at a church meeting, so I picked up my father's Bible to read and found myself reading the Book of Job. I was not Job, or one of his friends, or the devil, or God. Why was I drawn to this story and what did this story mean to me? Suddenly, it was as if God was answering me out of a whirlwind, asking me questions, showing me the limitations of my understanding. God's questions reminded me to be humble and think about how God influenced everything for a reason.

It was as if God could speak to me in the way the birds had communicated with me as a child sitting in a pram on the front porch of our house as a baby. The words of the texts talked about how God was intimately involved in the lives of all the animals. Through the words in the Bible, I could feel God explaining how God provided for each of these animals and could provide support for me. God was challenging me and reminding me of how limited my understanding was compared with God's.

That evening, I suddenly understood how God was involved in every aspect of what happened to me and all those around me. I may not understand why I was being put through all this hardship, but if I trusted in God, the result would be positive for me at the end of the day. I didn't know how but knew it would. I prayed and prayed into the night, not sure of the outcome, but knowing that some answer could come to me in my dreams if I only trusted in what I read. I had reached a turning point.

Day 164

Read: Job 40–42

After the Lord had said these things to Job, he said to Eliphaz the Temanite, "I am angry with you and your two friends, because you have not spoken the truth about me, as my servant Job has. So now take seven bulls and seven rams and go to my servant Job and sacrifice a burnt offering for yourselves. My servant Job will pray for you, and I will accept his prayer and not deal with you according to your folly. You have not spoken the truth about me, as my servant Job has." So Eliphaz the Temanite, Bildad the Shuhite and Zophar the Naamathite did what the Lord told them; and the Lord accepted Job's prayer.

—Job 42:7–9

I sat at my desk in the classroom as the other boys trickled in. My nemesis had to push some more—this time physically. He pushed, poked, and prodded, then threw a punch and before I knew it, we were in a full-blown fight. I had never fought anyone before, and it seemed to be an out-of-body experience. I was taller with a longer reach, and after only a few punches, he went down. I followed him and kept punching.

Suddenly, a teacher lifted me off him as he was bleeding on the floor. There were teachers and students gathered around us, and the headmaster appeared out of thin air, demanding to know what was going on. Several of the boys started to explain everything to the headmaster—the name-calling, the bullying, the teasing, the mock trial, and *Sending me to Coventry*. They told him it had been going on for over a year without me responding.

The headmaster had a teacher take the other boy to the school nurse to get checked out and sent me to his room to wait for him. When he came into the room, he sat down and just looked at me for a while. When he spoke, he wasn't angry; he was sad that for over a year, I had been bullied, teased, and taunted without anyone stopping it. He said he would talk with my parents, but I should know that I could come and talk with him at any time. My father came to the school and talked with him, then he and I travelled home together. I was worried because my blazer and my trousers were both torn, and I thought he and my mother would be upset with me.

He said, "Never mind. They can be fixed." And he gave me a hug.

Day 165

Read: Psalms 1–8

That person is like a tree planted by streams of water, which yields its fruit in season and whose leaf does not wither, whatever they do prospers.

—Psalms 1:3

The Saturday that I spent sitting with my father, talking about my pain from the last year, was one of the longest days of my life. My father was sad that I had felt I could not share what was going on with him or my mother. He told me that a healthy anger is okay to express, even though hitting the other boy was not good. He picked up his Bible and turned to the Psalms. He read from Psalm 1 and 2 and stopped.

He shared that his father had sent him to Australia to a boy's boarding school. He stayed with cousins he didn't know for the holidays. He felt totally alone, and the other boys were not exactly friendly to him either. He was only ten years old when his mother died. His sister, my Aunty Mary, was only four. My grandfather was left a widower at thirty-eight, with two children, living in a mining camp in Mexico. Grandfather's sister, my Great-aunt Edith, offered to raise his four-year-old, my Aunty Mary, and took her to live with her in Switzerland. My grandfather took my father down to Marseilles and put him on a boat, on his own at age ten, to sail to Australia. As he was leaving, my grandfather gave him a Bible to read on the trip and handwrote Psalm 121 on the flyleaf but also underlined Psalms 1 and 2, encouraging him to read them every day on the ship to Australia. My father suggested I read the Psalms every day for a while and showed me how I might walk in right relationship with God and "walk in righteousness." This walk was sometimes not an easy path, but one I tried to follow going forward.

Day 166

Read: Psalms 9–16

The Lord is a refuge for the oppressed, a stronghold in times of trouble.

—Psalms 9:9

Almost immediately, I was able to see the struggles shared in the Psalms were some of the struggles I shared in my daily life. Oppression and trouble had been part of my daily life for over a year, and here they were, written in the Psalms. The psalmist spoke with God about feeling pushed down and unable to grow as a person and certainly unable to be everything he could be. Between them, oppression and trouble had stopped me from enjoying my life for over a year and sent me toward an out-of-control tailspin.

What I had been missing was a solution to my problems, something to help protect me in this type of situation. Here it was, in the Psalms all along: "The Lord is a refuge for the oppressed, a stronghold in times of trouble." I realized understanding who God is was the solution I had been searching for. As I read more of the Psalms, I discovered that I could know and trust God more fully. Knowing "the Lord is my shelter and my refuge" was simply huge going forward. I knew I would not be able to fix everything every time; however, if I was honest with God, then, even in times of darkness, I could let God produce the strength I needed. That is God's specialty. If I am going through hard times, I will find God is not far away.

This was a huge part of my process that set the course for the next part of my life. Did I always remember? No. But somehow, I always found my way back to the roots of my faith, knowing God is there every time I breathe in and breathe out.

Day 167

Read: Psalms 17–20

Keep me as the apple of your eye; hide me in the shadow of your wings
from the wicked who are out to destroy me, from my mortal enemies
who surround me.

—Psalms 17:8–9

As I read the Psalms, vivid word pictures exploded in my head, which I drew on to help me ask for God's help when I felt in danger. When I felt I needed God's attention to what was going on in my life, a phrase, such as "Keep me as the apple of your eye," brought God closer to me. It felt like I was asking God to keep an eye on me and those around me.

A phrase, such as "hide me in the shadow of your wings," brought back memories of the birds I had seen growing up. They would settle down on their nests in our back garden and under the eaves of our front porch, protecting their eggs and their young from danger by spreading their wings over their nests to hide them from predators. Through reading the Psalms, I first saw a deeply loving side to God. In these verses, I first saw God's nature was to be loving, watchful, and protective of me and all creation.

I know I have blind spots and am sometimes not aware of hidden faults in my life, especially those lurking in my heart. Through the Psalms, I can ask to search my heart and have God show me behaviors and thoughts that could do with *cleaning up*. Most times, I read through the Psalms quietly in my head, but there are times when it is important to truly cry out to God for help and protection. Sometimes, I need to lift my voice and read the Psalms out loud to let God know I believe and want to fulfill God's plans for me. Sometimes I must shout them out, really loud, into the wind, from a mountain top, or at the confluence of two mighty rivers!

Day 168

Read: Psalms 21–25

Even though I walk through the darkest valley, I will fear no evil, for you are with me; your rod and your staff, they comfort me.

—Psalms 23:4

My father's suggestion to read through the Psalms led me to realize I am not alone on this journey; in fact, he had walked this way before me. It is comforting to feel I am walking in his footsteps as I read through the Bible every year. Psalm 23 is probably the most familiar psalm in the Book of Psalms. It could very well be the most familiar passage in the entire Bible. Later in life, I found myself turning to it by heart as I sat with people in hospital, or by their bedside, as they struggled to make sense of their lives.

Sometimes I have felt at a loss for words, yet the words of this psalm brought comfort when no other words could do. As I re-read the Psalms over the years, I felt something deeper. I believe they guided me to a way of living every day, which brought me into living in right relationship with God. It is as if the Psalms became a guide for daily use, a daily rule, not just when I experienced times of death, dying, or distress—but every day.

Visualizing God's role as a shepherd led me to realize I need never lack for anything; my needs will be met. I will have food to eat, water to drink. My basic necessities will be met. I will be kept safe and secure with shelter and protection, because that is what God does for us. Recognizing God's "goodness and steadfast love will follow me all the days of my life" reassures me every day. Accepting God's gift through the Psalms gives me the foundation of security as well as giving me a guide to praising God as part of my daily life.

Day 169

Read: Psalms 26–31

The Lord is my light and my salvation, whom shall, I fear? The Lord is the stronghold of my life, of whom shall I be afraid?

—Psalms 27:1

I spent an entire year of grammar school afraid. Afraid I would be shown as something I wasn't. Afraid of the bully who terrorized my daily life at school. Afraid of what others thought of me. Afraid to tell my parents or teachers what was going on. Afraid *constantly.* The list of things I feared was long and, with hindsight, quite irrational. Fear had undermined my faith and paralyzed me against doing many things I could have done.

In particular, fear had shaken my faith in God. When I read this psalm, I realized by accepting God as "my light and my salvation," I need not be afraid anymore. If God was my light and my salvation, my stronghold, then why should I be afraid? By letting go, I accepted that God could protect me from any enemies or bullies. I also found that through the Psalms, I could pray for others, especially those who needed prayers as they were going through some hardship or difficulty. By responding in prayer, I became more aware.

Later in life, prayer would be a focus of my life in chaplaincy as I responded to others. Sometimes, I would pray and not be sure if my prayers had been heard because I had become accustomed to hearing responses instantly by phone, email, or text message. However, I could be sure, through the Psalms, that God heard me when I prayed, "for he has heard my cry for mercy." By following what God says, whether through the Psalms or by signs, I could become all God created me to be, which is why I love a phrase shared at seminary many years later, "God is still speaking!"

Day 170

Read: Psalms 32–35

Many are the woes of the wicked, but the Lord's unfailing love surrounds the one who trusts in him.

—Psalms 32:10

When I understood God's intention was to guide me, to advise me, and to watch over me, I felt powerful after struggling with my fears for a long time. I always thanked my father for sharing the Psalms with me. My father also told me St. Augustine had posted these words over his bed so he would read them first every day. St. Paul quoted these verses in his letter to the Romans. My father's goal was to help me understand what I was reading so it could be relevant to my life going forward. He wanted me to understand by reading every day from the Bible, I was showing up every day for God.

Through these psalms, I was also in touch with myself, with what I needed to confess and be forgiven for, which could happen through the love of God. Thinking about this psalm being *of David* makes me realize David could have been confessing his affair with Bathsheba and subsequent murder of Uriah, which puts God's forgiveness into an intriguing context. These psalms also contain a lot of encouragement to sing and give praise. I asked my father: *What if I don't feel like singing joyfully?* I certainly hadn't felt like singing for a while. In fact, the bullying had stolen any joy out of my life for quite some time. My father encouraged me to simply trust the process, to ask God to open my heart in dark times, and then to praise God. My father reminded me of my childhood and our deacon at church, Desmond Tutu. Despite his experiences in South Africa, he always came across as joyful. In fact, he positively glowed at times, especially when he preached.

Day 171

Read: Psalms 36–39

How priceless is your unfailing love, O God! People take refuge in the shadow of your wings.

—Psalms 36:7

Describing God's love as reaching to the heavens and God's faithfulness as the skies, said to me that this God truly was "out of this world" or beyond anything I can understand, try to define, or put in a box. Realizing God's righteousness is as steady as the highest mountain and God's judgement is as deep as the ocean is comforting to me now, and was then too. However, the verse that jumped off the page to me was the second part of verse seven, "People take refuge in the shadow of your wings."

These words spoke to me from my earliest memory. I could find shelter with God, like the baby birds in the nests outside our window on the front porch when I was growing up, who found shelter under their mother's wings. They showed me that God's love for me is always there, arms open, ready to provide me shelter and care. Much of what the world considers success is temporary, and God does something different. God offers comfort when we are hurt and grieving. God guides us on when we are feeling lost and alone. I had to remind myself that God knew everything about me, faults and all, and loved me anyway.

When it looked as if my life was falling apart, I got through those tough times by trusting in God. I came out the other side, spiritually stronger with God's love. When reading these psalms, God heard me, even when I spoke silently or under my breath. God didn't stay at arm's length from me; rather, God knew exactly what I needed to experience, and, through my father's help, reached out and brought me comfort. This experience was a clear message to me to bring everything, good and bad, to God in prayer.

Day 172

Read: Psalms 40–45

As the deer pants for streams of water, so my soul pants for you, my God.
—Psalms 42:1

In reading these Psalms, I also felt like asking: Where was God when I was struggling and being bullied? I longed to know where God was when I was beaten up, mentally and physically. Through the Psalms, I came to understand where God was, where God is. The images through the Psalms showed me God in the people who visit those in prison or those sick in hospital. In the father who puts his arm around his son's shoulder when he is hurt or afraid. In the mother who holds her sick child while she prays for them, or the rescuers who put their own lives at risk to save people who are lost or hurt.

It became clearer to me than ever before that even when we are unable to fully sense the presence of God, God is always with us. The Psalms show me how to look at life when I am sad or downcast, or really brokenhearted. When I think back to my achievement of singing well in school——and how proud I was of what I achieved—I realize how small that was in comparison with everything that God does.

It is not like I didn't know that God was with me; however, in all my sadness, I couldn't experience God's presence anymore. I pushed down the memories of the amazing things God had done, all the things done for me and everybody else. In fact, if I stopped and tried to describe all the things God has created, there would be too many to list. I need to remember that even when God seems silent, God is in the boat with us in the storm. If the storm is going on inside of me, that is where God is going to be, bringing calm to my storm.

Day 173

Read: Psalms 46–50

God is our refuge and strength, an ever-present help in trouble.

—Psalms 46:1

When I was in my time of trouble, I didn't look in the Psalms. I couldn't be open to who God is. During this time, I had a false sense of calm when, actually, everything was falling to pieces around me. I could have turned to the one person always present with us—the one standing right beside us, ready to help and support us in our time of trouble. God is who the Psalms would have had me search for. It's right there, as clear as day, if I had looked.

My life circumstances could change—and they did—but God's love and protection remain constant. When I think how God cares for the bird on its nest or the flowers in my garden, I know God cares for me and is always ready to help me, if I just ask. Even saints have troubles, and one reason they became saints is because they overcame their troubles by believing in God.

Singing at school wasn't about me and the work I put into singing lessons. Singing was integral to my relationship with God. Singing at church for God wasn't just a means to an end or a part of a church service, but the songs reflected my joy at being in God's presence. There's a popular saying in spiritual circles: *Singing is praying twice.*

When we connect with the text in hymns and the psalms, we're not just singing the notes, but we are offering those words and tunes to God from our hearts and binding ourselves to one and other in community.

Day 174

Read: Psalms 51–57

Open my lips, Lord, and my mouth will declare your praise.
—Psalms 51:15

I prayed this psalm again and again as I failed to live up to the expectations I set for myself in life. Being forgiven for something I had done, or something I left undone, allowed me to keep moving forward in life while reminding me that there are consequences for my actions or inactions. This psalm helped me ask God for forgiveness, as if I was creating a completely new heart, a new spirit within me. In fact, the very words used here remind me of the writings in Genesis when God created the heavens and the earth— out of nothing.

Even when I felt surrounded by difficulties or pursued by my enemies at school, I could turn to the Psalms. I had readings that encouraged me to cry out and hand over things to God. *To let go and let God.* I may not immediately move out of the hostile situation I find myself in, but God will guide me until I can get through it and come out the other side. Realizing that when I am afraid, I can turn to God is huge. This knowledge helps me not be overwhelmed by anyone or anything. I take the Psalms at face value and put my trust in God.

If I put my trust in God, I am not afraid, no matter what *they* do. Before our deacon in London, Desmond Tutu, left to go home, we all gathered and prayed for him and his family. They were going back to South Africa, where they would be facing a very hostile time. His trust and faith in God shone through all our prayers with him, preparing him to preach truth to power.

Day 175

Read: Psalms 58–65

But I will sing of your strength, in the morning I will sing of your love.

—Psalms 59:16

If he could do it, I could do it. I went back to whistling every day as I went about my usual things, like my paper round. Without realizing it then, I took Deacon Tutu, who always seemed to find something to be positive about, as my example. No matter how tough his situation was, he had a way of turning it to praise God with a belief that God would make everything all right. After he returned to South Africa, he was threatened and discouraged in his work. Yet somehow, he always knew his safety and refuge for him and his family was in God's hands.

As I walked my paper round every morning, I whistled again as I delivered the papers—enjoying the early morning stillness in the neighborhood. Each day, I celebrated the gifts of being able to walk the streets in safety and share the new morning with the world. It was an incredible way to start the day, joyfully acknowledging God's presence and being thankful to God.

The Psalms also guided me to pray for others, always remembering the phrase, "taking refuge under the shadow of God's wings." I would sometimes find myself saying Psalm 61 out loud. It would remind me how I wanted God to care, not just for me, but for so many others I named over the years. Even when I was going through dry patches later in my life and longed to be back in communion with God, I had the memories of these days when I felt closer to God. These memories comforted me, especially as I began to understand that Jesus also knew God this way.

Day 176

Read: Psalms 66–69

A father to the fatherless, a defender of widows, is God in his holy dwelling.
—Psalms 68:4

My father shared how the Psalms in particular, and other passages from the Bible, were what he read on the ship as he traveled from Australia back to London. His father had wired him a ticket to meet him in London, where my father could go to university. However, the journey from Australia to London took over two months by ship, passing through the Suez Canal. When he arrived at the docks in London, the immigration service would not initially let him into the country, and his father was not there to meet him. His Aunt Edith and sister Mary came to the docks instead to explain to the officials he was coming to London to study at university.

At that time, my father had three passports: an American passport by birth, an English passport because of his father's birth, and an Australian passport because of his mother's birth. The officials explained to his aunt it was unusual for someone to travel with three passports. His aunt explained her brother, my grandfather, had come to London for medical treatment and sadly died from cancer while my father was traveling. My father was shocked. He really did not know his aunt well and hadn't seen his sister since she was tiny, over ten years before. The three of them sat in the immigration office while the officials decided what to do.

My father said he knew he was there for a reason, for a purpose, and he needed to trust in God in the way that the Israelites had. My father's aunt said the plan was for him to stay in London and go to university at Imperial College. This is what his father wanted him to do. The officials agreed and gave my father permission to enter Britain.

Day 177

Read: Psalm 70–73

My flesh and my heart may fail, but God is the strength of my heart and my portion forever.

—Psalms 73:26

When my father shared his story with me, I was stunned by the thought of him sitting, waiting for hours alone in an immigration room, not knowing why he was being held. Then his aunt and sister came into the room, not his father whom he expected to see. He was told his father had died in London while my father was traveling from Australia back to Britain. I struggled with making sense of it all in even then.

My father shared it was the Bible, and the Psalms in particular, that helped him get through some dark days and enjoy the light days all the more. He arrived in London to attend university with virtually only the clothes he stood up in and brought with him from Australia. He had none of the trappings of wealth that people traditionally looked for. His clothes were nice, but his treasures were the Bible my grandfather had written in, a crucifix (which I still have today), his love of God, and the knowledge that God would guide him on his path. His faith in God was the essence of where his goodness and compassion came from throughout his life.

Later in my life, I would experience Christians following the *Prosperity Gospel*. If I had not experienced my father's faith, I might have found it attractive with its promises of material wealth by following a self-appointed prophet. In reading this psalm, I couldn't help but notice the comparison between the two. However, the key is that God is a never-failing presence and source of strength to those who trust God and entrust themselves to God. In many ways, this psalm encourages us to remain outsiders in the modern American culture and to speak with a prophetic voice—to speak truth to power.

Day 178

Read: Psalms 74–77

I will cut off the horns of all the wicked, but the horns of the righteous will be lifted up.

—Psalms 75:10

Looking back through my journals from different years, I found similar memories in and through the readings. I often thanked God in response to something God had either done or had a hand in. However, this psalm encouraged me to simply worship God. Nothing more, nothing less. To simply worship God for being God. There were times when my heart was overflowing with thanks for knowing God and how special that was. When I was singing at church, I was lifting my voice in praise to God because I was just plain grateful for how God had been revealed to me in so many different ways.

There is a long list going through my head of all the ways God has been revealed to me over the years, which I read throughout my journals and notes. Because I like singing, I know there is nothing more wonderful than hearing voices raised in praise and worship in church. In some ways, singing strengthens my understanding of God. Some of these psalms encouraged me to reflect on God performing miracles, like leading the Israelites out of Egypt by the hands of Moses and Aaron. They also encouraged me to think about times when I cried out for help, remembering what God had done for others, and then believing God could do that for me too.

For nearly fifty years, I had jotted down these thoughts and memories, and I could see a pattern in my responses to these scriptures, readings, and psalms. Again and again, I saw how reading the Bible every day strengthened my resolve in how I lived my life and gave me hope for the future.

Day 179

Read: Psalms 78–79

They would not be like their ancestors, a stubborn and rebellious generation, whose hearts were not loyal to God, whose spirits were not faithful to him.

—Psalms 78:8

These same journals have shown me the mistakes and errors I made in my life. Yet, in the Psalms, I find that God stayed faithful even when the Israelites—or I—messed up. This psalm encourages sharing the knowledge of God with future generations so they can avoid making the same mistakes we have—to give them a knowledge of the law so they can also put their trust in God. There is a hope expressed in the Psalms that we will not make the same mistakes our ancestors did.

When I came to America in the 1990s, I did not know the history of the indigenous peoples. My knowledge of them was more or less limited to the movies and TV shows I watched in England. They were still called *Red Indians* in England until fairly recently, to differentiate them from Indians from India. Imagine how I felt when I discovered my great-grandfather, who had mined silver ore in Colorado, had written with his partner to the US Government to get the indigenous peoples moved off land they wanted to mine. It took several years, but eventually by the summer of 1880, they were removed by making the tribe walk 350 miles to a 1.9 million acre reservation in Utah near the Uintah Reservation. It was named the Ouray Reservation.

Growing up in England, I had never heard this story nor my great-grandfather's role in writing to the president for his help. The president committed over 1,000 US troops to make it happen. The Psalms let me look at both sides of a story and see how things could have been done differently, and maybe, still could today with reparations and reconciliation.

Day 180

Read: Psalms 80–85

Restore us, Lord God Almighty; make your face shine on us, that we may be saved.

—Psalms 80:19

One huge change I experienced when moving to America was the number of churches and different denominations. When I was at seminary, it wasn't a seminary for only Episcopalians. It was a United Church of Christ seminary, which our diocesan bishop felt was adequate for our forming as future priests. However, he decided that some of the seminarians—who did not have an Anglican background as I did—needed to polish up their Anglican heritage, and he sent them off for another year at an Episcopal Seminary elsewhere in the country as they completed their Masters of Divinity.

I relished how many different denominations worshipped and studied at my UCC seminary. We not only had United Church of Christ, but we also had Episcopalians, Baptists, Roman Catholics, Lutherans, Methodists, Disciples of Christ, Presbyterians, and many more. Somehow, we all got along and enjoyed sharing the communion table with different denominations. I didn't see the rival mentality that I saw in the outside world, in which denominations sometimes see each other as competitors, making us weaker and less effective than we might be. Rather, each seminarian grew from knowing and sharing with the other denominations, gaining grace to pray for and support other churches and our brothers and sisters in ministry at seminary and beyond.

As I continue reading this group of Psalms, I noticed the writer talked about a specific place to worship God. In my journals, I noted many different places where I felt I could worship God—not just one place. Everywhere I could reach out and talk with God and feel God's presence was a place of worship to me. It made my whole life a form of pilgrimage.

Day 181

Read: Psalms 86–89

Among the gods there is none like you, Lord; no deeds can compare with yours.
—Psalms 86:8

I find different things make themselves known to me from different psalms at different times in my fifty years of journaling. However, this verse from Psalm 86 jumped out at me several times. Living in America is very different from living in Britain. What I was not prepared for in America was the diversity of *Christian* faiths, from the televangelists to the fact that I discovered there were nearly three hundred other churches from different denominations within a three-mile radius of my current church. Many, I had never heard of. When you add in other places of worship, there are nearly four hundred places of worship within the three-mile radius.

This verse from the Psalms jumps out at me every year when I read it. I could pick any one of nearly four hundred different versions of *God* to worship; it is the God of Abraham and Jesus I have chosen, or maybe who chose me. God touches my life in so many ways I cannot count. God is not able to be confined in a box, which explains why I have always thought outside of the box—until I realized that, actually, there is no box, because God is even bigger than that.

Many people believe our one true purpose in life is to worship God, and I struggled with the narrowness of this concept until I realized my mother prayed all day every day, while doing the washing, making meals, cleaning, or just hanging out with neighbors. She kept the habit of praying all day, every day, because she had read the little prayer book by Brother Lawrence and realized prayer comes from the heart, and what better way to show it than in everyday actions.

Day 182

Read: Psalm 90–95

Satisfy us in the morning with your unfailing love, that we may sing for joy and be glad all our days.

—Psalms 90:14

When I started ministry as a chaplain, I began by working with my parish. I was then given an opportunity at a hospital as well, a large level-one trauma hospital in St. Louis. As a part-time chaplain who was studying full-time at seminary, I worked shifts at night and weekends. Each night, I would walk several circuits around the hospital, checking-in with each of the units and touching base with the staff to see what their needs were for the night. When full, over 1250 beds could be occupied, and I could walk over ten miles as I made my rounds.

Invariably, I would be called to a particular area for an emergency call, either the Emergency department, one of the ICUs, Labor and Delivery, or the cancer wards. At night, this hospital's practice was to have only one chaplain present, compared with two dozen chaplains during the day. Over the next fifteen to twenty years, at this hospital and then several others, I was present with over 2,000 people as they transitioned and died. Each death was different; each family grieved differently. Some were unexpected; some were anticipated.

Whenever I read this psalm, it brings back those experiences I shared with these families. I remember the conversations I shared with patients before death, and always with the families afterward. Knowing we all die, the psalmist encourages us to make the most of every day, because we know our days will not last for long. Many families shared with me their loved one's death made them think about what was important in their own life. The psalm encourages us to do just that and ask for compassion to be able to share God's steadfast love so that we can live by faith, hope, and most importantly, love.

Day 183

Read: Psalm 96–102

Sing to the Lord, praise his name; proclaim his salvation day after day.
—Psalms 96:2

    In my journals, I can see the opportunities presented to me each and every day to share the good news of my faith. Some days I failed when I should have shared the good news and didn't, but each day as I wake up, I know I'm starting with a clean slate from yesterday and an opportunity to do better. Every day I remember that Deacon Tutu taught us as children back in London to look for God in everyone we met each day, from the garbage collector to the Queen. He said that under the skin, we all shared in the love of God and were created in God's image.

    In 2004, when I started working with the church in Ferguson, Missouri, I saw how church doesn't happen inside the four walls of the building. Rather, church happens out in our community, in our neighborhoods, and in our workplaces as we share with others what God has done for us, what God has done for the whole world, and what God continues to do. It's not always easy to share with some of my neighbors, yet I keep hitting reset and working at it harder, trusting God will guide my words and actions.

    I remind myself with this psalm that even if things are not going well, and I am stressed out by life, I can still praise God. I ground my faith in praise of who God is, not just in what God does. When I focus on God's character and attributes, praising God comes naturally. Recently, our diocese changed the name of the newsletter it publishes to "Proclaim," and I thought how apt these verses are in this psalm as we are encouraged to *publish* or *proclaim* how God does amazing things in our lives.

Day 184

Read: Psalm 103–105

He makes grass grow for the cattle, and plants for people to cultivate,
bringing forth food from the earth.

—Psalms 104:14

One of my earliest memories is of being in my secondhand Silver Cross pram on my parent's front porch and *talking* with the birds that would come and visit with me while I was put outside for fresh air and a nap. Mostly, two robins perched on the handle and looked down at me, whimsically tilting their heads from side to side. They had a nest under the eaves of the porch, and probably wondered what this noisy object was doing, sitting outside on their porch.

Now, in my garden in Ferguson, I have a plethora of different birds who love the trees and Missouri wildflowers I've been growing. I have managed to create a positive bird, butterfly, and bee habitat in my garden, and I love it. The variety of birds amazes me as each is so different, from the cardinals to the doves, from the robins to the finches—and the finches are a multitude of colors, quite a menagerie. When I read this psalm, I feel the power of God's creation, not just for animals, but also for me as God forms me for whatever purpose God needs.

This group of psalms challenges us to search for God, not just in nature and ourselves, but to look carefully and thoroughly. I believe these psalms encourage us to search with our whole heart every day, then live life as God wants us to do, trusting in God, not just ourselves. Through continual searching, the Psalms reveal God's character and strength to all of us.

Reading the Bible from Genesis to Revelation every day through the year shows us a way of following *The Way* in our daily lives, and each day, it brings us more understanding of God and ourselves, and each year, a new understanding

Day 185

Read: Psalm 106–107

Praise the Lord. Give thanks to the Lord, for he is good; his love endures forever.

—Psalms 106:1

This psalm looks back over the history of Israel, highlighting the times when the people were disobedient to God and how God stayed faithful to them and had mercy on them. When I looked back through my journals, I noticed a trend. My personal evolution was pretty slow and very much a gradual process, so it was hard to see changes as they were happening. My journals provide a way I can see and acknowledge positive changes I made in the way I lived my life.

These trips through my writings make me want to stop, give thanks, and make a list of all the good things that have happened in my life, even when the steps in my life didn't look as if they were a good thing at all. I think about all the people I prayed for over the last thirty-plus years and the experiences that happened in their lives. Some struggled from sadness, pain, and addiction, and God reached into their hearts and lives to share in their progress. I also see the lives I have touched as a chaplain and as a human being and the wisdom I have been shown along the way—the growth I have been gifted over the past decades.

Keeping a journal over the last thirty-plus years and reading through the Bible every year has given me a focus and insight into how God works in our lives, not as some grey-haired grandfather figure, or some spirit up in the sky, but as a God who loves us and wants us to realize we are okay just as we are.

God loves us just as we are.

When the going gets tough, we can call out to God and feel heard.

Day 186

Read: Psalm 108–114

Awake, harp and lyre! I will awaken the dawn.

—Psalms 108:2

At what point did I start reading the Bible and morning prayer every day? I found when this happened in my journals. Interestingly, it did not start at times when I had the time to do so; it started when I didn't, waking to deliver papers in my local neighborhood. "Awake, harp and lyre! I will awaken the dawn." Just like the psalm says.

As my life became more complicated or *busy*, there were days, weeks, and months when I didn't read every day. Then, I would remember and find myself reading the Bible or saying a prayer and journaling as I woke up in the morning. As I grew older and my life more complicated, I created a routine of waking early to read morning prayer and my Bible every day before the day poured in over me, giving myself time to journal too. This practice became part of my own *rules of life* so I could reach out every day to consistently seek God before the day imploded on me with all my day-to-day responsibilities.

Sharing my daily discipline with others was another huge step. Identifying myself publicly with friends and family in this way didn't happen overnight. At first, I kept it to myself, just reading the Bible from cover to cover, from Genesis to Revelation. I didn't want to make it a big deal initially, then I realized it wasn't about me. It was about God—following the early teachings of Jesus and the followers of The Way—and praising God above absolutely everything else.

Day 187

Read: Psalms 115–118

The stone the builders rejected has become the cornerstone; the Lord has done this, and it is marvelous in our eyes.

—Psalms 118:22–23

There were a lot of days when I didn't exactly wake up like a ray of sunshine in my *happy place*. I wrote about dark days when I felt under the weather emotionally, or even physically unwell. There were days when my life seemed hopeless, and everything weighed heavily on my heart. There were days when I felt my prayers were not being noticed by anybody, especially God.

When I was young, it was my psoriasis that tormented me a lot. As I grew older, I seemed to constantly have something wrong with my gut. When I stop to think, really think about it, God creates everything new every day. I can sit on my front porch and see the plants, birds, and insects waking up to new blades of grass, new tomatoes growing, new flowers raising their heads to the morning sun.

If everything is new, so is God's presence in my life. We are created new each day, and I can give thanks for being created anew. The world is so beautiful each and every day, and it is a new opportunity for me to trust God and work with God on whatever ails me. I also noticed in later journals, I started to see more of the presence of Jesus in the Psalms. "The stone the builders rejected has become the cornerstone," is shared with us by Jesus later in the Bible and links us to older texts so we may realize how God is sharing this story and understanding with us. Even when I felt rejected, I saw how I could become something more going forward, so I would continue to explore God's purpose for me each and every day.

Day 188

Read: Psalm 119: 1–88

May your unfailing love be my comfort, according to your promise to your servant.

—Psalms 119:76

When I discerned my call to be a chaplain in the late 1990s, I realized God's purpose for me at that moment in time. I prayed I would be worthy of this new challenge in my life. I knew I needed to *let go and let God* guide me on this new path. I trusted that God would show me the way to be everything God could see in me. At that time, I believe God placed several people in my life to guide me, friends who were already in ministry as priests and deacons.

I also received the guidance of the brothers at the Society of St. John the Evangelist in Boston, who reminded me of my sister's godfather in England, a benedictine monk with whom I had spent time on retreat. The brothers shared much wisdom with me, but what stood out then and now was how they sat with people at different times, sometimes with words and more often, without words. Several of them shared variations of this psalm, particularly this verse of the psalm. The psalmist prayed with faithfulness, love, and compassion. I found myself sharing it, too, whether it was with a patient discovering the diagnosis of cancer or a parent with the loss of a child or the struggle with mental depression for another or the loss of a parent to a child.

It is a powerful prayer to share, and it brought comfort many times to whomever I was with. This prayer encapsulates that God is full of love and mercy and is there to bring comfort in time of need. For many of them, it brought God's presence into their lives for a moment in time.

Day 189

Read: Psalm 119: 89–176

*I have strayed like a lost sheep. Seek your servant, for I have not
forgotten your commands.*

—Psalms 119:176

I can see how often I strayed from following God faithfully—how
often I was a lost sheep. Yet every time, something, somebody, somewhere
brought me back to being present with God. I know when I worked for
the BBC, I was led astray in my personal relationships many times because
I didn't value myself or respect myself, which led me to not value others
as I should have.

Today, I am a person who looks for the other lost sheep and intercedes
for them, bringing them back to God or showing them a path they can
follow to return home safely. It could be a family member struggling with
addiction, or a friend struggling with poor life decisions, or a neighbor
struggling with loneliness in their life.

I place myself where they can see me and reach out to me so that I
can reveal God to them in whatever way makes sense to them, letting God
transform them through God's love for us. My role is to simply open their
hearts and pray God will bring them out of whatever darkness they are in,
so they can share in God's light and love. God works on earth through us
as we are God's hands, eyes, ears, and hearts. This understanding guides me
in my prayers for others and guides me in partnering with God to see how
people can find understanding and love in their lives, which can transform
them in ways they may never have imagined. Praying for them and with
them—and then staying out of the way—is what I learned as a chaplain
and from being a follower of The Way.

Day 190

Read: Psalm 120–132

I lift up my eyes to the mountains, where does my help come from?
—Psalms 121:1

It is hard to wrap my head around my father's experience of being only ten years old when his mother died and his father sent him to live with his cousins in Australia. They traveled from the mining camp where they had lived in Pachuca, Mexico, to Vera Cruz, where they stopped to bury his mother. Then, they sailed to England and crossed by ferry to France.

Next, they traveled by train to Paris, and my father, his sister, and my grandfather met up with my Great-aunt Edith. She took his four-year-old sister, Mary, to live with her in Geneva, and they took my father to Marseilles to catch the ship to Australia. Sitting in Paris with his two children and sister, my grandfather took out two Bibles—one for each of them, inscribing Psalm 121 inside each cover. He told my father that whenever he got sad or felt lonely, he should read this psalm, and it would remind him of his father and sister and the mountains where he grew up in Durango, Colorado.

My father never saw his father, my grandfather, alive again, as he died in London while my father was traveling back from Australia. This psalm was one that my father would say over me as a baby, and for us, it was a psalm that assured me that no matter where I was—whether I was traveling by foot or by plane, by sea or by air, whether I was awake or asleep—I was not alone. I have shared it with many others during my life: with my children, my friends, my loved ones. I whispered it to my father as he made his journey to his final resting place on the banks of the River Tweed in Scotland.

Day 191

Read: Psalm 133–139

I go up to the heavens, you are there; if I make my bed in the depths,
you are there.

—Psalms 139:8

When my son Charles was little, I would sit and read with him every night before he fell asleep. For many of those years, I read him a book, *The Runaway Bunny*, by Margaret Wise Brown, which is beautifully illustrated by Clement Hurd. I would alternate it with *Goodnight Moon,* and woe betide me if I skipped a word or phrase as he would immediately correct me. I'm not sure when I realized the parallel between Psalm 139 and this book, yet when I did, it was obvious to me.

As my son grew older, he would say his prayers after we had finished reading, praying for everyone he knew. He ended by including himself in the prayers. After praying for his grandparents, his mother, his sister, and me, he would add, "thank you for me." I firmly believe that over time this prayerful practice helped him keep a positive attitude about his self-worth and self-esteem.

Years before, I read this psalm back in London and took great comfort in the words and the thoughts it stirred up. I often felt that I wasn't enough or that someone would find me out and show me up as a fraud. Yet, each time, this psalm calmed me down and helped me refocus on doing my best at whatever job I was doing. Each time, it helped me overcome my *imposter syndrome*, as I took strength from knowing that I was known, not just by family or friends, but by God.

God knows us fully, so God will not let us *get away*, just like the mother bunny would not let her little runaway bunny get away.

Day 192

Read: Psalm 140–145

Do not let my heart be drawn to what is evil so that I take part in wicked deeds along with those who are evildoers; do not let me eat their delicacies.

—Psalms 141:4

Sometimes a job I had taken on didn't turn out to be what I had expected, and I had to compromise as I was asked to shelve my personal moral standards to fit in with whatever the job required. I couldn't easily do that. This problem increased as I got older, and the jobs were higher profile. I felt sometimes I was destroying myself from the inside out as I compromised one way or another.

After coming to the US, I found myself sitting with a group of guys I had little in common with several years in a row, and I realized how the words of the Psalms could guide me in a way David understood. These guys brought up lots of temptations: simply drinking to excess, making deals which only benefited a wealthy few, or ignoring those who were doing the work and not being rewarded for it.

I knew God had promised to help me overcome temptation wherever it happened if I was open to listening for God—sometimes in strange crowds of people. By sitting and talking with other friends through church, I was able to resist the temptations put before me and walk a straight path as I overcame the problems in my life. These friends also helped me overcome the desire to just acquire new stuff, when I knew that physical things would never satisfy the longing in my heart for peace and happiness.

As I became more and more involved in the church, and in ministry as a chaplain, I realized experiencing oneness with God was what made me feel fulfilled. The temptations of wanting stuff for my personal happiness dropped away. I really only needed God in my life to guide me to peace and happiness.

Day 193

Read: Psalm 146–150

Let them praise the name of the Lord, for his name alone is exalted; his splendor is above the earth and the heavens.

—Psalms 148:13

Every year, I notice something new about the verses, and I am drawn to Psalm 148. I guess it is the tree hugger in me. When I worked for the BBC World Service, I spent some time working with people from the Indian subcontinent. I was fascinated by their history and heard many incredible stories. One story was about women who protected sacred trees in their community by literally hugging them so they could not be chopped down for the construction of a new palace. The soldiers accompanying the workers decapitated them. Each time they did so, more women stepped forward until 365 women had been massacred, at which point the Maharaja building his new palace relented and called for a permanent ban on chopping down the native khejri tree.

In case you think this was a long time ago, this happened at the same time George Washington was born in America, and Benjamin Franklin founded the first American library in Philadelphia. What struck me, though, was that the women of Bishnoi believed God was above all in sovereignty over everything in their lives and in nature. When the psalmist says, "God's splendor is above the earth and the heavens," the psalmist is recognizing God's place in the great scheme of things. The psalm seems to state that theology and ecology are inseparable. It also has clear implications for how we structure humanity.

In America, the Declaration of Independence states, "All men are created equal," yet it is clear only a few people actually believe this, or act like they believe this. Yet this psalm does offer us a theological foundation for making the effort to build bridges and bring change, not just in America, but across the world.

Day 194

Read: Proverbs 1–3

For the Lord gives wisdom; from his mouth comes knowledge and understanding.

—Proverbs 2:6

As I read through my journals, I can't help but notice how often things cropped up in my life where others suggested I do things that could lead me down different paths than I planned to take. Sometimes their suggestion seemed like a little thing, yet each time, I felt I lost my way. When I was younger, I could turn to my parents to ask their advice. As I got older, I realized the Bible had lots of the answers, if I only knew where to look.

From Proverbs, I learned the value in seeking wisdom and understanding. As I looked through these chapters, I could find ways to keep myself out of trouble and guide my decisions. What was harder was recognizing *who* was leading me astray and guiding me down the wrong path. If I looked back at the example my father set for me, I could see living humbly and honestly was the way to go.

When I first met and talked with my parents' neighbor, Lord Home, I was taken by how quiet and unassuming he was. I would never have known he was a peer of the realm, a former prime minister who sat in the room with British Prime Minister Neville Chamberlin as he negotiated with Adolf Hitler for a "Peace for Our Time" agreement. Britain used this time to rearm and prepare for war with Germany. He was truly blessed in many ways, but his humility, honesty, and perseverance shone through his manner and conversation. His encouragement to me to run for elected office in Scotland in the late 1980s never faltered and, though I was unsuccessful, it was a great honor to call him my friend and learn so much from him.

Day 195

Read: Proverbs 4–6

I instruct you in the way of wisdom and lead you along straight paths.
—Proverbs 4:11

Within a month of starting to work at the small church in Ferguson, I was asked to lead a Bible class for a group of women. Most of the women were English and had come to America by marrying GIs during World War II. Sitting and sharing the Bible with them was just wonderful. We sat in armchairs in the church library, drinking tea and snacking on cookies. Most of the time, they were sharing the stories of their lives with me, as prompted by our reading that day.

One of the women asked where my parents had been during the war. They moved out of London to stay in a cottage on a large estate near Newbury. My mother had three young daughters at that time under the age of six, was pregnant with my brother, and the cottage had no gas, electricity, or running water. It had an outhouse, or privy, in the yard and a well to draw water from. It did have a nice garden with swings for the children, and they were far from the bombing in London. My father cycled to the nearby town of Newbury and caught the train to London each day.

One of the women started to share stories I knew about my mother and sisters. I certainly did not expect to hear familiar family stories from a woman sitting in Ferguson. It turned out she had been the cook at the big house and walked up the lane by that cottage every day. She got to know my mother and sisters and babysat them sometimes to give my mother a break. Listening to her share about my family brought me to a place where I felt God was showing me I was supposed to be.

Day 196

Read: Proverbs 7–9

My son, keep my words and store up my commands within you.

—Proverbs 7:1

Over the next few months and years, this group of women shared their lives with me. The wisdom of their lives was incredible. Their stories of falling in love and following their American GIs back to America were amazing. Some of them shared the shock of all the different things they experienced coming from a war-torn country to a country that had an abundance of everything. They struggled with adjusting to different money, different foods, and overall different lives.

The constant for them was this church. Most of them had come to the church in the 1950s after the war. They found that they could meet other women from Britain and forge a bond. The women who had grown up locally accepted them and showed them the ropes about things that were very different for them. Food was common ground, though, and they swapped recipes from Britain with recipes from America.

As they had children, they also helped each other with schools and American traditions. Most of the British women didn't know about the Fourth of July or Thanksgiving, though they had great recipes for cakes and sandwiches, so the annual English Tea became a staple event of this church. By sharing wisdom with each other, they were aided in making good choices. As they settled into a rhythm, this shared wisdom brought knowledge, understanding, and common worship at church. They offered each other nourishment and understanding. Their stories, rich with drama, showed me how they lived out their faith with each other through the church. They understood the wisdom of the proverbs without anyone having to point it out to them. Instead, they grasped it by living it.

Day 197

Read: Proverbs 10–12

The fruit of the righteous is a tree of life, and the one who is wise saves lives.
—Proverbs 11:30

My middle sister, Cathy, had a nickname, and even these women thousands of miles away in America knew her nickname, "Trouble!" One lady at church shared the story of how my sister had been playing on the swing in the garden, going higher and higher. Told by my mother to stop going so high, she had gone even higher. It was a hot summer's day, and she only had pants on as she swung so high she lost her balance and flew off the swing into a large patch of stinging nettles. Covered with welts and stings, she had to have calamine lotion spread all over her to relieve the pain. Yet, the next day she was back out there doing it again and trying to swing higher than ever.

Listening to this woman from the church in Ferguson sharing a story about my sister, who was only five at the time, I remembered all the other times she had pushed the envelope with my parents. My middle sister brought the drama of boyfriends, late nights, missing trips, calls to school, detentions, running away, running off to Switzerland, marrying a stranger, and having a child—many, many adventures as the wind blew through her life and she through ours. All the way through, she could return to the sanctuary my parents created for us, a safe place for each of us. She found she could leave her troubles at the door and be safe and sound at home. We didn't love her any less for it. If anything, we loved her more for being who she was. Her death left a large void in all our lives and a stillness that made us ask, *Who inherited the wind?* But left us hearing nothing.

Day 198

Read: Proverbs 13–15

A happy heart makes the face cheerful, but heartache crushes the spirit. The discerning heart seeks knowledge, but the mouth of a fool feeds on folly. All the days of the oppressed are wretched, but the cheerful heart has a continual feast.

—Proverbs 15:13–15

My sister Cathy had a big heart, and though she got herself into lots of strange and unexpected situations because of it, she always opened her heart to others and looked for the best in people she met. We can tell a lot about a person by their heart, and their heart is what God sees, beyond the surface of our lives. My sister had such a heart. Whether for people or animals, justice or injustice, she would look into her heart and champion others who had been disenfranchised or abused.

Most of the time, she shared a happy heart, though, sometimes she had what she called her *black dog* days, when she struggled as her spirit was crushed by circumstances beyond her control. She constantly searched to know more about everything, and no fact was too insignificant for her to want to find, even if it took her down some strange paths with stranger still friends.

However, when she was in a room, she lit it up as if she had brought the prodigal feast to the family, no matter whose home it was. Even when a terminal illness caught up with her, she laughed and continued to enjoy the company of friends and family, bringing laughter and fun to everyone she was around. Infuriating at times with her impracticability, she lit up a room and brought laughter and happiness to everyone. Truly, her happy heart brought a continual feast to us. I always felt God laughed with her and smiled as she laughed too. Even in her difficult times, I felt God lifted her up to make her journey easier and her heart lighter—and our hearts lighter too.

Day 199

Read: Proverbs 16–18

Gracious words are a honeycomb, sweet to the soul and healing to the bones.
—Proverbs 16:24

I am not sure when I realized the power of words—the power to lift someone up or smash them down. Words can soothe the wildest animal or scare the living daylight out of a person. These proverbs encourage me to seek guidance from God before I attempt to implement any of my own plans. By seeking God's guidance, I will work through the plans in my head and heart and come to the best decision.

To say the right thing to someone—the honest thing, the calming thing—is not easy at times. Doing so with integrity, humility, and righteousness is often even harder. The image of bringing honey to my words means bringing life-giving food to someone who needs to hear words of kindness. Many times, I have sat with people in hospital corridors and by bedsides through the night when a loved one is dying. I have sat and listened to their words, and my response has been to offer few words, thoughtful words, kind words to soothe their souls and their hearts as their grief and pain peaks. I strive for words that promote positive energy and help give them strength to take the next step forward in their lives.

It is only by asking God to fill me with kind and nourishing words I can truly be present to others every day when they need these words the most. My mother and father recognized how difficult this was for me as a child growing up, and for many years, I carried a small card on which my mother had written, *Lord, fill my mouth with worthwhile stuff, and close it when I've said enough.*

Day 200

Read: Proverbs 19–21

Whoever is kind to the poor lends to the Lord, and he will reward them for what they have done.

—Proverbs 19:17

Throughout my readings of the Bible, I have seen that God cares about the poor. My parents lived through World War II, and because my father was a conscientious objector on religious grounds, he lost his job. Instead, he was put to work on a government project, where his skills as an industrial chemist could best benefit the war effort. My parents went through a period from 1939 to 1949 when they had almost no money and were blessed to be helped by others.

When the nighttime bombing of London directly affected their lives—destroying where they lived—a friend through the church reached out and helped them move to the country. The cottage they moved to did not have gas, electric, or running water, but it also did not have bombs! They scraped through those years, making ends meet.

When I moved to Ferguson, I found that one of the parishioners who knew them during the war, regularly dropped off leftovers to them from the big house where she was the cook. My parents never forgot the assistance they received at this time and applied the lessons from it to everything they did in their lives. Their actions of caring for others, whether a meal for a neighbor, a ride to church, clothes for a neighbor's child, or books and pencils for school, were ways they found of helping and feeding others. My father used to say: *How can you expect children to learn or someone to work, if they have an empty belly or are too cold to stop their teeth chattering?* Several times, he gave away his own winter coat to help someone from church, and each time he would say they had a need for it, and he shared his good fortune of having a coat with them.

Day 201

Read: Proverbs 22–23

A good name is more desirable than great riches; to be esteemed is better than silver or gold.

—Proverbs 22:1

When I look at the ups and downs of my life, I am eternally grateful for the way my parents raised me. Their very practical, down-to-earth wisdom transcends time and offers me valuable guidance for my personal growth, a way to live ethically, and a way to have healthy relationships with others. Remarkably, they shared how important a good reputation was, long before I saw others losing their reputations by not living as ethically as they could. I am glad they taught me moral values and the importance of doing everything I could for anyone who was poor or in need. They taught me if I wanted to be in right relationship with God, then this is what I had to do.

My parents always guided us with love, even if they were correcting something we had done wrong. I learned their lessons and applied them in my own life later. What I like about these proverbs is that I find new things to like each year I read them. They are extremely practical and relevant thousands of years after they were written down to share with the people of Israel. Clearly the teachings they share can lead to living a purposeful life with values that can stand the test of time.

Day 202

Read: Proverbs 24–26

If your enemy is hungry, give him food to eat; if he is thirsty, give him water to drink.

—Proverbs 25:21

Over the last few years, there has been so much trouble in the world. It's like it is spinning faster out of control every day. Here in Proverbs, we are encouraged to give our enemy food to eat and water to drink. When I stop and think about it, it makes sense. The first thing we do if a disaster hits a friend or family is comfort them by bringing them food and water. Every day, we see people doing this as part of life.

At the same time, we see some people who would rather cut off the next shipment of grain, or the next free breakfast for a child at school, or healthcare for women. Thankfully, this selfishness is often matched by someone else stepping up and sourcing grain elsewhere or a person fundraising to provide the meals children need.

Proverbs encourage us to see the value of wisdom to build a strong and balanced life. It challenges us to seek reconciliation rather than confrontation, and to treat our enemies with kindness rather than exacting revenge. Over the last few years in my journals, I wrote that Proverbs guide us against engaging in quarrels and gossip, emphasizing how powerful words are and how they can hurt others.

If I can channel what my parents taught me and reinforce it with the words from Proverbs, then I can resist getting sucked into the *black hole* of social media and its destructive nature. I can seek ways to make discussions online positive rather than negative. This is one positive way to help with my own personal growth and in building meaningful relationships with others. It can also help heal my local community.

Day 203

Read: Proverbs 27–29

Do not boast about tomorrow, for you do not know what a day may bring.
Let someone else praise you, and not your own mouth; an outsider, and not
your own lips.

—Proverbs 27:1–2

I was working really long hours at the BBC, going above and beyond what I needed to do in order to get the best soundbites for the foreign language services to share with their listeners. Many of my predecessors had focused only on what the English-speaking World Service wanted to cover. I was scheduled to attend each of the political party conferences, so I researched all the elected members of parliament and found out which ones were fluent, or slightly fluent, in a foreign language. I reached out to each of them, requesting a meeting with them during their party conference so that I could provide an opportunity for them to broadcast in a foreign language.

At that time in Britain, we had three major parties and three weeklong national conferences. All three conferences went well, and the language services appreciated the good coverage. They were able to interview members of parliament in their own languages and gain a better insight into the political system and how democracy worked in Britain. After three weeks of intense work and long hours, all my immediate boss said was I had created a nightmare expectation for anyone who followed me.

Over the following weeks, I shut down, did my basic work, and nothing more. Then I was summoned to see the managing director of the BBC World Service. I really thought I was in trouble. However, he had received thank-you letters from every single one of our forty language services, and a letter from the British Foreign Office, praising us on our outstanding multilingual coverage of how British democracy worked during the three-party political conferences. The Foreign Secretary and Prime Minister were both impressed with our broadcast coverage of our democratic process and wanted to thank all involved.

Day 204

Read: Proverbs 30–31

A wife of noble character who can find? She is worth far more than rubies.
—Proverbs 31:10

Anyone who has really been involved in church knows it is run, managed, cleaned, prepared, and survives because of countless women who have dedicated their time and energy to supporting the church. From an early age, I realized this by watching my mother, godmother, and the other women at church. I've reminded myself of this over the last twenty years with the women at my current church, who do so many things to make the church run smoothly.

In between my involvement with churches, I saw women making sure businesses run properly, radio stations run well, and political departments and campaigns run smoothly. In fact, everywhere I have worked—from hospitals to parliament—I have seen the behind-the-scenes work of women, making things happen. In the last twenty years, I have seen women step up and challenge the status quo of society in ways I could not have imagined, powerfully leading us to change our relationships with each other and our communities. It has been inspiring to see a group of women saying they are *praying with their feet* as they march through a city, or the capital of the United States, or even the capitals of cities across the world. Standing up and walking peacefully shows they care about each other and their rights as human beings.

It didn't surprise me to learn from a national park guide last summer about the role of women at Mesa Verde in Southern Colorado. Their matriarchal society was industrious and kind to others while caring for the needy with everything from food to shelter, which is echoed today in Meals-on-Wheels and food pantries.

This chapter from Proverbs reminds me of so many women who have provided good examples of how to live my life and be supportive to others.

Day 205

Read: Ecclesiastes 1–4

There is a time for everything, and a season for every activity under the heavens.

—Ecclesiastes 3:1

One of the amazing things about reading the Bible in small bites every day is the opportunity to journal about it and then to be able to look back over years of events, times, struggles, successes, failures, and see them in the context of the same words from the Bible. The one constant in all my journaling and writing is the Bible. These words from Ecclesiastes were there whether I was studying at university, working for the BBC, campaigning with Prime Minister Thatcher, traveling to America, sitting with a dying patient, holding the hand of a single mother delivering her first child, or crying over the loss of a young man in the streets of the neighborhood I had just moved into.

Time is relative. Time always keeps moving forward; we all change and grow older. When I was really young, I had no idea there was a cycle of life. I was simply present in the moment, the *right now*, and didn't think about yesterday or tomorrow.

As I grew older sitting with my grandmother, she reminded me that each phase of life should be treated with love and respect. When she shared her story with me and I stored it away, I realized I was creating my own story. Each day was another day forward, another day to savor and store up for myself. Looking back over the last years, there have been challenging and difficult times, but I have always known they were part of the cycle of life. I could see how I constantly prepared myself for the next phase and was ready to meet it when it arrived. Understanding God's timing really has brought me a degree of fulfillment, even when I could only see uncertainties.

Day 206

Read: Ecclesiastes 5–8

Whoever loves money never has enough; whoever loves wealth is never satisfied with their income.

—Ecclesiastes 5:10

I listened to my grandmother as she talked about her childhood, working from sunrise to sunset as a seven-year-old child. Carrying things up and down six flights of stairs. Scrubbing floors, washing linens, emptying chamber pots. One might expect her to be angry at what happened to her. After all, her parents had sold her into service. She had no choice, but amazingly she wasn't angry. She talked about all the things she saw that she had never seen when she lived with her parents. She talked of the wealth of the family she worked for and all the nice things they had. She spoke of the children who had lessons at home and how she would sometimes listen on the stairs as they were being taught by a tutor. She shared the big house had so many rooms, so many floors, and her parents' home had just one room for her and her siblings.

At one point in time, creating an abundance had become a driving force in my day-to-day life, and that drive certainly didn't equate to happiness. As I experienced my second divorce, I saw how the pursuit of wealth and possessions during this marriage had led me astray from my core values. My journals reminded me I cannot take earthly possessions with me into the next life. Finding ways to simplify my life, with the help of some really good friends from church, grounded me as I followed a path into chaplaincy and pastoral care of others. I found in time, I could not only sleep well but also could be present for others in a way I had not been available to be for several years.

Day 207

Read: Ecclesiastes 9–12

Moreover, no one knows when their hour will come.

—Ecclesiastes 9:12

My grandmother pointed out that I would often say how I would do something *one day*, which was sometime between that moment and the future. Often, this was something I longed to do or said I was committed to do, like lose weight, get fit, be healthier, finish my book. She pointed out I would use this phrase about helping someone or starting a new ministry or program.

She found there were two places we could not go. We cannot go back to the past, or despite the film of the same name, jump *back to the future!* All we truly have is today. When I look at my journal entries for these chapters in Ecclesiastes, I see they reflect on the unpredictable nature of life and death. I write that we should enjoy life and do good while we have the chance. In past reflections, I challenged myself to find one thing I could do that day—generously from my heart, without condition—to help someone or make their life easier.

As I grew older, I also appreciated the challenges my grandmother faced all those years ago, and my parents too. Ultimately, I know I will face similar physical and spiritual challenges as I age and be held accountable for my actions. What I read now, though, are the insights these words offered into living a meaningful and purposeful life while acknowledging how fragile life is, how fragile our earthly existence can be.

Day 208

Read: Song of Songs 1–8

Have you seen the one my heart loves? Scarcely had I passed them when I found the one my heart loves.

—Song of Songs 3:3–4

My grandmother seemed nervous when I walked into her room. Normally, she would be sitting in her high back chair with her Bible on her lap. This time, she closed the Bible as I came in. It turned out she was reading the Song of Solomon and thought it might be a bit *racy* for a teenage boy. I laughed, assuring her I had read it years before when my sisters were giggling over it. All three of them read it because our parents thought it could help guide them as they started dating.

I told her I thought it was an excellent poem about love and the depth of human connection between a man and a woman. My journals over the last thirty years reflect my regret over never finding love to the depth expressed by King Solomon—before he took hundreds of wives and concubines. Rather, I wrote of my sadness at being betrayed several times, which left me guarded and struggling with this guide in the Bible as to how a marriage should work.

Now, I see this text as patriarchal writing, reflecting a rigid view of marriage between a man and a woman; whereas, I now see and experience—through friends—marriage as a relationship between two people who love each other, no matter their gender. Over the years, so many of my friends were in complicated relationships, yet would have totally identified with the core of this book from the Bible. Over the last few years, each time I have read these words, I expressed sadness about what could have been in my relationships. Yet, it always gives me hope, being the never-ending romantic I am, that one day I will experience this love again.

Day 209

Read: Isaiah 1–4

I reared children and brought them up, but they have rebelled against me.

—Isaiah 1:2

My grandmother asked me why the prophet was so angry with the people. She wondered if it was a bit like how she would get angry sometimes in the past with my mother and her siblings when they didn't do what she asked them to do. *Was it like that?* she asked.

We sat in silence for a while, each deep in thought, until I suggested to her it was different, but the same. Different in that the prophet was focused on how the people were corrupt and following empty rituals. At the same time, it showed God as a loving parent who promised to forgive them if they repented. I felt God was looking for ways to forgive the people who were no longer listening, and the prophet could see days ahead when they would listen, and nations would gather in Jerusalem and have peace.

Unlike my grandmother's children, the people God was talking about through the prophet had to experience a lot more before they could seek forgiveness. At this point in the book of Isaiah, they were still too arrogant, not listening to God. They needed to experience oppression and exile before they would seek forgiveness.

As usual, my grandmother expected it would be women left to pick up the pieces, and they would be essential to any forgiveness of God's people. We discussed how this was also about moral accountability, accepting the consequences of our actions, and yet still holding on to the hope of salvation and renewal if we repent and ask forgiveness.

How many times have I asked for forgiveness of others, especially when I wasn't listening, to them or to God?

Day 210

Read: Isaiah 5–8

Whom shall I send? And who will go for us? And I said, "Here am I. Send me!"
—Isaiah 6:8

I remembered sitting with a Russian broadcaster at the BBC. We were recording his weekly commentary, "Notes from an Observer," which he recorded in several Slavic languages so that different East European Services could broadcast them. It was always remarkable to work with him and see how he could speak comfortably in several different languages.

On this occasion, sitting in the BBC cafeteria late at night, I asked him if he had a copy of his "Notes" in English I could read. It was written in a way that surprised me. Instead of being confrontational, particularly with the Russians, his words encouraged them to see what was happening in Britain and Europe as they were not experiencing the same in their own countries because of their government. He shared his opinions, demonstrating Britain was not an enemy. Rather, he said, it was a society made up of people just like the ones he was broadcasting to, people who wanted to live their lives in peace.

He was not the only one who answered the call to broadcast peace to others, which was one of the magical things about working for the BBC World Service. At that time, we were working in over forty languages. Many of our broadcasters were former diplomats or government members; some were professors or teachers. All of them loved broadcasting and were responding to the need for broadcasting the truth to other countries. Even the building we broadcast from had a statue over the entrance symbolizing Anglo-American friendship and the words, "To the Friendship of the English-speaking Peoples," complementing the BBC motto, which is: "Nation Shall Speak Peace Unto Nation."

Day 211

Read: Isaiah 9–12

For to us a child is born, to us a son is given, and the government will be on his shoulders. And he will be called Wonderful Counselor, Mighty God, Everlasting Father, Prince of Peace.

—Isaiah 9:6

Looking over my journal entries again and again, year after year, I ask myself: *What did Jesus think when he read these words? Did he know what lay ahead of him? Did he know his mother's family history?* I always remind myself that Jesus, though clearly having grown up in the peasant class of the population, was clearly brilliant by the time we get to read about him. Jesus' knowledge of the scriptures in the Jewish Bible was clearly extensive.

We see this later in his use of language and his ability to quote scripture extensively. I wonder if he sat with his mother or even his grandmother much like I did to read and discuss the Bible.

I remember discussing this with my grandmother during one of the times she opened up about her family and my grandfather's family on my mother's side. She dug out pictures and showed me brothers and sisters, aunts and uncles long gone. She stopped quite suddenly and said she thought Jesus' mother would have shared her history, how she and Jesus were of the family of David. That made sense to me as Jewish family histories are passed down through the maternal line in the same way as other tribal nations across the Middle East had done for centuries. I only had to look back at what I had read earlier that year—when sometimes it felt like all I was reading was a list of names in the Chronicles—to realize how important ancestry was to the Jewish nation.

My grandmother liked that the words came back to us later to describe Jesus. She felt it meant so much of what we were reading together was true. I listened to her and sat at her feet while she sat and smiled, a memory I'll always have.

Day 212

Read: Isaiah 13–17

The Lord Almighty has sworn, "Surely, as I have planned, so it will be, and as I have purposed, so it will happen."
—Isaiah 14:24

I almost can't believe how many times in my journals I saw what I planned to do wasn't happening! My grandmother had an expression: *If you want to make God laugh, tell God your plans!* Her words seemed appropriate as I turned the pages of my entries from different years, different places, different jobs, different marriages! Yet, through it all, God seemed to have a plan even when mine was flying out the window.

When my first marriage came to an end through the infidelity of my wife, I was able to throw myself into my work at the BBC and help others in ways I had never considered. When my second marriage ended, I was able to draw on my inner strength, give myself over to God, repurpose my life, study and grow in my faith in seminary, and become a chaplain serving those in great need. As my second marriage ended, I was able to be present for my children in ways I never could be for the children of my first marriage, and I felt God guiding me in how to be there for them.

When I realized my life ahead was going to be financially troubled, I was guided by friends through the difficult times. Friends helped me find a home and a way of life, simpler and more fulfilling than before. When my plans were flying out the window, I needed to trust God to have a plan for me that I could honor and reach out my hand to take into the future. Again and again, I had to humble myself and put my trust in God.

Day 213

Read: Isaiah 18–22

He will be a father to those who live in Jerusalem and to the people of Judah.
—Isaiah 22:21

There have been so many wars around the world over the years. I wrote about so many wars in my journals. Most of the time, we like to think we are at peace in the world; however, because I spent so long with the BBC World Service, I pray every day for countries and people far away who are experiencing wars and uprisings across our world. Each night, when I tune in to the BBC, I hear of another country where an uprising or war is taking place across the world from the Congo to the Sudan, from Albania to Iraq, from East Timor to Lebanon, from Sinai to Syria, from Afghanistan to Ukraine.

Each time I read this section of Isaiah, I realize there is nothing new under the sun. The fighting between humankind is constantly starting and stopping every day as countries and the people governing them lose direction and understanding of who they are. I see how often wars are started from a place of pure greed or belief one side or another is right and everybody else is wrong. From a distance, it is easy to see it ties in with a desire of nations to place pride before anything, and a disobedience to God's plan for the world.

However, when I read on in Isaiah, I see a glimmer of hope, an opportunity to repent, and a path to aligning the warring nations with God's will and purpose. It gives me hope there are solutions out there to the wars and fighting, which hopefully more level heads will consider. So, I continue to pray each night and each day for peace in our world.

Day 214

Read: Isaiah 23–27

Open the gates that the righteous nation may enter, the nation that keeps faith.
—Isaiah 26:2

When I pray each day for peace, I also pray that warring nations find themselves again. When I sat with my grandmother, we talked about this. I felt the people who were at war, who had lost their right relationship with God, had to find a way to put their trust in God again and commit themselves to being back in a right relationship with God. If they could only concentrate on finding that right relationship with God and stay focused on it, then they could find a way to end their wars.

When fighting a war, people are thinking about many different things, and I realized there were parallels in my own life. I often find myself running over things in my mind, replaying the list of my responsibilities, tasks, and scheduled events I have committed to, which doesn't include thinking about other people's problems, their tragedies, and all the things going wrong in the world every day. When I can stop myself, calm my mind, and refocus, I can clearly see God is my rock and refuge in times of trouble.

If mine, then why not for everyone? This truth creates a possibility for me to be a conduit between those I pray for who are struggling, in fear, homeless, hungry, or in need, and God. I am no longer committing to solving the world's problems on my own; rather, I am trusting God to guide my thoughts and prayers, and the minds of others, to find ways to heal and end their wars and fighting. I am not saying I do nothing! I seek guidance from praying with God to find the solutions I can share with others.

Day 215

Read: Isaiah 28–30

Yet the Lord longs to be gracious to you; therefore, he will rise up to show you compassion.

—Isaiah 30:18

I only have to think about the last thirty to forty years of my life, and I can see times when I messed up, times when I wouldn't listen to anybody, and times when I was so stubborn about something that I missed the opportunity of a lifetime. I can also see the times when I was not open to what God had in mind and was led astray in all sorts of different ways.

I am not talking about going out and robbing a bank, but about not listening to what is going on around me, not being as perceptive as usual, not listening to other's problems, and being self-focused and self-pitying. Yet even when I was rejecting God's call to me, it is clear to me now God was always open to my returning. If this was true for me, then surely it is true for humanity as a whole.

In these words of Isaiah, I see God opening up to all of us, no matter what we have done, what we are resisting, what we have hardened our hearts to. God's desire is to receive us and give us healing and love. What an amazing gift to us today and every day! God shares our problems and difficulties, no matter where we are in our lives, whatever mess we have gotten into. However bleak and forlorn our outlook is, God is there to hold us and heal us. Only through God can we heal our souls, calm our spirits, and love ourselves again so we may love others. If we are quiet, still, peaceful, calm, and confident in God, we can experience the strength and love of God, which leads us to the peace which passes all understanding.

Day 216

Read: Isaiah 31–35

Be strong, do not fear; your God will come, he will come with vengeance;
with divine retribution he will come to save you.

—Isaiah 35:4

I am not sure when I first realized to be in the right relationship meant being righteous. It may have been when I sat with my grandmother, and she shared she wanted to be in right standing with God. She used to laugh and say the reason she read something from the Bible every day was to "cram for her finals." I would quickly say she had plenty of time to do that, and in fact, she lived with my parents for about another thirty years, up into her nineties.

She had a point though. Righteousness is being in right relationship with God and happens when we put our trust in God and live our lives reflecting that. Living in America, I witness the pressure on people to believe they are right in their own eyes; therefore, they must be right. In America, many believe they are right, so accordingly, they think they can do whatever they think is right.

My grandmother would never have thought that. She felt to be righteous meant being right in the eyes of God and that included being of good character, having a clear conscience, being of good conduct, and living up to one's word. Righteousness is a God-centered attribute that we can only reach with God's help.

A lot of these chapters in Isaiah are warning the people about the consequences of not following God's teachings. Yet in Isaiah, the prophet constantly wants the people to understand how to come back into right relationship with God and how much God wants that too. If the people of Israel, then we too! Throughout these chapters, despite the harsh imagery, there are hints of righteousness and, ultimately, peace.

Day 217

Read: Isaiah 36–41

The time will surely come when everything in your palace, and all that your predecessors have stored up until this day, will be carried off to Babylon.

—Isaiah 39:6

Just when we think everything is going okay, the prophet shares their downfall and exile to Babylon. My grandmother thought this was a bit like after the war. People who had fought in different countries saw both the wealth of those countries and the poverty of others. People started to see the large differences between countries that were rich and had great wealth and those that didn't.

I noticed this later in my life with the people who broadcast for the BBC in the foreign language services. Some of them came from countries wealthier than Britain. Others, not so much. I was the specialist studio manager for an area of the world that included all the countries from Vietnam to Afghanistan. Some of the broadcasters were formerly government employees in their country; others were teachers, doctors, or lawyers. The one thing they had in common, though, was they were *privileged* in their own countries. As more people traveled back and forth between countries, others came and shared their views, which often contradicted the status quo.

When countries changed governments with coups or elections, the privileged class seemed to do okay no matter what. I realized when the people of Israel were taken away to Babylon, it was mainly the elite and privileged class with all their belongings and wealth that were taken, leaving behind the peasant class to work the fields and continue life much as before. They are not talked about in this passage as they didn't matter to the people who wrote the book and recounted the stories. A good lesson here.

Day 218

Read: Isaiah 42–44

When you walk through the fire, you will not be burned; the flames will not set you ablaze.

—Isaiah 43:2

My grandmother often repeated her stories about her life, about being sold into service by her parents because she had too many brothers and sisters for them to feed. They lived in great poverty in a Dickensian part of London at the turn of the 1900s. She was only seven when she was sold into service to a family.

I struggle wrapping my head around her story, but she said *what didn't break her, made her stronger*. She felt it helped develop her character and learn to persevere, and she felt it brought her closer to God. She learned the disciplines of sacrifice and its benefits. In turn, this discipline made her a better person. She was prepared to go through these challenges to reach her full potential.

I have faced challenges, bullying, loneliness, and even persecution, and there were times when I wanted to give up. There were also people put into my life to test me, yet they became the very people to smooth off my rough edges. When I meditate on this text, there are words that jump out at me, particularly *When* and *through*. It is not a matter of *if* something will happen in my life, but *when* it will happen, and then, I can ask: How will God guide me through?

It doesn't matter how tough or deep my problems are because God has committed to helping me through them to the other side, which brings comfort to me whenever I experience challenges or see challenges around the world. God helped me as I went through a divorce, job loss, bankruptcy, and illness. Hope was always there. Since there was hope, I could pray and give thanks to God for it.

Day 219

Read: Isaiah 45–48

I have made you and I will carry you; I will sustain you and I will rescue you.
—Isaiah 46:4

My parents were convinced growing up that I would become an architect. From when I could first draw, I drew pictures of houses. I spent years of my life struggling with difficult math problems, taking extra math courses in high school—which I didn't like, but told myself I needed to become an architect. At university, I went through a difficult time as I was marrying, separating, reuniting, divorcing—all the while studying for a degree in architecture. With two friends, I worked hard on a project, entered it in a competition, and won the 1973 Royal Academy Award for Architecture from the Members of the British Institution.

Then, I suddenly hit a brick wall. I spent a year working in two different architects' offices—one large, one small—and realized I hated the work in both. Fortunately, I had a mentor who taught History of Architecture, and he helped me see that the skills I learned as I trained to be an architect could be used in many different ways. He suggested we talk about and discuss other careers or opportunities. He started by saying if I still wanted to finish as an architect I could, but . . . and he let the remaining words float away into the ether.

I realized then that God wanted me to use my gifts to communicate. I still had a lot to learn. In fact, I learned something new every day—about myself, about others, about the world—and still do so to this day. It was then I applied, and was accepted, to work as a studio manager with the BBC World Service. It was as if a connection to the universe closed, and another opened. Lots of things fell into place and made sense in a way they never had before. God had been there all along.

Day 220

Read: Isaiah 49–53

He said to me, "You are my servant, Israel, in whom I will display my splendor."
—Isaiah 49:3

Knowing God has a plan is one thing. Understanding and accepting it is another. The next years of my life were spent working at the BBC and struggling to understand if I had a call at all. The words of Isaiah challenged the people of Israel to look back at their history with Abraham and Sarah and see God's promises fulfilled through them.

I looked back at what my parents had shared with me and what their parents had shared with them. I remembered how my father sat and read from the Bible every day, how my grandmother sat and read her Bible every afternoon, and how I was able to help her read it. I remember my mother reading the Bible with her women's group each week, sharing their troubles and woes.

The common denominator was the Bible. In those years of working at the BBC, I felt the call to open the Bible again, read it, and journal my thoughts every day. Despite my best intentions, I lapsed many times over the next few years, distracted by opportunities from work or relationships. Reading the Bible and journaling my thoughts took second place. When I read the journals from that time, though, I highlighted different things each time I read the same chapters of the Bible. As my life changed, my understanding of the Bible changed also. More and more, I saw the Bible as a human product that tells us how our religious ancestors saw things, how they explained things, but not how God sees things.

Imagine my surprise when, years later, I heard theologian Marcus Borg say the same thing in a guest lecture at Eden Seminary in St. Louis, a long way from the BBC studios in Bush House in London.

Day 221

Read: Isaiah 54–58

I live in a high and holy place, but also with the one who is contrite and lowly in spirit, to revive the spirit of the lowly and to revive the heart of the contrite.

—Isaiah 57:15

Inside my father's Bible, my grandfather had handwritten Psalm 121. He had written it as he hoped it would sustain my father memories of growing up happily in Durango and Silverton, Colorado. Reading it also reminded my father that God was in a high and holy place. In fact, my father realized God is everywhere, not needing a house or a building, but rather existing within us.

The power of these words is in the living of them, honestly and openly. At different times in my life, I have lived in a house, an apartment or flat, a tent, my car, and a bench in a park. Yet everywhere I have lived, everywhere I have laid my head to rest, I have known God is with me. At times, I believe I am unworthy of God's love, yet God loves me anyway. I have put pride before a fall more than once in my life, yet releasing myself into God's care has always been possible. I find myself daily asking God to help me grow in humility, to weed out my arrogance or privileged attitude—even as I pray for others I care about, whether I know them or not. I need to prepare the road in my heart every day as it is often blocked with obstacles to simply loving God.

My journal thirty years ago contained these words, "I am no longer my own, but yours. Put me to what you will, place me with whom you will. Let me be put to work for you or set aside for you. I freely surrender all things to your glory and service" (Wesleyan Covenant Prayer, modern. UMC Hymnal 1989).

I think I had been reading John Wesley. I was certainly channeling his spirit.

Day 222

Read: Isaiah 59–63

He has sent me to bind up the brokenhearted, to proclaim freedom for the captives and release from darkness for the prisoners.

—Isaiah 61:1

When I read stories from the Old Testament, I remind myself Jesus only had the Jewish scriptures. Indeed, his followers sought to place his ministry in the Gospel stories in order to fulfill particular Old Testament prophecies. When I read of an "anointed servant of the Lord who will proclaim good news to the poor, bind up the brokenhearted, proclaim freedom to the captives, release from darkness the prisoners," this servant sounds a lot like Jesus.

However, living in a world surrounded by these issues still, what I have seen and noted in my journals are the stories of ordinary people doing amazing things. Growing up, I recall the amazing work and ministry done by Rev. Trevor Huddleston and his stories of life in Sophiatown, which he shared at our kitchen table. His ministry to overturn apartheid in South Africa—first in South Africa, then back in the UK—by starting the anti-apartheid movement with Bishop Ambrose Reeves and others. Then, I met his protégé whom he helped come to London to complete his theological studies, Desmond Tutu. His powerful and joyous sermons and message that he shared with our church in North London transformed the members of our church.

These experiences opened my mind to listening to the stories of prophets of our time. My father and I talked about many of them up until his death in 1992, and we always shared their stories with each other. Through my father, I came to know many stories from Mother Theresa to Gandhi, from Martin Luther King, Jr. to St. Oscar Romero, from Dietrich Bonhoeffer to St. Maximilian Kolbe. However, my father's greatest gift was encouraging me to see beyond these people and find God in everyone I meet—and the things they do every day.

Day 223

Read: Isaiah 64–66

See, I will create new heavens and a new earth.

—Isaiah 65:17

In my journals, I find days when things were not going well. In fact, I see weeks, months, and even years when things looked particularly bleak. Then, each year I would come to this chapter of Isaiah and hear again the promises of hope, restoration, and our purpose in the life of our world. The "new heaven and a new earth" suggests a complete transformation of the world, one in which all problems will be replaced with opportunities for a new beginning.

As the years have passed, we seem to be beset by climate change, wildfires, floods, storms, and more. I now see this passage speaks not only to the world's climate, but our spirituality too. As my life has gone up and down, as friends have come and gone, as family has passed away and been reborn in the next generations, I can see these words in a broader perspective. Each trip through the Bible opens new insights and clarity.

We are part of the creation, so, if God is renewing creation as the prophet proclaims, then God is renewing us as well. After all the judgement and challenges thrown at us through these chapters, God simply wants us to have a humble and contrite heart. This is where reading through the Bible every day helped me remember another text that overlaps the words of Isaiah, the words shared on his inauguration day by former President Jimmy Carter from the book of Micah, "He hath showed me, O man, what is good; and what the Lord does require of thee, but to do justly, and to love mercy, and to walk humbly with thy God." (Micah 6:8)

Day 224

Read: Jeremiah 1–3

Before I formed you in the womb I knew you, before you were born, I set you apart; I appointed you as a prophet to the nations.

—Jeremiah 1:5

I remember being involved in church from the time I was little. As a child, I straightened the prayer books and hymnals in the pews after services were over. I carried the flowers to whomever was supposed to receive them after church. I helped lay the places for parish breakfast. Later, I was involved in the services, first as a boat boy, carrying the incense for the thurifer, then as an acolyte, then a choir boy, then a lector.

Early one Sunday morning, I heard someone coming into the church. I heard them call my name. There was no one there, not even the priest had arrived yet. I thought I must have been hearing noises in the old building and ignored it. I didn't mention it to anyone. In my late teens, I heard it again when I was upset about the way my life seemed to be shaping up. I went to church on a weekday morning and sat in the lady chapel on the side of the church. I had been sitting and praying for a while and thought I heard someone come into the building—and then heard them call my name. Again, there was no one there.

Many years later in America as I went through a painful divorce, I went to my local church and sat in the side chapel as I had nowhere to sleep. The doors had an electronic lock that locked me in at 10 p.m. I sat there, praying for guidance through the night. Then in the early hours, I heard someone call my name—softly but clearly—but there was nobody there. This time I shared it with someone.

Day 225

Read: Jeremiah 4–6

If you can find but one person who deals honestly and seeks the truth, I will forgive this city.

—Jeremiah 5:1

I was sitting alone in church, listening. Was it the wind in the trees outside or a creaky floor or window? As I reviewed old journals, I found a pattern I had not seen before with this text, this book, this prophet. Again and again, year after year, these texts reached out to me, calling me back to church, to the spirit of church. My reflections were questioning, not answering, what my actions were at that time. Listening—just listening, not speaking or saying anything out loud—was not something I found easy to do.

These texts challenged me to ask who I thought God was and what was the character of God. Portraying God as sovereign over creation and the nations, these chapters bridge thoughts between the Old Testament and the New Testament. Through Jeremiah, God speaks, and the course of history changes. God appears to have the power to pluck up and pull down, while building up and planting with us, as well as with other nations.

To me, each year, it seemed like a giant pendulum swinging back and forth, first rising up, then crushing down, and then rising up again. Through it all is a path of mercy for others and for myself. When I read about what was happening in my life at different times and how I reacted to it, Jeremiah's guidance was often front and center. I sometimes saw the inevitable disaster coming my way and looked for ways to humble myself, though it might not be enough. Seeing corruption all around me often left me struggling with what I should do: *How do I stay honest when all around me is falling apart?*

Day 226

Read: Jeremiah 7–9

If you do not oppress the foreigner, the fatherless or the widow and do not shed innocent blood in this place.

—Jeremiah 7:6

There was a time when I felt I was doing well in a new job with the BBC—my colleagues and bosses seemed nice and positive about my work—however, God reminded me through Jeremiah to not trust deceptive words. When I questioned myself, I realized I had not listened enough to what people were saying and was only hearing what I wanted to hear, rather than what God was sharing with me.

This also woke me up from being misled by other gods and *shiny things*. The BBC management was very good at telling you one thing while actually planning another. They didn't want us to see the truth, mainly because they were not living up to even the first commandment. After all, if we didn't exploit others, where was the *good* program that would attract viewers and listeners?

I struggled with this practice at different times, in different positions within the BBC. One year, the news position I held involved editors who wanted stories to be as salacious as possible, or they wouldn't attract enough listeners. Another year, different editors on another program wanted the story to show others in the worse light possible. When I challenged this, they went around me to broadcast their story—not the honest story, in my opinion. My journals showed me how difficult it was to live this life honestly, consistently reflecting the guidance of a prophet like Jeremiah.

Day 227

Read: Jeremiah 10–13

But God made the earth by his power; he founded the world by his wisdom and stretched out the heavens by his understanding.

—Jeremiah 10:12

A recurring theme in my journals, year after year, is a wakeup call to not get distracted by humanmade idols, but to remember to follow the teachings of my parents, godparents, and ultimately, God's teachings. Easier said than done sometimes. At different times in my life, I was led astray by new friends, tempting me with different gods. The hardest one to resist is the god of money. So many people I worked with over the years are primarily driven by how much money they can make. When they meet someone like me, to whom money is not the primary driver in a career or calling, they are not sure how to handle it. By constantly reminding me of what they have by being paid more, they try to draw me in to following their God of money.

Thankfully, through prayer, I realized their lifestyle was taking me away from God. I was able to turn back to one God, the living god, the God who made the earth and stretched out the heavens. If God is beyond manipulation, as Jeremiah says, then God is concerned for the well-being of creation and humankind and to be trusted. Many times in these readings, Jeremiah raises the question of false idols and idolatry.

In one of my journal entries, I wrote about sitting at the confluence of the Mississippi and Missouri Rivers, watching the two big rivers come together as one. I remembered how the indigenous peoples worshiped a river god as opposed to the one, true God. Sitting and praying there, I understood how they could worship a river god, as the power of the two rivers was huge. However, I knew in my heart that God created everything I could see, and I fully trusted in creation.

Day 228

Read: Jeremiah 14–17

When your words came, I ate them; they were my joy and my heart's delight,
for I bear your name, Lord God Almighty.

—Jeremiah 15:16

"When your words came, I ate them." Not just eating the words, but each time I read the pages in my journals, I devoured the words. I ate them up. I consumed them. It was as if I had a hearty and healthy appetite for the words of God. In Jeremiah, I saw the need to do this every day, as if I was being given instructions on how to share this book.

Each day, I need to read a few pages of the Bible. Each day, I need to meditate and journal about the reading. Each day, I receive nutrition and sustenance from words in the Bible to guide me in my life. Realizing the instructions for this book, *Bible 365,* are in Jeremiah didn't come at first. It took decades for it to sink in, and for me to understood what these texts meant. At first, I read on my own or asked my parents questions. Later, I asked my godparents, then I asked clergy, or through my sister's godfather, monks on retreat at Buckfast Abbey. Later, when I worked at the BBC recording religious programs, I met Reverend John Stott, who has been described as an architect of twentieth century evangelicalism who shaped the faith of a generation, and he challenged me to think about things differently.

When I moved to America in 1992, my new parish priest challenged me to look deeper and study the Bible in a new diocesan program formed to encourage us to study the Bible. Then another priest shared that he felt I should explore a call to ministry at seminary in St. Louis. All these events led me to a side chapel of a church, sitting through a dark night of the soul, praying, listening, and being open to hear the still small voice in the night.

Day 229

Read: Jeremiah 18–22

This is the word that came to Jeremiah from the Lord: "Go down to the potter's house, and there I will give you my message."

—Jeremiah 18:1–2

Life plays tricks on you. In 2003, I searched for a place to sit, pray, and be safe. My searching brought me to a chapel attached to a church in a suburb of St. Louis. I had worshipped at this church when I first moved to St. Louis, and the chapel was added a few years later. It was a quiet place. At 10 p.m., automatic locks on the door clicked to tell me I was safely locked in. I sat quietly, praying and reading through my Bible. I could feel the hands of the potter working the clay of me, forming something new from something old and broken. So much was going on in my life, my work, my marriage, my very being.

My parents, grandparents, and godparents had all passed away. My brother and sisters were back in the UK and out of touch with my life in America. The beautiful stained-glass windows of the chapel let in the soft glow of evening light as if looking through trees. Creation was all around me. I also had my prayer book given me by my godmother at my confirmation, an English Catholic Prayer Book, used by our church in London in the 1950s–60s. The familiarity of the prayers was comforting to read. As the night rolled on, my prayers explored more and more of my inner thoughts. Gradually I calmed my mind, sat, and meditated.

In the early morning light, I heard the click of the locks opening, and then a feeling came over me—a feeling of being safe, of knowing what I had known for a long time and fought a long time. I was called to serve others in ministry, in hospitals and pastoral care. God was remolding me as a chaplain.

Day 230

Read: Jeremiah 23–25

They will be my people, and I will be their God, for they will return to me with all their heart.

—Jeremiah 24:7

I spent a good deal of time with several different priests in our community. Their guidance and support were critical in my moving from working in the business world to hearing my call to become a chaplain. One helped me find somewhere to live during the transition of the divorce from my second wife. Another helped me find a good therapist, a Scottish woman, who could identify with me culturally as well as spiritually. Another helped me find a new parish home where I could be accepted for simply who I am. Another started me in the process of discussions with the bishop of the diocese I lived in.

After my divorce was final, I began to move on. My role as a parent became even more important than previously, as I sought to give my children all the stability I could. I also started working as a chaplain both in hospitals and in a small parish in north St. Louis County. There was a lot of turmoil in my life. Spending part of every day journaling, sitting in prayer and Bible study, centered me and helped me be more open to all the changes in my life, as every day brought something new.

Seminary plucks students apart and builds them back up. For me, this process confirmed I was called to serve in ministry as a hospital chaplain, and I spent the three years at seminary strengthening those skillsets, which included earning units of clinical pastoral care from two different hospitals. Gradually I found my calling, and my eyes were opened to how I could bring God's purpose for me into both hospitals and church. I was being brought back to who I was, who God created, and how I could serve others.

Day 231

Read: Jeremiah 26–29

You will seek me and find me when you seek me with all your heart.

—Jeremiah 29:13

Journaling every day, reading the Bible, praying and meditating every day, sounds great—until things go wrong. There were times when my life was going smoothly, seemingly moving forward. Other times I struggled and could not make heads nor tails of my life or what its purpose might be. It is comforting to think that somebody else has our back. These words always spoke to me that someone, somewhere, has a plan or a thought about what my purpose in life is.

These words also always spoke to me about going back into the rhythm of life: of praying, reading the Bible, and meditating on the Word. I often found this happening when I was already stretched to the limit and thought I couldn't add another thing to my day. Yet by doing just that—adding more to my day—space opened up, peace opened up, my heart opened up, and God opened a door in my life to step through in ways I could never have imagined.

It takes courage to step through the door, trusting God has guided me to it for a reason. Several times, the doorway didn't seem the right one at first, yet each time, one door led to another and kept moving me forward. Sometimes I hung back, yet each time, trusting God led me forward. Over the years, there have been a lot of doors leading me to new relationships, friendships, and opportunities. Sometimes when I hold my journals in my hands, I can feel God's hand in my life; sometimes I can see God's influence. Yet, at the time I was journaling, I was facing the unknown as I stepped through a door, crossing the threshold of the next story of my life.

Day 232

Read: Jeremiah 30–31

Write in a book all the words I have spoken to you.

—Jeremiah 30:2

I went to a performance of Shakespeare performed live outdoors. The performance happened on the terrace of a large country house to the North of London. Powerfully, it was in the open air, using the terraces and walls of the existing country house as its stage. Shakespeare's words transported us back to another time and place, back in history, to the court of Queen Elizabeth I. This old country house had not hosted a performance like this for centuries, though the play felt like it had always meant to be performed this way.

I always felt this was like Jeremiah being told by God to write down a story in the book so that in times to come, others could look back and know they were always meant to be there, living their lives as God's people. And if Jeremiah, what of me? What of anyone else who reads the Bible? Hearing Jeremiah saying that God "will break the yoke off our necks and tear off our bonds" means so much to so many who have suffered. These are words of faith, hope, and love, not just for the people of Israel and Judah, but for everyone.

After reading these same chapters in a different year, I noted I was sitting alone in a divorce court with no friends or family, and I felt beaten up by my soon-to-be ex-wife. These words in Jeremiah brought me comfort and hope, hope I could rebuild my relationships, and hope for my future to be restored. A period of great change was sweeping through my life then, and was each time I looked through my journal, yet the words in Jeremiah gave me hope that whatever came my way I would be able to face it with God at my side.

Day 233

Read: Jeremiah 32–34

Then the word of the Lord came to Jeremiah: "I am the Lord, the God of all mankind. Is anything too hard for me?"
—Jeremiah 32:26–27

A word or phrase can jump off the page when you are reading the Bible every day. A passage can sound different when hearing it on a Sunday, sitting in church. Several times in my journals, I found I was scared of what was going on in my life. Many years ago, I was suffering as my first marriage fell apart. I struggled to find a way to heal the broken relationship with my first wife. No matter how hard I prayed about it, everything seemed to stay broken. I felt the problems in my marriage were too difficult, even for God.

Then I read these words, and they jumped off the page at me. Nothing in my life is beyond God's reach. Nothing is too large or too difficult. I might not understand why God hasn't answered me or shown me what I needed to do, but by praying and sharing my difficulty with God, an answer can be found. I might not receive the answer I expected or thought I would get, but it could lead me forward in my life.

In my journals, I see this happening again and again. Often the answers were not what I expected or wanted, but answers they were, each time opening new ways forward. When I was alone in a foreign land, deserted by someone I had loved deeply and not knowing how to move forward, I prayed and talked to God about what was facing me. No prayer was too hard for God to answer, no temptation to powerful to deliver me from, no sadness too deep to relieve me from. Each time, prayer, meditation, and journaling brought me closer to God and closer to the answer to what was going on in my life.

Day 234

Read: Jeremiah 35–37

Please pray to the Lord our God for us.

–Jeremiah 37:3

These chapters from Jeremiah puzzled me at first. Several days each year, I thought there was a lot of hope in what Jeremiah shared with us; then there was this. It made me stop and wonder how I fit into what was being shared. Clearly, if I lived an abstemious life and didn't get drunk or stopped drinking completely, then I could be like the Rekabites, a nomadic people who abstained from alcohol and other *indulgences.* Not easy for someone growing up in England in the 1960s, though my parents set a good example with the occasional glass of sherry before a meal and a glass of wine with the meal—nothing to excess. One of my sisters, though, ran and managed a pub for many years, and drinking with her was a cultural norm. Even at the BBC, there was a social club in the basement of the building we worked in, allowing us to drink every day.

When I was going through a difficult time after my first divorce, sitting in the social club in the evening was a way of passing the time with others, avoiding being on my own. I could drink every evening, which became a habit. Fortunately for me, a good friend sat with me one evening and talked to me about how I might need to break the habit. He shared how he had gone to Alcoholics Anonymous, and that organization had helped him. As I was due to take a break from work, I decided to visit my sister's godfather, a Benedictine monk. Being on retreat at the monastery, in a different routine, re-energized my prayer, Bible study, and journaling habits, which in turn, helped me break the habit I had slipped into of drinking every evening.

Day 235

Read: Jeremiah 38–41

This city will certainly be given into the hands of the army of the king of Babylon, who will capture it.

—Jeremiah 38:3

My journal entries over the years were extremely varied about these readings from Jeremiah. One year, all I put down was a row of exclamation marks. Another year, I questioned the relevance to my living and working in London. Another year, as I watched the recapture of an invaded Kuwait and the violence taking place, I commented in my journals how similar it must have been for the people left behind. What I did see was that the people in charge were either executed or taken away as prisoners. Those left behind were the women and children and those working the fields, pushing their boats out to fish, growing crops, herding sheep and goats—the sheepherder, the blacksmith, the carpenter, the fisherman, the baker, in other words, the poor. Who speaks for them? Who prophesies to them?

Over the last fifty years, there have been so many wars, famines, and disasters. Each time, those left behind had to fend for themselves as well as they could. I am more familiar with some of these events than others. More recently, I was sitting with a priest from South Sudan who had come to seminary in America, listening to his life story of being an orphan and refugee from his youth. Yet, he still managed to be trained and called to become a priest. I can only wonder what God's plans mean to him. He would share his stories with us, of the things he had seen, and his eyes would well up. He could have stayed in America and been safe; rather, he returned to South Sudan. His call, his ministry, is not an easy one; however, since he has returned to South Sudan, he has not only survived but also flourished with God's help.

Day 236

Read: Jeremiah 42–45

". . . for I will bring disaster on all people," declares the Lord, "but wherever you go I will let you escape with your life."

—Jeremiah 45:5

The priest from South Sudan shared with us how important it was to return to his home. He needed to return to help lead a peace between North and South Sudan, not as a politician, but as a leader in the church. North and South Sudan had split mainly on religious differences between Muslims in the North and Christians in the South. By returning and leading his community in the South, he believed prayer could make a difference. Our diocese set out to help him in any way we could, and Christians from a diocese in England traveled to help however they could.

Reading how Jeremiah talked with Baruch made me think about the whole mess the remnant of Judah had gotten itself into. How much it was prepared to give up to just be safe! I wondered about the migrants who travel up through Africa to the Mediterranean coast, then make the dangerous crossing to attempt to travel to Europe where they believe they will be safe and better off. Many migrants die on the way. More than that, it is clear they give up so much of their beliefs and lives from their original countries. Many of them even change their faith on the journey and lose their faith of origin. Some of them travel back years later to see the families they left behind, finding it almost impossible to fit back in, no longer having the common knowledge, faith, and experiences.

How does this writing in the Bible from so long ago influence my thinking about the wars currently happening? Letting people escape with their lives when everything is destroyed is not easy either.

Day 237

Read: Jeremiah 46–48

Jacob will again have peace and security, and no one will make him afraid.
—Jeremiah 46:27

In the midst of all the retribution and fall of the countries who overcome Israel and Judah, there is still the promise to Israel that God will not desert them, and Jeremiah is no exception. When I journaled about this in 1977, I felt this reflected the work being done by President Jimmy Carter, the Prime Minister of Israel, Menachem Begin, and the President of Egypt, Anwar Sadat. Their efforts resulted in the Camp David peace agreement. It was as if they had taken a leaf out of the Bible to give Israel peace and security from the nations who had surrounded them and attempted to destroy them; their actions resulted in the *Six-Day War*. Peace was not easily won and cost the life of the Egyptian president a few years later.

When I read these chapters now, I think and pray about how to resolve conflict around the world and how peace can be introduced into the situation. Over the last fifty years, I have prayed about different parts of the world from the Falklands to Vietnam, from Kuwait to the Congo, from Iraq to Afghanistan, from Sudan to Ukraine. Being aware of the conflicts has helped me not feel helpless about what happens in the world. Praying for resolution to conflict and peace may seem futile, but I believe the power of prayer exists and can move mountains. Most of the time, I pray for the combatants to see how they can come to a peaceful resolution. I am not asking God to intercede and magically stop the wars, but rather to show the combatants how much we are all alike, so we can settle our differences with our words, not by force. True then, and true now.

Day 238

"In those days, at that time," declares the Lord, "the people of Israel and the people of Judah together will go in tears to seek the Lord their God."

—Jeremiah 50:4

When I was younger, I read the stories from scripture and wondered what it would have been like to have been in the middle of the stories. I was drawn to the history forged out of Israel and Judah, and Jesus' place in all this. As I grew older, I was journaling on a park bench in a public garden overlooking the river Thames, when something different happened. I felt free to think for the first time in a long time. Free to be myself. Free, but also realizing with two young children, my twin boys, my life had totally changed for the better. I deeply loved them, yet at the same time, I was being kept away from them except for limited visits. They were going to have a new stepfather in their lives. How was I going to both be in their lives, yet not the dominant father part of their lives?

The words of Jeremiah jumped off the page as riverboats went up and down the river, as buses passed by, as people walked through the park, and I sat quietly. The key was to stay connected to God. It was easy to lose sight of the commitment to keep my relationship with God safe and strong. When I lost sight of the commitment, it led me to wrong decisions. When I did not stay focused on keeping a daily relationship with God through journaling, praying and reading the Bible, I lost sight of God's purpose for me.

Reading through the Bible every day, meditating and journaling on it, makes a difference. It makes it possible to be able to be present to God, open to God's purpose for me and others.

Day 239

Read: Jeremiah 51–52

Do not lose heart or be afraid when rumors are heard in the land; one rumor comes this year, another the next, rumors of violence in the land and of ruler against ruler.

—Jeremiah 51:46

To me, Jeremiah seems focused on how and why God is sending Israel into captivity, what it did wrong, and how God judged them. Over the years, I dove deeper about how God was sovereign—not just over Israel, other nations, and other kingdoms, but the whole world. I could see how God reached out, judged, and punished Israel, but also how having used Babylon, God then judged and punished them too.

God went further still, judging and punishing anyone who worked against God—any nation, any empire, or any individual. Throughout the Bible, Babylon, who had been God's agent of power over Israel, became a threat to God's power. The prophets spoke before Babylon came to power, and their voices seemed to give authority to God over Babylon and any other nation. This played out in violence across our world between nations and between individuals.

The ultimate power lies with God. So often though, we see force chosen instead of negotiating and diplomacy. We witness senseless wars between countries; we see people shot because of road rage or carjackings; we see lives being taken for no reason. If God is in control and created our world for us to live in, then we must be open to listening, mediating, and praying. Sometimes it's hard to live by this practice; sometimes the headlines bring us to tears. This is a practice I believe God wants us to live by.

Day 240

Read: Lamentations 1:1–3:36

The Lord is good to those whose hope is in him, to the one who seeks him; it is good to wait quietly for the salvation of the Lord.
—Lamentations 3:25–26

When I was little, we went to church every day during the week leading up to Easter, called Holy Week. It seemed exhausting to a child when we had to be there for so many services. My mother, godmother, and the other ladies of the church also seemed to be constantly changing things around. Moving flowers out. Bringing candles in. Changing the color of the linens. Washing robes. It was an incredibly busy week without a break for anyone, especially not to sit with God.

On the Wednesday before Easter, everything came to a grinding halt; everything would stop. Candles were lit in church, and people would come in and sit down in silence. Simply sit in silence. A bell rang. The priest stood in front of everyone, and we started. A service flowed from within the soul of the church made up of nine readings, many from Lamentations, Psalms, canticles, responses, antiphons, and other readings with lots of breaks and silences between the readings. It was as if between each reading, each response, we were waiting to hear God's response, waiting for that *still, small voice* of God in the midst of all the rushing. In that busy time, we took a moment of time to wait, and watch, and listen.

As I got older, I sought out a church on the evening of Holy Wednesday to find a community who shared this service, known as Tenebrae. When I still lived in London, I could find one most years and join, for a moment, with a community of souls who sat, watched, and waited to hear God's still, small voice.

Day 241

Read: Lamentations 3:37–5:22

You, Lord, reign forever; your throne endures from generation to generation.
—Lamentations 5:19

When I moved to America, I didn't initially find a church that shared the *Tenebrae* service. When I found myself assisting at a church in North St. Louis County, I suggested sharing this experience. However, the idea of adding another service to the already busy Easter week schedule didn't sit well. Instead, I visited another church that was holding this service and took the opportunity to slow down the busy pace of Easter week for a moment.

Because I had planted the seed of the idea, my own church talked about it and decided to introduce a new Sunday evening service reflecting this spirit. We based it on the Celtic tradition from Iona in Scotland. This Celtic service on a Sunday evening created a peaceful end to the week for our community—a time to listen for that still, small voice as we prepared to go back into the fast-moving culture of the week. It also brought us together to share readings from Lamentations, which enabled us to be ready to sit and listen for God's voice to guide us in our ministry going forward when we had a time of trouble in our community a few years later. God's purpose for us as community came through to us by sitting quietly in the moment. It was comforting to realize that in an ever-changing world, with change happening on a daily basis, God doesn't change.

In so many ways, God's mercy is always the same, and God's grace is too. However, what does truly change is our *perception* of how God moves in our lives. These changes are really in us, not God, as we open ourselves up more and more to change. How we interact with God, how we experience God might change, but we are the ones changing.

Day 242

Read: Ezekiel 1–4

And whether they listen or fail to listen, for they are a rebellious people, they will know that a prophet has been among them.

—Ezekiel 2:5

Living in a community in a time of unrest and change is challenging. The year was 2014, and Ferguson, Missouri, erupted in a storm of pain, protest, and violence. I wrote about violence in the streets, broken windows, torches, and men wearing body armor who sat on rooftops. Our city was hurting. It was not clear to any of us what would happen. Would our homes burn to the ground? Each night for weeks, people walked in the streets. They walked past my home and threw bricks through windows. Each night, they chanted in the streets as helicopters hovered overhead. Each night, my home shook as the helicopters hovered. And then I heard a voice: "Do not be afraid." First a whisper and then a roar.

Those walking through the streets each night were praying, praying with their feet. Every day, people swept up the broken glass. Every day, broken windows were boarded up. Then people came out of their homes and painted the boards, painted the streets with prayers of peace. People spoke out every day, and every night people protested. We gathered at church and prayed. We asked for help, and people provided food to feed our community, as all the shops in our community were closed or boarded up.

Our little church became the little church that could. We heard God's voice and provided a safe haven for food and for people. Every day for weeks, we served food free to whoever needed it. Despite having nothing to start with, we never ran out. Each time food was running low, more food arrived, and we shared it with others. Everyone got served. No one went hungry or thirsty. At the end of each day, when we cleared up each evening, we still had food. And we prayed prayers of thanks.

Day 243

Read: Ezekiel 5–8

Son of man, have you seen what the elders of Israel are doing in the darkness, each at the shrine of his own idol.

—Ezekiel 8:12

Nights turned into days. Days turned into weeks. My journals from these days and nights were full, confused, painful, and soul-searching. I was blessed in seminary to be taught by a wonderful man, a man who gently challenged my thinking and assumptions. My class with him was in Black studies, and I was one of three white students in his predominately black class. One of my colleagues dropped out early on, leaving two of us to complete the course.

The course was not easy as it challenged everything I had been raised to understand, and my fellow students had life experiences totally different from my own. I struggled to identify with their experiences of growing up in a racially segregated America. I had no good points of reference, so I sat and listened to find references that spoke to me and could guide me. This professor challenged my core being and my foundational thinking. He challenged me to walk a mile in another's shoes, and to pray as I did so. In fact, to pray with my feet. Slowly, I was able to realize, listen to, and share in the grief and trauma my fellow students had experienced simply growing up in America. It was all so different from my own upbringing in England.

As each day and night merged into one, my home shook as people trod the path between the two streets of pain. I saw firsthand the suffering in the faces and bodies of the protestors as they marched from one street to another, much like the Israelites wandering in the desert, searching for a place to grieve their losses and find themselves. As they prayed with their feet, I could listen and be open to feeling their pain and then search myself for how I could change.

Day 244

Read: Ezekiel 9–12

They will eat their food in anxiety and drink their water in despair, for their land will be stripped of everything in it because of the violence of all who live there.

—Ezekiel 12:19

Our church became a place where not only could folks be fed physically, but with prayer, they could be fed spiritually. The most common emotion shared was anger—anger from people pressed down for centuries, boiling over in the streets of my hometown. Anger from people who felt everything they had spent their lives working for was being randomly destroyed. Two conflicting positions prayed to one God. Confused and uncertain of what the future might hold, they did not know what they would wake up to each day. People said they had to move. People said they wanted to move. People said nothing. People said a lot.

On any given day, I sat with people I had never met before, or who I had known for several years, and the same, but different, expressions of fear and anger where shared. Through it all, a still small voice spoke inside of me, asking me to stay calm, speak out against violence, and pray for peace. I challenged myself, though, as to what that might mean. Clearly it meant different things to different people.

God did not make it easy. I could hear my grandmother saying, "Stephen, if it was easy, God wouldn't have asked you to do it!" I could laugh in the middle of all this tumult and mayhem, as I experienced my grandmother's calming presence and the fond memory of her sitting in her chair with her Bible on her lap. I shared with others that I read the Bible every day and invited them to join me. The response was slow at first, then more people picked up the habit, turning to reading and working at understanding what the scriptures mean and how they speak to us today.

Day 245

Read: Ezekiel 13–15

The word of the Lord came to me: "Son of man, how is the wood of a vine different from that of a branch from any of the trees in the forest?"
—Ezekiel 15:1–2

So many people shared their grief, their loss, and their fears that the church became a place of crying, of weeping, of gnashing of teeth. Yet through it all, a seed was planted. At first, I could only sense it, but soon I could feel the presence changing. The broken windows and looted buildings gave way to swept sidewalks and painted artwork on our boarded-up city. People could be seen sitting and talking to each other—sometimes heatedly, sometimes calmly, but talking *with* each other, not *at* each other. They shared their concerns, hopes, and dreams for the future with a lot of *what if* moments happening on street corners and sidewalks.

I listened to people as they shared their hurt and pain, often having nothing to do with this moment, but stemming from pain and grief over many, many years. I listened as people shared their stories of lost hope, lost innocence, lost joy. I listened as they shared their pain of lacking a place to sleep, or a meal to eat, or somewhere to wash and clean their clothes or even themselves. I listened as they shared how they felt God didn't hear them, or how God didn't care, and then the same people gave thanks to God for finding them food and shelter. I listened as they spoke of losing everything they had worked for, and how their children wanted them to move away from this pain and grief. I listened as they said they were staying to rebuild their lives, and the lives of others, in a new, kinder image of God.

I listened. I wept. I prayed.

Day 246

Read: Ezekiel 16–17

I dry up the green tree and make the dry tree flourish. I the Lord have spoken, and I will do it.

—Ezekiel 17:24

How many times over those weeks and months did I write in my journals about the hopes and fears, the dreams and visions, of people around me? Slowly, we realized that change was happening. The constant in all our lives became change. Each day, there were new stories of change. Some stories were met with great sadness as people moved away, leaving homes they had lived in for many years. Some stories were met with great joy as new families became part of the community. Businesses opened, businesses closed, change happened. Through it all, individual people came together to grow a new community. Some still harked back to the old days and how they were missed. Others embraced the challenges of rebuilding and finding a new way of being community, experiencing a new loving God in everything they did.

Through it all, I saw entries in my journals about hope, faith, and love—the most important one being love. Change can be almost imperceptible or sudden and violent. Both types of changes happened over the following years, and my entries reflecting these readings confirmed the changes and positives ultimately seen: a new business here, a new neighbor there, a new organization recognizing that black women are at greater risk of death from childbirth than white women, and a health facility opening its doors and sharing space to create a safe harbor for women to midwife childbirth. A church shared unused space to provide a safe space for women who were traumatized and violently damaged by life, helping them restore their lives, giving them hope for their future. Small local farms grew and provided local food to anyone in the community. People were fed, physically and spiritually.

Day 247

Read: Ezekiel 18–20

Are my ways unjust, people of Israel? Is it not your ways that are unjust?

Ezekiel 18:29

The writing of Ezekiel stands out many times in different ways in my reflections. Some years, I realized I was not living up to my own expectations. At other times, I saw those around me were not living up to the expectations I had for them. Sometimes, people did things I thought were unjust and unpleasant to others. Other times, I saw I also could be unjust and not fair with others. Each time I realized I was being unjust, I worked hard to make amends and to change.

This was not always true with others around me though. Realizing others saw nothing wrong with infidelity was hard. To see people robbing each other both physically and emotionally was heartbreaking. I saw people starving on the one hand, and others throwing away food as it spoiled on the other. I saw children struggling to find clothes to wear in cold weather, while others wore incredibly expensive fashion statements oblivious to others' needs. Over the years, I have seen the culture change as a relationship with God seemed to mean less and less to more and more people.

Fairness, compassion, and love for neighbor no longer seem to be top of mind for many people across the world. In different years, my journal entries picked up on different experiences of this playing out across society. Some years, I could identify strongly with those who had nothing. Other years, I could see through the eyes of those with abundance and in denial of other's needs. In different years, my entries opened my eyes and heart more to the scriptures, showing me how to be in right relationship with God, every day, every way.

Day 248

Read: Ezekiel 21–22

The people of the land practice extortion and commit robbery; they oppress the poor and needy and mistreat the foreigner, denying them justice.
—Ezekiel 22:29

Watching on the news as immigrants cross borders, escaping from famines and wars, searching for a better future for themselves and their families, it strikes me how the story doesn't change, just the people. In my journals, I wrote about the people of the Sudan, South Sudan, who were being persecuted by the people of North Sudan. My friend who had trained in ministry had returned to his home area in South Sudan, yet the war continued. A group of people traveled out of our diocese to help and were joined by a group from England. After several years, the two parts of the whole country split, and South Sudan became its own country. My friend was consecrated a bishop in charge of several churches, making up a new diocese.

Yet the famine, the war, the suffering, did not go away with this change. The poor are always with us. Governments were still corrupt, and soldiers still terrorized the people and abused them. Their daily struggles to survive continued. We did what we could to help; however, they ultimately worked at building churches and schools to help themselves. Slowly, things changed. Less people left to travel to other countries, and some who had journeyed away came back. They no longer worshipped where they had; rather, they found new places to worship, to grow food, and to share the scriptures with each other. The stories in the Bible came alive to them as they grew their food to survive next to their church and in their community. They could relate to both the Old and New Testament stories as they reflected their own life experiences. Listening to the stories from Sudan brought the stories in the Bible to life.

Day 249

Read: Ezekiel 23–24

*Ezekiel will be a sign to you; you will do just as he has done. When this
happens, you will know that I am the Sovereign Lord.*

—Ezekiel 24:24

One year when reading Ezekiel, I wrote entries about the Sudan. Another
year, I wrote entries about television evangelists in America leading their
flock down the wrong path. A flood hit an area of Texas where floods had
not happened before, and the usual helpers from the Red Cross and FEMA
rushed in to help. In contrast, a televangelist said he would not open up his
sanctuary to people who had been displaced by the flood because he was not
equipped to help. All the people wanted was to find somewhere dry, out of
the rain, where they could lay their head and keep their children safe. Yet
the televangelist said no. He did move his cars and airplanes to safer ground
to protect them, but the people he had no room for.

I struggled with his message, which he was sharing with others. I
needed to let God deal with this and not judge the televangelist myself. I
acknowledged there might be circumstances I was unaware of, so I needed
to step back and not judge him. Then another year in my journals, I was
in the same predicament. *Can we open our church as a warming center in
the winter or are there reasons we cannot?* I jumped to all the reasons why we
couldn't do it first, not the reasons why we should do it.

How can we make it happen? What can we overcome to truly reach
out and be somewhere the hungry, tired, and cold can come and rest and
recharge themselves? How can we make the impossible possible? How can
we change our hearts, so we can change our actions too?

Day 250

Read: Ezekiel 25–27

They will set up their camps and pitch their tents among you; they will eat your fruit and drink your milk.

—Ezekiel 25:4

One of my earliest journals mentioned how things changed in the 1960s in London and for our family. My eldest sister wanted to marry and, as she was under twenty-one, she needed parental consent. Because my parents did not believe she should marry a divorced man, they refused on religious grounds. Their future son-in-law took them to court. The judge went on record saying that she felt my parents held an outdated view of marriage, and she felt they should not refuse on religious grounds. She granted my sister the right to marry in a civil marriage. My parents were initially saddened by this as they felt it undermined their religious beliefs completely; however, they still reached out after the marriage to help my sister and her husband however they could.

I saw how the culture in the 1960s was changing and the laws of the church—whether it was marriage, sex, homosexuality, or other things previously believed to be against God's wishes—were all about to change. As I read my journals from the1970s and 1980s, I saw the changes coming faster and faster. At the same time, attendance at traditional places of worship dropped across Europe and the West as a whole. Today, if asked what they would say about their religious denomination, the largest group in North America is the *nones*—people who claim to not believe in any organized religion.

The established religious views from the Bible are less accepted than ever before. Personally, I know reading through the Bible daily can help open your mind about all these issues in a way that those who only quote sections to support their arguments rarely accept.

Day 251

Read: Ezekiel 28–30

They will live there in safety and will build houses and plant vineyards.
—Ezekiel 28:26

My journals from the late 1970s reflect what was going on in both my life and in the world. I went through a separation and divorce from my first wife. What was harder still was the daily separation from my twin sons. Initially, I only got to see them at weekends, then it became every other weekend, gradually building walls that would always stay between us. When I reached out, connection was often not wanted, and I was increasingly alienated from both my sons. I attempted to bridge that when I moved to America in the 1990s, encouraging one of them to visit and study in St. Louis for a semester or two. Sadly, it didn't work out, and he returned to study in England.

Even though he didn't stay, it was a time of growth for me. I felt the future was good, and my faith was stronger. Yet there was a nagging doubt that something wasn't right. I joined a Bible study group through my church, then our diocese started a school for ministry, which included Bible study as part of their program. Gradually I was feeling an awakening in wanting to go deeper in study of the Bible. At the same time, my full-time career was changing me into someone I wasn't. This transition came to a head after several years when I was asked to hide the truth, and I couldn't in all honesty say what they wanted me to say as I knew the truth. After going back and forth over this, I negotiated a time of separation that would be long enough for me to truly consider what I would do as I discerned my next steps through patience and prayer.

Day 252

Read: Ezekiel 31–33

When all this comes true, and it surely will, then they will know that a prophet has been among them.

—Ezekiel 33:33

I read about one year when I decided to make a stand for the truth. As I perused other journals, I discovered I had stood up for the truth before in my life, not once, but several times. On several occasions, I stood up for the truth, and people around me ignored what I said, continuing to follow the path they had chosen.

Early in life, I told my sister I could not understand why she wanted to hurt my parents by marrying someone they did not approve of, especially as she knew it went against their beliefs and faith. She did it anyway. At school, I challenged a group to not bully someone. They continued to bully anyway. At the BBC, I challenged a group of journalists who were misreporting a story without fully checking the facts. They misreported the story anyway. In a job here in America, I challenged my boss to tell the truth about a plant closure, which was more about his personal greed than the need for the plant to close. He closed the plant anyway. I shared with my second wife her infidelity was forgivable if she didn't continue it. She continued it anyway.

Seeing the repetition linked to these daily readings came as a surprise to me as I looked back over the years, yet through it all, there was a constant that echoed in the words, "They will know that I am the Lord."

Reading through the struggle facing Ezekiel has given me a lot of strength to persevere.

Day 253

Read: Ezekiel 34–36

They will live in safety, and no one will make them afraid.

—Ezekiel 34:28

Hope is a strong emotion. Through all my times of trouble, I held out hope for better things to happen—a better marriage, a better job, a better life. Finally, I realized I was just moving the same issues around the board. Taking time to discern what I was called to do, what I was called to be, was something I had never done before. It wasn't easy work. I knew I wanted to make a positive difference with my life, in the lives of others, or even the world at large. In the 1990s, my thoughts crystallized : I wanted to bring an awareness of God's presence to every person in the world.

Inside my head, I could hear my grandmother saying, "Baby steps, take baby steps, but do so boldly." I met with various people over a period of a year, gently asking and listening for advice. Gradually, I discerned a call to chaplaincy within the framework of my church and denomination. At times, I looked beyond my denomination; however, the Episcopal church was a good fit and reflected my beliefs.

Finding I was not called to be a parish priest was a surprise to me; however, being a chaplain for a parish and for several hospitals was a calling I truly recognized. It quickly became clear God was calling to me to minister to people who were experiencing great pain and suffering through sickness and death. I was surprised, though, as I was to minister to women giving birth, sometimes through great difficulty and alone. Gradually I accepted the call to be present at birth to death, from first breath to last breath. *Breathe in, God within me. Breathe out, God around me.* Truly, an incredible gift and blessing.

Day 254

Read: Ezekiel 37–39

I will put breath in you, and you will come to life. Then you will know that I am the Lord.

—Ezekiel 37:6

In accepting the call to be a chaplain, I was able to pour my whole self into my work. Through my ministry, my productivity, creativity, and reliability were expressed as a whole. Unlike any previous time, I was fulfilling a purpose that ran deeper in me than I had ever experienced. I became aware of my soul's purpose, what God desired of me. However, balancing the demands of being a father and a chaplain were not easy. By reading the Bible and journaling every day, I was able to bring structure and balance to my life, which had been missing.

I went on retreat with the monks at the Society of St. John the Evangelist in Boston and spent time discerning my calling with them. Listening and praying with them about my call was enlightening and energizing. Gradually, it began to take shape, and suddenly, it just was. I could not imagine doing anything else.

My life truly changed as time passed, and I felt the closeness of the Spirit in the time spent with others. Many years before, my mother had given me one of my father's business cards with a few words from her on the back, "Lord, fill my words with worthwhile stuff, and stop me when I've said enough." These words could be applied in my role as a chaplain whereas, "Lord, take me where you want me to go; Let me meet who you want me to meet; Tell me what you want me to say, and Keep me out of your way."

Later on, I would hear these words again shared by a chaplain who died at the Twin Towers in New York City.

Day 255

Read: Ezekiel 40–42

Son of man, look carefully and listen closely and pay attention to everything I am going to show you, for that is why you have been brought here.

—Ezekiel 40:4

Looking back over my years as a chaplain, I see how everything I had done in my life before was brought to bear in the ministry of chaplaincy. Suddenly understanding and living in harmony with my soul's purpose brought me to a place where I felt like a useful member of humanity. In finding my purpose and focusing on building the life I was called to, I felt my daily rule of life take on a new significance. The more I did this work, the more I changed, and the more I was aware of the change.

Quite a lot of people were surprised by the path I chose, yet I found it less important to worry about what others thought than the fact it truly was my calling. I worked long hours at night and on weekends and covered multiple shifts for others. At the same time, I was also able to return to full-time study at a seminary in St. Louis where I worked for a Master of Divinity degree. While there, I started a small group to read through the Bible in a year. Combined with a group at the church in North St. Louis County, this group quickly became something different from what and how people had studied the Bible before. No judgments were made of anyone, and everyone voiced their thoughts and feelings about how the Bible was currently relevant to them.

A group of young people studying at a nearby college visited our church, and several of them asked to follow me via the internet and Facebook from their home countries. So, reading the Bible from Genesis to Revelation each year and journaling about it spread to Mexico, Thailand, Vietnam, and even Mongolia.

Day 256

Read: Ezekiel 43–45

*Then the man brought me by way of the north gate to the front of the temple.
I looked and saw the glory of the Lord filling the temple of the Lord, and I
fell facedown.*

—Ezekiel 44:4

Several members of our small church commented on the different
experiences they were having. Suddenly the focus was not only on the New
Testament readings—in particular the gospel readings— and we were reading
parts of the Bible some of the group had never read before. Many of the Bible
study group only read what we heard on Sundays in church. They started
asking more questions about the purpose of the Bible and the stories in both
parts of it, spotting connections they had never seen before. Several times
members of the group shared they had wondered about a specific reading
from the Bible, but no one would sit and discuss it with them.

One older member of the church said she had always felt ashamed to ask
her questions because she didn't want people to think she was uneducated.
Like my grandmother, she had never gone to school in England where she,
too, grew up. She also entered service, working in a kitchen of a big house
from when she was only eleven years old. As we discussed her questions,
she started sobbing. The woman sitting next to her reached out, and in a
moment we all did, and comforted her through this moment.

Over that year, in parallel to working as a chaplain, this ministry of
sharing the Bible became a large part of my life in the several groups we
grew around small tables at church, in homes, and online. It wasn't easy,
and I often felt completely drained after we closed our Bibles for the day.

The common practice in churches today is to focus on scriptures only
during worship or in short-term Bible studies during holy seasons, such
as Advent and Lent. These groups proved the value of ploughing through
the Bible in a year as we reflected a fundamental truth: Our lives go where
we focus our attention.

Day 257

Read: Ezekiel 46–48

Every month they will bear fruit, because the water from the sanctuary flows to them. Their fruit will serve for food and their leaves for healing.

—Ezekiel 47:12

This method of studying the Bible went through the entire year and kept finding new outlets through friends, and friends of friends, who shared the readings and the method of studying. Groups started at other churches, and they shared it across many different churches. Our practice really wasn't anything new, just small groups of people sitting and reading together, breaking bread together, and praying together.

Several people commented that being in a house church reached them differently than being in church on Sunday morning. In some cases, sitting in a small group was preferred by people who felt lost in a church on a Sunday morning. Over the years, many people shared their experiences of participating in these groups, and I quietly journaled about their journeys as well as my own. Clearly, we met a need, a hunger I had not been aware of before.

Much like Ezekiel, I saw how the church could be rebuilt and renewed in ways I had not seen before. There was so much abundance in the church we could share with others, if only we were truly open to doing so. One thing I liked about this program in its first year was its lack of structure and leadership, allowing anyone to speak and share equally. I was just a guide on the way, on the path, to open the book and read from where we had stopped last time. I stood at the door and welcomed them in. Others wanted to structure it, formalize it, put it in a box, shape it into something they could control, which led to me stepping away from it after a while, and returning to the basics of one small group.

Day 258

Read: Daniel 1–3

You have given me wisdom and power, you have made known to me what
we asked of you, you have made known to us the dream of the king.
—Daniel 2:23

I have always remembered my dreams. I often experience vivid dreams that feel so real I can't separate them from reality. I've woken up in the middle of the night, sweating and twisting and turning and running in my dreams. When I started keeping a journal again in my late teens, I found that if I was quick, I could jot down in the journal a few thoughts from my dreams before I lost them and still get more sleep.

Over time, I realized dreams were another way of understanding life and the challenges we face in our lives. My dreams became a way for me to work out in my head whatever was troubling me or challenging me, and through my dreams, I often came to understand deep and mysterious things in my life—things that seemed unseeable, unknowable, or unsearchable to my awake mind during the day.

At night, my mind sifts and searches until it finds what it is looking for to share with me. What I found incredible was I don't do anything to create this. I do not do it on my own. It was, and is, the Spirit doing something within me that I can only marvel at.

No matter what I was going through—a problem at work or in my marriage or with my children—I was able to hand it over during sleep to let it hum away in my head until morning when, by trusting in the process, what I needed was revealed to me.

Day 259

Read: Daniel 4–6

Three times a day he got down on his knees and prayed, giving thanks to his God, just as he had done before.

—Daniel 6:10

There were times I lapsed in my daily prayer, reading the Bible, or journaling. Again and again, I turned back to praying, sitting quietly, reading the Bible, and journaling. Each time I returned it was in reaction to things going on in my life, and each time, my spiritual practice brought me peace and clarity in what to do and how to be. It's almost impossible to share in an explainable way how much it worked for me in my life. From simple childhood concerns to matters of great world importance, each situation was important at the time.

As a child, I struggled with my family, appearing to be pulled apart by the actions of my sisters or brother, and I turned inward to reading and praying to be present for them and my parents in whatever way could help the situation. It wasn't that I did anything to change what was happening; rather, I was open to whatever change our family was going through at the time.

As I grew up, when I struggled with the challenges of my work, sitting for a while, thinking and praying about the challenge put in front of me, it helped me gain clarity in my search for solutions to the problems I was facing. In 1987, I was appointed as Director of Communications for the British Conservative Party and guided the broadcasting campaign for Prime Minister Margaret Thatcher to her third consecutive victory. In 1990, I joined Shandwick as an advisor to the UK Government and Prime Minister John Major concerning the Public Relations response to the First Gulf War. My public relations advice each morning, which was shared with the Prime Minister and the cabinet, could make or break lives. Stopping myself for a few moments as I wrote my morning briefing, taking time to think and pray about my actions, made it possible for me to be centered as I shared my thoughts and words with others.

Day 260

Now, our God, hear the prayers and petitions of your servant.
—Daniel 9:17

Reading the Bible every day sounds a lot easier than it sometimes is. The method I developed of picking up reading where I left off each day was good because it didn't put me under pressure to *catch up* in my reading. I continued to read at the same pace. I never felt pressure from reading the Bible, only a calmness that allowed me to meditate on scripture and my life. As I meditated, my eyes and ears opened to whatever was going on in and around me. I was able to focus on problems at home when I was young, or the struggles with my first marriage, or the challenges in working at the BBC, or the disappointment of a second failed marriage. All these situations could be put in perspective by journaling for a while and reading the Bible.

As the challenges in work became more critical, especially when I started working for the Prime Minister, my time spent reading the Bible became more essential to steadying my thinking about my contribution to her election campaign. Sitting for a short while each day meditating on the Bible cleared my head and my mind. I was able to bring all of myself to bear on the day's challenges and find solutions to the problems we faced. I shared with the Prime Minister that it was part of my daily practice to do this, and she shared with me, that as a daughter of a Wesleyan Methodist lay preacher, she had always found strength in reading the Bible too. It became a common bridge between us as I helped her campaign successfully in the 1987 General Election.

Day 261

Read: Daniel 10–12

Many will be purified, made spotless and refined, but the wicked will continue to be wicked. None of the wicked will understand, but those who are wise will understand.

—Daniel 12:10

Daniel's prophecies are not easy to understand. Some might even say they are not relevant to our lives today. Yet each time I read them, I hear the voices of young people who have been taken from their homes to another country—those who are keeping their original faith and culture alive while living in a strange land. Throughout my life, I have seen wars and struggles take place around the world.

When I worked at the BBC World Service, I saw firsthand young people who had been brought to Britain who still worked at keeping their original culture and religion alive in their lives. Not an easy task when surrounded by all the temptations of a society very different from their own. Their efforts made me look long and hard at my own life and how I lived it and worshipped in it. By continuing to be present to God through reading scripture and praying, I could make a difference with my life. I didn't always get it. I didn't always understand. However, I always realized it was through these two acts of worship I could make a real difference in the world.

It would take several years and journeying to another country until I could hear and accept God's call, God's ministry, through prayer. *Come to me* is more than a phrase when translated through prayer and reading scripture. These words brought me to chaplaincy and pastoral ministry for nearly twenty years of my life, humbly serving in whatever way I could. Sitting, listening, praying, and simply being with someone as they search their lives for meaning is still the most humbling experience I have had as I listen to the call to *come.*

Day 262

Read: Hosea 1–7

Therefore I will block her path with thornbushes; I will wall her in so that she cannot find her way.

—Hosea 2:6

I hadn't thought of my relationship with my first wife, or my second wife, in the way that Hosea described his wife and her actions, though both of them fell out of love with me and in love with someone else. So, I guess there are similarities. Both times, I prayed we could overcome unfaithfulness, find common ground, and repair our relationship. Each time, in my case, it did not happen and led to divorce. Each time, my partner could not see the destructive path she was on and how it would affect our relationship. Each time, I felt I wanted to build a wall around us both to protect us from what was leading her astray. Each time, I realized I could only be responsible for my own actions and learned I could not be responsible for the actions of another. No matter what I thought or prayed, the marriages imploded, ending with divorce and sadness.

Particularly with my second wife, I hoped talking with her lover and getting him to lose interest, to stop luring her into an unhealthy relationship would make a difference. It didn't. When I look back in my journals at those times, there was little to comfort me in this experience. What I did find was a way of handling my emotions through difficult times. Knowing that the world goes on and God has a way of loving me through thick and thin helped me get through some rough spots. Both times, I was led to therapy with outside help to guide my recovery. Each time, there were different lessons to learn, different experiences to grow from. Each time my faith helped me rediscover my North Star.

Day 263

Read: Hosea 8–14

Say to him: "Forgive all our sins and receive us graciously, that we may offer the fruit of our lips."

—Hosea 14:2

Instead of building walls to protect me from my wife, I built walls to protect myself from any destructive influences. I did the same for my children. With my first marriage, I was not too successful at that, ultimately leading to a broken relationship with my twin sons. But, I learned from experience. When my second marriage broke down, I worked hard to maintain a more healthy, open, and honest relationship with my children. I was able to offer some degree of protection to them through the experience. I didn't offer as much as I would have liked if I had successfully saved the marriage; however, I did provide much more than I did at the end of the first marriage. This protection enabled me to keep a healthier relationship with my children from my second marriage.

However, life is messy, and when you are down in the weeds, it can be quite difficult. Prayer, meditation, and journaling can make a huge difference. The message of hope in the final chapter of Hosea helped me understand how God's love endures despite our actions, and the possibility of reconciliation through repentance and staying faithful to God is always there. Somehow knowing this helped me be in right relationship with both God and my children. It was enlightening to look back in my journals and see this scenario had happened before—how I repeated my actions, making the same mistakes, with one person and then again with another. Initially not being able to explain my reactions was one reason I searched back through years of journals. The words of Hosea jumped out at me as if to say, A*gain, really!* and remind me that ultimately what helps me most in life is that God is love.

Day 264

Read: Joel 1–3

But the Lord will be a refuge for his people, a stronghold for the people of Israel.

—Joel 3:16

When I was going through my first divorce, the people of Poland were establishing the Solidarity anti-communist movement as a viable opposition to the communist government. Several of my friends in the BBC had family and relatives who died during the protests and struggle against the communists. While I supported them, I was also struggling with the aftermath of my divorce, child custody rights, and financial implications of the divorce.

One thing I was aware of, though, was how different the church in Poland was to the church I had grown up with. I thought about the work of Father Huddleston, who had planted a seed in my mind as a child about the evil of apartheid in South Africa. The way communism kept people down, rather than raising them up, was clearly wrong to me. It was also true of the way the law treated the rights of fathers in a divorce at that time in England. I often thought to myself: *It is only through experience that we can learn about the world and ourselves.* I was unable to see my twin sons frequently, so I decided to visit my sister's godfather at the monastery where he lived as a monk. I spent time in prayer, searching for answers, yet heard only the silence. Gradually, I realized I had to trust something bigger than myself, which I called God, though I felt it was something even more than that. It was like looking through a glass darkly all the time, with small glimpses of something better from time to time. Something better was out there. I just couldn't see it or find it until I prayed about it. I needed to return to making God the center of my life, which was harder than I thought.

Day 265

Read: Amos 1–5

He who made the Pleiades and Orion, who turns midnight into dawn and darkens day into night, who calls for the waters of the sea and pours them out over the face of the land, the Lord is his name.

—Amos 5:8

As I searched for hope after my first divorce in the 1980s, I began going to church more regularly in London and found support in my life that had been missing. I could help the church I was attending and help the people who attended there also. I put to use skills I didn't realize I had: from something as normal as cooking a parish breakfast to helping find housing solutions for a new immigrant family in our community. The more I returned to prayer and reading the Bible every day, the more I was guided in my life.

It didn't make me popular, though. When I was producing a BBC news program and felt the journalists were biased against the police, I asked them to check their facts and reach out to the authorities for feedback, which they hadn't done. When they didn't, I reached out—which they resented, as doing so might have jeopardized their story. While their story was solid, the input from the authorities gave it balance and told the other side of the story, which ultimately made the news less of a *gotcha* piece and a better-balanced story. They didn't all agree, feeling I had undermined the drama of their story, making it a more truthful, explainable, and in their view, *boring* piece.

Truth became important to me and would become a regular part of my life, both in my work and personal life. However, truth is often relative, and ordinary people do not know the truth of many situations. People in power, including myself, can be economical with the truth. I struggled with this *truth* for several years.

Day 266

Read: Amos 6–9

"The days are coming," declares the Lord, "when the reaper will be overtaken by the plowman and the planter by the one treading grapes."
—Amos 9:13

One of the benefits of reading the Bible every day is how it calls me back to the truth of what God is—and isn't. American New Testament scholar and theologian Marcus Borg said, "The Bible is a human product: it tells us how our religious ancestors saw things, not how God sees things" (Borg 2014). The more I read the Bible, particularly the books of the Old Testament, I realize Jesus only had the books of the Old Testament. The stories Jesus shares with us from the Bible give us word pictures of God's power and strength. I increasingly saw the comparison between the time of Amos and our own time—the rich getting richer and the poor getting poorer until God acts.

The people of Amos' time were separating the *haves* from the *have-nots* and rewarding the people who had plenty with more, while taking from the people who had little and struggled. Amos recognized prosperity scripture and how unfair it was. Eventually, there was a promise of hope and restoration for both the temple and the people if they turned back to the word of Amos and of God. Reading Amos' view of social injustice and unrepentant sin seems relevant to our time. Not only do the extremely wealthy not see anything wrong with having incomes far in excess of anyone else, but they consistently want more, while forcing the poor to become poorer. It is as if they have forgotten where everything comes from—that they did not create it all themselves.

In the time of Amos, impending destruction and exile would arrive before they could fulfill a promise of restoration. I am not sure what that means for us today.

Day 267

Read: Obadiah, Jonah 1–4

He said: "In my distress I called to the Lord, and he answered me. From deep in the realm of the dead I called for help, and you listened to my cry."

—Jonah 2:2

Putting the years of arguing with God calling me toward ministry into words hits me in my gut, which is ironic as I have Crohn's disease. I spent years studying to be an architect, working in broadcasting, working with government, with large corporations, until—until it dawned on me in a small chapel in a suburb of St. Louis, seeking shelter in the night from a failed marriage with nowhere to lay my head, that the voice in my head speaking softly to me was, in fact, calling me to ministry for God. Some will say they always saw me in ministry, and others will say they never saw me in ministry. Much like how Jonah fought against going to Nineveh, I went backward and forward, fighting this call.

I can hear the arguments I had with God. *I'm not worthy. I'm not right. I'm not the person you think I am. I talk too much. I don't listen enough. Surely there are lots of people better than me at this.* That night, I realized I was just the sort of person God needed. My prayers were a cry from the heart: deep, guttural, and sincere. I prayed this sort of prayer many times in the next fifteen to twenty years as I sat with patients in hospitals, in emergency rooms, in the middle of the street outside a hospital, or even when asked to baptize and help lift a brittle-bone baby from a mother's womb. I cried these prayers as I sat holding the hands of a grieving parent or hugging a grieving child.

There is nowhere where prayers cannot be heard, and no one better than Jonah to guide us in praying to God, the ultimate grantor of second chances.

Day 268

Read: Micah 1–7

And what does the Lord require of you? To act justly and to love mercy and to walk humbly with your God.

—Micah 6:8

Each time I read Micah, I find something new—some phrase or sentence strikes me in a different way. One time, the verses in chapter 3 caught my ear. The Yom Kippur war took place as I was studying architecture in London and separated from my first wife. My life was a hot mess. Yet in Israel, I could feel them fighting for their lives.

I even took a break from work at the BBC World Service to catch the inauguration of Jimmy Carter—hearing him quote a verse from the sixth chapter of Micah, and amazingly, seeing him walk up Pennsylvania Avenue, hand-in-hand with his wife and daughter as if he was out for an afternoon stroll in a park. There was so much hope in America at that time, especially when he announced a war on poverty instead of a war on another country.

When I was working on a children's program at the BBC, I heard the words of Micah being quoted by President Jimmy Carter during the signing of the Egypt-Israel peace treaty, encouraging people who had fought to beat their swords into plowshares and their spears into pruning hooks. It was as if he prayed for a new revival of faith across America.

Seeing and hearing President Carter that day affected me deeply in ways I would not recognize for several years and were part of the realization I came to in the small chapel in the St. Louis suburb on the night I realized my call to chaplaincy:

To act justly and to love mercy and to walk humbly with my God.

Day 269

Read: Nahum 1–3

Look, there on the mountains, the feet of one who brings good news, who proclaims peace!

—Nahum 1:15

My parents got married in London just before the outbreak of the Second World War. Their marriage was followed a year later by the birth of their first daughter and two more daughters over the next three years. They moved from an apartment to a small house, then as the bombing of London got more intense, they moved to a cottage in the country, on the grounds of Highclere Castle near Newbury.

When I worked with the church in North St. Louis County, one of the members was a GI bride who shared her stories of working in the Highclere Castle kitchen during the beginning of the war and meeting my mother, and even of babysitting my sisters on occasion. Growing up in North London after the war, all I knew about the war was what was shared with me or what I overheard as a child. What I did hear was how almost everybody expected to lose the war to Germany, especially after the nearly 300,000 allied troops had been evacuated from Dunkirk.

Much like Nineveh, Germany seemed to roll over everybody in its way. However, my father told me everybody hoped they could still win, so they reached out to America for help. They really felt that God was on their side, especially after the truth started to come out about the Holocaust. America's support left me with an impression of America as a welcoming and helpful country where I hoped to travel later in life, especially as my father had been born in Durango, Colorado. Though, I didn't expect to move here permanently and live here for part of my life, nor did I expect to hear God's call to ministry as a chaplain here. All of which shows me how God moves in mysterious ways!

Day 270

Read: Habakkuk 1–3, Zephaniah 1–3

Lord, I have heard of your fame; I stand in awe of your deeds, Lord.
—Habakkuk 3:2

In certain situations, I struggled with being patient and trusting the process. The older I get, the more I notice the unjust things done to so many people across the entire country, and indeed the whole world. I love this country; however, I found people all around me were negative about almost everything. So, I took time out to sit in a quiet space, the small downstairs chapel in my current church, surrounded by the old stained-glass windows saved from the rebuilding of the church nearly seventy years ago. Sitting there, I cleared my mind and thought about the church above me, which had experienced huge change over that time: the aftermath of World War II, the wars in Korea, in Vietnam, in Iraq, in Afghanistan, against terrorism, and so much more.

I let my mind calm down and clear, then I looked around me in the light of the chapel from the backlights to the stained-glass. All the light in the chapel streamed through the old images and names—the names of former church wardens and souls who had windows dedicated to their lives. Ordinary saints who had gone before me. All these people had stood for something. Their lives mattered to their families and friends. I understood. I needed to be *for*, rather than just *against* something.

How could I pray with my feet and make a difference in the world? By taking baby steps at first, I could accept others and not be sucked in by their negativity. I could push back with positivity. I could see how one size doesn't fit all, whether for politics or religion. To be accepting of others was crucial, and being positive about my own beliefs would attract others. And it did.

Day 271

Read: Haggai 1–2

Because of my house, which remains a ruin, while each of you is busy with your own house.

—Haggai 1:9

The chapel under the church is small. It can seat about thirty people. It is dark, peaceful, and calm, with traditional Tiffany style stained-glass windows from the 1800s. The space embodies peace and rest. In fact, after the death of a young black man in our town in 2014, it became a place for quiet prayer. People gathered to just sit with their thoughts and their lives, and pray.

Upstairs in our parish hall, we shared food and household supplies for free with whoever needed it. We served over a thousand bags of food a day at the beginning. All the local stores in a three-mile radius were boarded up. We became the *de facto* source of food, water, and household supplies. People reached out, supporting us from across the city, across the region, across the nation, and financially, from across the world. We shared what we had with other food pantries in our area and gradually disbursed all we had until the stores reopened.

People serving others upstairs came down every now and then to take a break—to sit, rest, pray, and refresh themselves spiritually. Our rector helped everybody who asked with whatever need they had, in whatever way we could. I did what I could to support him. I moved the week before to a home only seven doors away from the church, yet in those next weeks, I spent most of my time and energy at the church. We were rebuilding the church in God's image, feeding the hungry, giving water to those who were thirsty, inviting in the strangers in our community, clothing those who needed clothes, healing those who were sick, and visiting those who were arrested protesting.

The priority was rebuilding God's house, the church, which wasn't the building. It was, and still is, the people.

Day 272

Read: Zechariah 1–7

I will live among you, and you will know that the Lord Almighty has sent me to you.

—Zechariah 2:12

Within a three-mile radius of our church are more than two hundred places of worship. For a few weeks in August of 2014, many of them were shut or closed during the time of unrest. Our church stayed open as we provided shelter and a place to heal. Two other churches also reached out to the community, providing places for people to wash and clean themselves and to rest awhile. I looked around me in the parish hall and saw people from many other churches, helping, serving, sharing, and just being with each other. I could feel the presence of God walking among us. I looked around me, and wherever I looked were moments of pure grace. Many different churches came together to bring healing and comfort to the community as a whole.

No longer was our church the country club it had become in the 1950s; rather, it was the raw church of the streets of Jerusalem as it struggled to search for its identity. Weeks earlier, we had been discussing our shrinking church, our dying church, our church that had lost its way. Here we were, alive and being *church* itself. It was not about us; it was about God. We were finding ourselves and our purpose. Some responded positively within our flock, others not. Some could see God's hand in what was going on, others not.

As the dust settled, some people stopped attending church on Sunday, and others came instead. We felt we had a message of hope, restoration, and renewal because we trusted in God to provide and support us in our time of need, and we felt we had returned to God in ways we could not have imagined weeks before.

Day 273

Read: Zechariah 8–14

See, your king comes to you, righteous and victorious, lowly and riding on a donkey, on a colt, the foal of a donkey.

—Zechariah 9:9

The early followers of Jesus were Jews, as was Jesus, and they looked for guidance from the Old Testament stories. I was challenged by this prophecy in Zechariah many times, over many years. It was all a bit too neat, as if tied up in a bow. However, I noted several times over different years, there seemed to be more underneath these visions than could be captured in the texts. Beyond the normal status quo was the opportunity to find a time of peace and fulfillment that could only come from a place of love.

I also noted, here and there, an increasing awareness of a different view of God than I held as a child. I noted I was questioning the view of who or what God is more and more. Through questioning, I changed my view of who Jesus was also—who he was and what he meant to the early followers of his way, The Way.

Each year as I read through the Bible, I found myself reading these books at the end of the Old Testament and anticipating reading the familiar stories of Jesus that I had been told as a child. These stories were shared with me by my parents, my grandmother, my godparents, priests, and clergy at all the churches I attended over the years. We based our daily lives around these familiar stories—our rituals each day, each week, each month, each year—culminating in the two great feasts of Christmas and Easter. As I read the Bible more and more, though, my beliefs were changing, my heart was opening, and my very being was changing to become something else.

Day 274

Read: Malachi 1–4

Remember the law of my servant Moses, the decrees and laws I gave him at Horeb for all Israel.

—Malachi 4:4

Reading Malachi when I was younger, I often found myself struggling to see how the prophets were relevant to me. As I moved from my teen years into my young adult years and experienced marriage, an unfaithful wife, a sad divorce, a period of loneliness and emptiness before remarrying, and again being deceived and divorced, the prophetic messages became more understandable. I might not have committed all the actions the prophets challenged Israel about; however, I could see each year how I failed one thing or another.

As I moved from my adult years into my time working as a chaplain and with the church, I saw the encouragement and call to faithfulness in both worship and following God's commandments. I can see this call was one of the reasons we started a daily morning prayer service at church. We met every day to share prayer and time together in a small group. I noted more and more in my journals how Malachi's words emphasized the importance of being sincere in daily worship.

The early followers of Jesus felt this time was imminent, and that aspect carried over into expectations in the Gospel stories. Sometimes, I feel we are not responding to God's call to us to be, to believe, and to be open to love in the urgent way these stories share. We constantly question our being and the purpose for our being. For some, God is the answer. Some see God as eternal and infinite and humans as temporary human expressions of God. Our ancestors struggled with this, too, and wrote the stories in the Bible to help us see how they interpreted things, including God.

Day 275

Thus there were fourteen generations in all from Abraham to David, fourteen from David to the exile to Babylon, and fourteen from the exile to the Messiah.

—Matthew 1:17

My first wife gave birth to twin sons just over nine minutes apart. The first baby was named James; the second one was Matthew. The memory of their birth repeated each year in my journals. The first part of Matthew is so familiar with its long list of names and forty-two generations showing where the Messiah came from. I remember hearing it read to us every year as the church seasons moved ever onward.

My mother even created a large round calendar of the church year that had a rotatable pointer in the middle, like a clock, that moved relentlessly around the calendar each year. It listed the main Gospel readings for each week, and later, I would discover she had three calendars, one for each of the three years of the church's calendar.

Matthew's Gospel stories certainly received a lot of attention in our daily lives. My mother and grandmother quoted verses often, when something suited them. From the miraculous conception to the gifts of the wise men, they told me these stories as a child and dressed me up to reflect them for special Christmas services.

Later in life, I found deeper and more significant meaning in these first words of the New Testament. I understood why this story had been written, and who had written it. I understood it hadn't been written until many years after Jesus' death at a time when the early followers were struggling with the traditional Jews in their synagogues, which made more sense to me. What always spoke to me were the words from near the end of the fourth chapter where Matthew writes: *Jesus said, "Come, follow me."*

Day 276

Read: Matthew 5–6

He causes his sun to rise on the evil and the good and sends rain on the righteous and the unrighteous.

—Matthew 5:45

Many things in these chapters of Matthew feature in my thoughts and journals, from the beatitudes, to how to pray, to understanding how to turn the other cheek. The significance of these chapters on how I lived my life is enormous, as within the words here are teachings on ethics, prayer, discipleship, and how to be in right relationship with God. I think I was in my mid-forties before I realized I was constantly setting myself up for failure with a standard so high I could never attain it.

What was missing was humility—love and trust in God's care. As I understood the readings and teaching from that perspective, I saw how to live my life differently. This new understanding coincided with going to seminary and starting my ministry as a chaplain. It also coincided with my learning to listen more and speak less, something I had struggled with all my life and still do to this day. Sitting and actively listening to someone one-on-one—truly listening to them, even if they say nothing—became part of my core *ethos*. As I did so, I found I could be present with a person in their time of need in a manner I had never been available to be before.

This new perspective helped me process and let go of the deep pains and disappointments in my life. I could open my heart and soul to look at my own actions, to forgive others, and forgive myself. My journals over the past twenty years reflect the thoughts and words of healing I experienced and my desire to change, simplify, and seek ways to serve in whatever way I could. A simpler life.

Day 277

Read: Matthew 7–8

So, in everything, do to others what you would have them do to you, for this sums up the Law and the Prophets.

—Matthew 7:12

So many times, as I have explored what living in America actually is, I have been surprised at how people have twisted and distorted these words, *So in everything, do to others what you would have them do to you.* Probably the key to this lies in the cultural disparities in the legal system, which surprised me a lot. I was also surprised by how many televangelist prophets distorted the Gospel, promising everything to their viewers for the price of a small donation, instead of helping people understand what the scriptures really share with us. It was quickly apparent to me how Americans needed a voice to explain scripture in a way lay people could understand.

After I came to America, I found my father-in-law liked the English Anglican priest, John Stott, whom I had met several times in London at All Souls Church, Langham Place, next door to where I worked at BBC Broadcasting House. I heard him preach several times, and his voice had prompted me to think differently about my relationship with Jesus. He encouraged me to not keep Jesus at arm's length, but rather to invite him into my home to sit, listen, and talk by the fireside, much like my mother and grandmother had done. John Stott's writing and books helped shape my faith and understanding of what I came to believe. It was comforting to find my father-in-law shared my curiosity. Sharing with him that I saw the teachings of Jesus shared with us by Matthew could be applied to our lives today was more than comforting. When I later was divorced from his daughter, these teachings remained a bond we shared, a positive hope for the future for my children, his grandchildren.

Day 278

Read: Matthew 9–10

Anyone who welcomes you welcomes me, and anyone who welcomes me welcomes the one who sent me.

—Matthew 10:40

My first year out of college, I worked with a small architectural practice and then with a large practice. I was shocked at some of the ethical decisions taken by the people running the company. They seemed to be cheating each other, their clients, the planning authorities, and ultimately everyone. What made it worse was they didn't seem to care and regarded it as business as usual. When my two colleagues and I entered and won a competition to design an extension to a school, I had high expectations and dreams, but quickly the people who stepped in to ensure the extension was built saw it as simply a way to make more money and to *cheat* the system, instead of generating benefits for the handicapped children for whom it had been designed. None of the three of us are working as architects today as we became so disillusioned with the profession at the time.

Reading these passages later in life, I wrote of the impact I witnessed as I ministered as a chaplain in a hospital. Being able to sit and listen to patients or their families as they struggled with the crisis that had brought them to the hospital meant living the Gospel teaching and encouraging their faith in dark moments. Experiencing the comfort and hope my sitting with them brought was simply remarkable, and sometimes even miraculous. Holding a premature baby for a few moments as it took its first breath or holding the hand of a patient as they took their last breath became holy and amazing spaces to be invited into—holy spaces where God was welcomed through the love and faith we shared in that moment.

Day 279

Read: Matthew 11–12

Come to me, all you who are weary and burdened, and I will give you rest.
—Matthew 11:28

I have journaled many different perspectives of how this spoke to me, reached out to me, comforted me. One time, I was weighed down by *knowing* the unfaithfulness of my wife and *not knowing* how to respond. Another time, I was aware my father needed extra care after my mother had died, yet aware my sisters had *circled the wagons* around him to care for him, shutting me out of the process. Another time, I was overwhelmed with my struggle over a relationship with my son who knew how to say the most hurtful of things, yet whom I loved unconditionally. Another time I struggled as I faced shaming and bankruptcy by my ex-wife for being fiscally irresponsible.

Each time over the years, I experienced the invitation to come, share my heavy load, and allow God to give me rest. Whenever I read these verses from Matthew's Gospel, I breathed a sigh of relief. I could take a moment of time to rest and recharge. One time, I was visiting with the monks at the Society of St. John the Evangelist in Boston, when the brother I sat with shared with me it was okay to just rest, sleep, recharge, and hand all my problems and concerns to God. I would be shown The Way. I sat and prayed, prayers pouring out for others around the world, in the streets, in poverty, and in harm. Then, in the silence, I prayed for myself. In that moment, I experienced a calm flowing over and through me. I felt the peace which passes all understanding flowing through me in the holy space we had created together.

Day 280

Read: Matthew 13–14

This is why I speak to them in parables: "Though seeing, they do not see; though hearing, they do not hear or understand."
—Matthew 13:13

When I was young, I asked my parents to explain things, and they would patiently explain and give me answers to my questions. As I read the Gospels and the parables shared with the disciples, I saw the truth behind what Jesus said. He said if we are open to hearing what the Gospel says, then we can understand it. If we are not open to what it says, because it doesn't fit with our beliefs, then we will not *hear*.

Being receptive to spiritual truth opens the door to a deeper understanding, while resistance to what is being shared leads directly to becoming spiritually impoverished. This was never clearer to me than when I worked for a political party. I saw how policies could be made and enacted that could directly benefit people, and I naively believed people would create policies to help others. Quickly, I noted my sadness as policies were enacted that didn't meet those goals. Too often, policies helped a minority of people, frequently those who already had an abundance in their lives, and did not benefit those to whom an abundance would be a dream.

My journals allowed me a safe space to vent and process my thoughts without upsetting others; however, they did not create any progress in changing the views of those in power. As I opened my thoughts and my heart up to truly understanding the meaning behind the parables, I found ways of sharing with others. Some were open to hearing and others not, much like the sower in the field. Being open to change made all the difference.

Day 281

Read: Matthew 15–17

Truly I tell you, if you have faith as small as a mustard seed, you can say to this mountain, "Move from here to there," and it will move. Nothing will be impossible for you.

—Matthew 17:20

I see my parents' influence on me in accepting a traditional view of Jesus and church, and my journaling as a child was simple. In my teens, I asked more difficult questions, and more often than not, got no answer. As I married for the first time and had children, my questions became more basic and yet more complex at the same time. As I experienced my first marriage's failure and loss, I searched through my journal for answers and heard a deafening silence.

Now I see that I did hear, but I couldn't or wouldn't listen. *What you resist, persists.* In the interregnum between marriages, I was constantly searching in my journal entries, almost manically so, yet not listening or writing the right questions. With my second marriage and move to America, I began to listen again and ask the questions I truly needed to ask. I was better prepared when this second marriage failed to ask questions that reflected the Gospel and helped guide me through the challenges facing me. I explored the concept that my happiness was mixed up with others' happiness and my being at peace in the world was tied up with everyone else's peace. If others could not be at peace, then I could not be either.

I finally realized I could be the salt of the earth and bring out the flavor of what it is to be alive in the world. As I moved forward in my ministry of chaplaincy, I sat with people who were sick and was with them, no matter what demons they fought as their lives changed in the moment. I can have faith as small as a mustard seed and move a mountain, so everything is possible.

Day 282

Read: Matthew 18–19

Therefore, what God has joined together, let no one separate.
—Matthew 19:6

In my journals, I question what marriage is, what relationships are. *How could I live with broken friendships, broken relationships, broken marriages?* Again and again, these words jumped off the pages at me. At different times in my life, they spoke in different ways. In my teenage years, it was the marriages of my sisters and my parents that were reflected in my thoughts. I had concerns for my eldest sister who was physically and emotionally abused by her husband, yet stayed in the marriage as she believed she should try to keep it going, despite his repeated infidelity. My second sister also struggled with an abusive and deceptive husband who thought his infidelity didn't count, but woe betide her if she even talked with another man. My third sister despaired of, and struggled with, a husband who flirted with every woman he met and was constantly out of alignment with her, spiritually and emotionally.

My parents' relationship floated above these three sagas. I saw the strength they drew from their marriage and their deep relationship, even when they were frustrated with not being able to solve their children's problems. My brother and I seemed relatively normal in comparison, though, I now realize we became more guarded at sharing our lives with my parents or other members of the family. We were better at learning from their mistakes.

This history made my experiences of being betrayed by my first wife, and then again by my second wife, tougher to bear and harder to process. To help me going forward, I spent years exploring my part in these failures, learning from them, and journaling my thoughts and emotions to bring self-awareness and support in my healing.

Day 283

Read: Matthew 20–21

On the third day he will be raised to life!
—Matthew 20:19

These verses from Matthew's gospel are clear, and yet the disciples somehow didn't really get it. We still see them squabbling among themselves over who will sit on his right hand or his left hand. They still celebrated his entry to Jerusalem as if he was an earthly king. They still saw him being challenged by the religious authorities of the day about who authorized his teaching and did not understand his reply.

When I sat with this reading a few years ago as my second marriage crumbled around me, I had never felt more alone and vulnerable, a stranger in a foreign land. It was a time when I needed to let go, open my heart and my mind, and let God help me find my purpose in life. I felt like the son who had said *no* when asked to work in the vineyard; I was now ready and willing to work in the vineyard.

Even so, I don't think I was aware of what it would mean for me, my children, and the future. In my journals, I searched for the core of what these words could share with me, to guide me. Slowly, each year for the next few years, they did just that as I realized others could read through the Bible with me, sharing their thoughts, their dreams, their concerns, asking their questions, and searching for The Way. I found the rock that had been put in my way to halt my way of life had become the cornerstone of my life going forward. The joy of sharing this journey was like a pilgrimage, a journey alone, with others, and with God.

Day 284

Read: Matthew 22–23

Jesus replied: "'Love the Lord your God with all your heart and with all your soul and with all your mind.' This is the first and greatest commandment."
—Matthew 22:37

It was hard to find forgiveness in my heart after my second divorce. I felt betrayed and alone. I felt I was a failure. I spent hours going over everything I had done in my marriage and searched for what I could have done differently. I met with a therapist. I journaled about my thoughts and feelings. I gradually came to see that I could love my ex-wife, not in the way I had before, but truly love her as a child of God, as my neighbor, as my friend.

It wasn't easy at first, and the first years of journaling after our divorce showed the struggle I had with this text. When I tried to do things by myself, I felt overwhelmed and was tempted to write off the relationship. I tried listening to others, and they guided me to answers for my questions. It was as if others were answering my questions before I even asked them. It was first time I felt I could share the burden I carried with others and not simply carry the burden alone.

I was moving forward in my life and ministry in a positive way I had not experienced before. Through reading, sharing, and openly discussing these readings, I found a way to confront my fears, my concerns, and my beliefs. As my faith was challenged in various ways, I was guided forward in the ministry of chaplaincy. My eyes were opened to be available as a teacher to others, guiding them to an authentic faith with a humble, servant-hearted approach to God and each other. This ministry would be part of my purpose going forward.

Day 285

Read: Matthew 24–25

For I was hungry, and you gave me something to eat, I was thirsty, and you gave me something to drink, I was a stranger and you invited me in, I needed clothes, and you clothed me, I was sick, and you looked after me, I was in prison, and you came to visit me.

—Matthew 25:35–36

Every time I read these words, I remember a scene from when I was really young. It was an early winter's evening, and it had been raining all day. There was a knock on our front door at home in North London. My father got up and went to answer it, leaving my brother and I playing in the living room while my mother sat reading. We heard muffled voices, then the sound of the door on the hall closet opening and closing, more voices, then the front door closing. My father came back into the room and sat down.

My mother asked him who it was, and he replied, "It was a homeless gentleman who needed a winter coat, so I gave him mine."

My mother was upset at first and started to say they couldn't afford to replace my father's coat. It was nearly new and, and, and, and, and . . . and her words trailed off. Then she stopped herself.

After a slight pause my father simply said, "He needed it more than me."

Both of them looked at each other, and my mother got up, went over, and hugged him.

The examples my parents provided on how to live the life Jesus showed us have stayed with me all my life. At times, I have not always lived up to them as I wanted, and certainly, some of the examples around me set by others contradict this action. As I regrouped my life after my second divorce, I simplified my life, and at the same time, opened myself up to my parents' example more and more. I don't always succeed; after all, I will always be a work in progress, always still being formed in God's image.

Day 286

Read: Matthew 26

Jesus said, "Take and eat; this is my body." Then he took a cup, and when he had given thanks, he gave it to them, saying, "Drink from it, all of you. This is my blood of the covenant."
—Matthew 26:26–27

I spoke elsewhere in my journals of when I was a child, and we were visited by Father Trevor Huddleston. During a meal with us, he took his bread, broke it, said the words of the eucharist, and shared it with us. He then raised a glass of wine, prayed over it, and shared it with us, bringing the presence of Jesus into our meal celebrating his return from Africa.

Several years later, I was having supper with my sister's godfather, who was also a monk and priest, when he did the same, and we shared communion within our simple meal. On a visit to Brick Lane in the 1980s, I shared a meal with an elderly man from India who had asked to meet with me. We sat in a small little café, chatting about his life and travels from South India. As it was getting on in the day, we decided to share a meal when he picked up his bread, broke it, blessed it, then shared it with me in a moment of communion. He was someone I barely knew, yet it felt like I had always known him.

After my first divorce, I spent time sitting in the early evenings in a small park near the BBC's Bush House. It was a quiet place in the midst of all the bustle of London commuters. I sat on a bench and watched people walking by or just sat and meditated. On one occasion, another man sat on the same bench and opened his sandwiches to eat. After a few mouthfuls, he turned to me, asking me if I would like something to eat. He took his bread, broke it, and gave it to me in a way that fed me for days to come.

Day 287

Read: Matthew 27–28

"Eli, Eli, lema sabachthani?" that is, "My God, my God, why have you forsaken me?"

—Matthew 27:46

Each year, I have heard these words in a church preparing for Easter. Each year, I have sat with the words, sat with my feelings. When I was young, I listened and watched my parents' reaction. As I grew older, I explored what these words spoke to me. I struggled with accepting it at face value as the recollection of someone who saw this moment. After all, this Gospel was written more than seventy years after Jesus' death, an oral story handed down from person to person.

Then something changed. I was sitting alone, at the end of the day, in a hospital chapel. I needed to process what had happened that day. I had just experienced an amazing moment in time. Due to certain complications, I had been asked to attend the cesarean section of a patient. As the doctor opened the patient, I was asked to baptize the baby while it still lay in the open womb. Because my hands were there baptizing the baby, I helped lift the baby from the open womb. I did so, and the doctors and nurses took the child from me. The baby lived for a while but sadly passed away after a short time.

Much later, I was sitting alone in the chapel, refocusing myself. I looked up from prayer to see the evening sun shining through the stained-glass windows onto the tabernacle on the wall next to the altar in which the consecrated host was kept. I suddenly remembered these words and felt a presence with me, comforting me as I had comforted the parents earlier. I was not alone in that moment; I knew God's presence was with me, and with those parents, and with the baby who had only lived a short while.

Day 288

Read: Mark 1–3

"Come, follow me," Jesus said, "and I will send you out to fish for people."
—Mark 1:17

I see the rush and excitement in the writing of Mark's Gospel. He can't wait to share the *Good News*, jumping over the birth and baptism of Jesus to Jesus starting his ministry. I always liked this opening, these words, this passion. It seemed so lacking in my life and the lives of those around me. I kept thinking how wonderful it would be to have that energy when, in only three years of active ministry, Jesus changed the world. It was as if Mark sensed this passion, this urgency.

I journaled about meeting John Stott at the church next to the BBC, All Souls Church, Langham Place. The conversation we had that evening was transformational in the way I thought about the Bible, its purpose, its meaning, and what it meant to me. I didn't agree with everything he said, nor did he agree with me. He answered my questions with ones of his own, probing my thoughts for more questions, always more questions. He spoke always with a sense of urgency as if the clock was ticking, and, of course, it was.

Much later, when I moved to America, I discovered my parents-in-law had not only read and listened to John Stott but had invited him to speak in St. Louis. He had stayed in their home, and they helped fund a tour for him. His writing and our conversations led me to realize I needed to *go with the flow* instead of *struggling against the current*, and I do think he helped me realize the universe had a natural flow that I could flow with. That flow took me down several tributaries, detours, and soul-searching, but eventually I got there—like Mark, but not as quickly.

Day 289

Read: Mark 4–5

But to those on the outside everything is said in parables so that, they may be ever seeing but never perceiving, and ever hearing but never understanding; otherwise, they might turn and be forgiven!

—Mark 4:11–12

Mark's Gospel goes at breakneck speed to share stories of parables, stories of healing, and real events in my life reflected this. I was dealing with local politics and working for the BBC, struggling to find myself and my sense of direction. My father suggested I spend time with my sister's godfather at the monastery in Devon, not to see if there was a *fit*, but rather to gain clarity about where I was going in my life. My time there was spent in prayer and walks along the banks of the River Dart, listening to Brother Arthur as he shared thoughts about life and the famous Buckfast bees.

I seemed to be surrounded with parables in my life and no clear direction. Slowly though, I started to gain clarity and saw more of my purpose in life at that time. A lot of my work with the BBC required me to think about problems and how to solve them. I got involved with one section of the World Service that broadcasted from Burma (now Myanmar) to Pakistan and then transferred to another unit specializing in selecting actuality to rebroadcast for the language services.

I spent time writing and directing a children's program for six months and then a news program for another six months. I was always seeking to know if *this venture* held the answer to my purpose in life. I helped some friends put a band together and sang lead vocals with them for about six months, but that experience still did not answer my call. I switched for a while to working for a commercial pop radio station, producing their breakfast show and editing their news output. But, I was still left searching.

Day 290

Read: Mark 6–7

A prophet is not without honor except in his own town, among his relatives and in his own home.

—Mark 6:4

Each time I visited with my family after my first divorce, I felt estranged from them. I couldn't see how what I was doing related to them at all. My life was full, yet empty of purpose. I seemed to be driven, yet was handling a huge emptiness inside. If I tried talking with my parents about it, I couldn't find the words to describe what I was searching for. I continued to read, pray, and journal every day, looking for something in the daily readings from the Bible, yet not hearing anything, even when they were great stories of Jesus ministry.

Every two weeks, my life turned on its head, and I drove the two hours up to Milton Keynes on a Friday evening and picked up my twin sons for the weekend. We did all sorts of things in London, and then on the Sunday evening I drove the two hours back to Milton Keynes, and later to Northampton after they moved. I drove back down the motorway on those Sunday evenings.

Then, I wrote in my journals how we had spent our weekend. How little time I was allowed to spend with them. How distant I was becoming to them as they grew up and had friends in their hometown. It was harder for me to see the balance between my life in London and the changing relationship with my sons, especially as my first ex-wife worked harder and harder to separate me from them. Over the years, my journals from these days reflect a lot of pain and soul-searching. These entries contrast dramatically with my journals years later as I started working in hospital chaplaincy in St. Louis, and I had a positive relationship with my two children from my second marriage.

Day 291

Read: Mark 8–9

*I have compassion for these people; they have already been with me three days
and have nothing to eat.*

—Mark 8:2

When I went through my first divorce, I was working at the BBC. It's
hard to remember now, but after I had given my ex-wife money needed to
pay the mortgage and feed and clothe the twins, there did not seem to be
a lot left to live on. I sort of hung out around the BBC building to use the
bathrooms to shower and the couches to crash on. I lost a lot of weight, and
clearly it showed, though, I thought nobody noticed how much I was there.

The woman in charge of our cafeteria noticed and shared her concern
with my colleague. He came in the middle of a night to sit and talk with
me. I opened up to him, and, as he worked with human resources, he set
about arranging to help me through this time.

He said, "There is enough to go around for everyone, and we can surely
help you through this time."

After a few months, the courts finalized how much I needed to give to
support my ex-wife and twins, and it became tax deductible, which helped
me get back on my feet again. The first thing I did was to thank the colleague
who had reached out to help me and taught me there was always enough.
Later that year, I persuaded the woman in the BBC cafeteria to allow me to
pay for meals for some homeless people who hung out along the Embankment
area of London, just by Bush House. Some other colleagues joined in, and
we were able to share a Christmas meal with several of the homeless in the
warmth of the BBC cafeteria. This created a bridge to finding ways to help
them because, after all, there is always enough to share.

Day 292

Read: Mark 10–11

And when you stand praying, if you hold anything against anyone, forgive them, so that your Father in heaven may forgive you your sins.

—Mark 11:.25

I sat in St. Martin-in-the-Fields church and listened to a concert and let my soul heal. I listened to an organ recital in St. Clement Danes Church and realized I was feeling better in my heart about things. Finally, I found myself sitting in St. Paul's Cathedral, listening to the choir singing and remembering hearing my mother addressing the Mother's Union women when I was very young.

I called my godmother and talked with her about everything for hours. She felt nursing my grudges against my ex-wife and my high school friend was not helping me. In fact, it was hurting me. She said I needed to find a way to let go and let God heal it.

In my journal, I noticed these words from Jesus seemed to be countercultural; however, I found it to be at the very core of what Jesus calls us to. Holding grudges separated me from having a right relationship with God; it stopped me from being honest in my prayers and stopped God from being able to help and heal me. It was as if a lightbulb went off as I realized God provides me with the grace to both experience forgiveness and to forgive others.

As I sat in the different churches near the BBC, a healing started that I would work at for several years until I felt I truly had forgiven my ex-wife, my friend, and myself for the pain we had all experienced. Sitting in church, my shoulders suddenly felt a huge weight had been taken off them. I thanked God for my godmother.

Day 293

Read: Mark 12–13

The second is this: "Love your neighbor as yourself." There is no commandment greater than these.

—Mark 12:31

My godparents, Joy and Ken, were a wonderful couple, and they had a deeply loving relationship. From my birth, they were actively involved in my life. When things were too much for my mother, Aunty Joy would appear, as if out of thin air, and sweep me up to look after me. When my mother spent time in a psych ward of a hospital, Aunty Joy stepped in to make sure I was taken care of. As I grew up, she came with Uncle Ken to school events, even when my own parents couldn't.

She arranged for her sister to teach me to play the piano and made sure I got to my piano lessons with my new pieces studied each week. To do that, she had to take a bus from her home to my parents', then take me on a bus to her sister's home, sit and wait while I took my lesson, then bring me home—and go home after that. As children, I don't think we realize how much others do for us.

As I had my own children, I realized what a love she had for me that was not initiated by birth, but by Jesus. To me, she and Uncle Ken epitomized *loving your neighbor as yourself.* The fact that I could turn and talk to her about my pain and my brokenness before I could talk with my own parents was telling. The closeness and trust I felt for her, the value I placed on her advice, and the depth of understanding she had were true blessings. Loving God first was something she instilled in me. Loving your neighbor as yourself was something she showed me in her life every day.

Day 294

Read: Mark 14

She broke the jar and poured the perfume on his head.

—Mark 14:3

Different parts of this chapter from Mark jump out over the years. Again and again, this story of the woman breaking open a jar of expensive perfume and pouring it over Jesus' head, anointing him as if for burial, is the section that hits me. Over the years, I have been helped and supported by many people, many women. Their kindness and gifts of kindness have sustained me at some of my darkest times. There have been meals that fed me. A pillow to rest my head on. A walk on a riverbank to talk and listen. There have been times when I could not see my way out of the path my life was following, and a friend stepped in and showed me the way forward, the light to guide my path into the future.

In the action by this woman, I recognize the love she felt for Jesus and the sadness she had for his approaching death. It was as if she could see what the disciples couldn't, as if she deeply listened to him. She seemed to accept what would happen while the disciples were in deep denial. Some of these people were deeply religious. Others were not religious at all, yet underlying their spirit was a primal reaction to another person struggling with life and needing support to get them through a dark time.

More than anything else, this passage guided me as I searched for my path to understand how my gift, my broken jar, was the ability to be a chaplain in a hospital or a home for those who needed a friend to sit with them, to journey with them, to just be with them, as they searched for their paths.

Day 295

Read: Mark 15–16

"Do you want me to release to you the king of the Jews?" asked Pilate.
—Mark 15:9

I wondered what was going through Pilate's thoughts at this time. The story is vivid as much of Mark's writing is. Mark's style of telling this story leaves lots to think about. Pilate did not seem to let the facts bother him. He went with the crowd rather than his conscience. He appeased an angry mob—but at what price? I have noted times when decisions were made by friends, spouses, family, politicians, and business colleagues, and we all had to live with the subsequent consequences.

It is not easy to take the high road, or even to know what the high road is. Being true to God's Word is not easy as it requires us to know God's Word in the first place. Several times, I noted words from Shakespeare, "This above all: to thine own self be true, and it must follow, as the night the day, thou canst not then be false to any man" (*Hamlet*, 1.3).

It seems strange to me that words from one of the shallower characters in Shakespeare stuck with me and are inexplicably connected with Pilate sending Jesus to his death. I was struggling with decisions others were making, and finding I was out of sorts with their choices. I struggled to not just please others, to simply go along with crowd. I searched for a way to remain true to my beliefs, to remain authentic, and to be clear enough in my beliefs to share them with others.

Through those struggles, I found that as I have remained authentic, I have higher self-esteem, and generally, even after conflict, felt happier knowing I stuck to my inner voice and followed my heart and intuition.

Day 296

Read: Luke 1

And Mary said: "My soul glorifies the Lord, and my spirit rejoices in God my Savior, for he has been mindful of the humble state of his servant."
—Luke 1:46–48

How did Luke know about the conception and pregnancy stories of Elizabeth and Mary? Who shared those stories with him? Who were his sources? Growing up in a household of mainly women, I was often ignored as I sat playing on the floor with my toys. I listened to what my mother and grandmother talked about, or my mother and my sisters, or my sisters with each other. I realized early on that if I just sat there quietly, I could learn a lot by listening.

I learned about all the women's illnesses, whether natural events like my sisters going through puberty or my aunt having cancer. I listened to my mother and godmother talking about their *ailments* or about the health or pregnancy of someone at church. When I traveled with my mother to Mother's Union groups, or Young Wives groups, I sat and listened while they talked about everything from contraception to birthing babies. I never heard any men talk about these things, ever!

This part of my history made me more than curious as to who had shared these stories with Luke. Was it because he had a medical background that he was party to these conversations? I believe it must have been Mary who shared these stories with Luke. It also helped confirm for me the role women play in our faith, and the debt we owe them for all they go through. Even though they lived in a patriarchal society, it is clear women were a lot more influential in the completion of the story of Jesus than many men would have us believe. I only had to listen to my mother, grandmother, godmother, and the all the other women at church to understand this.

Day 297

Read: Luke 2–3

For my eyes have seen your salvation, which you have prepared in the sight of all nations: a light for revelation to the Gentiles, and the glory of your people Israel.

—Luke 2:30–32

As I finished seminary, I was given the opportunity to be a hospital chaplain for both the Emergency Room and Labor and Delivery in the hospital. With every delivery, I recognized the gift of the life as it took its first breath in and breath out, breathing God within them, and breathing God around them. The uniqueness of this experience was immediately evident to me for every woman delivering her child. I also swiftly recognized the privilege I felt, sharing this moment in time with them.

I was surprised how often the mother was on her own as she prepared to deliver her baby and how often they wanted the company of a chaplain to sit with them as they prepared for this amazing moment. Some asked me to stay with them through the delivery and gripped my hand or my arm while doing so.

Something amazing happened each time I was present at a birth. I got a glimpse of God that lit up everyone who experienced it. It reminded me of what Desmond Tutu had said to me when I was only a child, "Look at everyone you meet, see God in them, feel the Spirit in them, and find Jesus inside."

Each birth was different, yet each birth welcomed God into the world, again. Many people in the hospital were too busy to see this; they were too distracted by being busy to stop and look. If I looked for God in these everyday moments, drawing close to the child and mother through prayer, then I truly caught a glimpse of God entering the world. These moments strengthened my own faith as I helped strengthen others.

Day 298

Read: Luke 4–5

It is not the healthy who need a doctor, but the sick. I have not come to call the righteous, but sinners to repentance.

—Luke 5:31–32

World War I took its toll on the men in England, killing 42 percent of the adult male population in *the war to end all wars*. Then the Second Word War happened, and more men were taken, leaving women alone at home. Our church was maintained by the women who worshipped there. As men returned from war service, they took over the roles of running the church again, yet the influence of the women was significant.

When the women of the church gathered to talk about the mission of the church, we increasingly looked for ways to help people. Sometimes we helped a single mother with small children who needed help, sometimes an old lady who was forgetful or frail. Sometimes, a young woman had come to London from the country and lost her way. Sometimes, there were children who had lost their parents.

I was shown how the people of the church who lived most closely to Jesus' teachings were the same people who reached out to help others no matter who they were or what they had done. When my godmother found that children in detention were not being allowed to celebrate their birthdays, she campaigned to visit them with a cake, a card, and a present. Pairs of women would visit with these young people and follow up with them. I came across a mention of a release party for a sixteen-year-old who had never had new clothes. As a church, we clothed him and then helped him as he went forward.

I saw this same hope in Ferguson when they did the same type of ministry in Missouri.

Day 299

Read: Luke 6–7

They are like a man building a house, who dug down deep and laid the foundation on rock. When a flood came, the torrent struck that house but could not shake it, because it was well built.

—Luke 6:48

We were sitting together in the living room of a parishioner's home, a small group of diverse backgrounds and ages. The common thing between us was we all liked the idea of reading the Bible from cover to cover, from Genesis to Revelation. The others had some involvement with either their own church or with the church I attended. How exciting it was to be gathering to study together!

As we started our journey, I sensed differences in the group. Some wanted to study the readings passively. Others wanted to find ways to act on their new knowledge of faith. I struggled with how to balance putting new insights into action and the changes involved. Jesus had the same issues, and his parables provided good foundations to build on.

I shared stories from discussions I had with John Stott years before to show the need to be grounded in trust and obedience to God's teachings. Only then, could we stand the inevitable challenges and difficulties we face in life from personal struggles to external adversities. This practice of putting our reading of the Bible into practice involved a significant degree of personal transformation.

As I shared what we were doing on Facebook, with our weekly Bible study groups at church, and through email, others were attracted to the program. This practice answered an unmet need from people to actively engage with their faith. It called for a commitment to live out the principles of love, compassion, forgiveness, and righteousness learned from reading through the Bible from cover to cover, from Genesis to Revelation. Together, we had found a way to weather life's storms.

Day 300

Read: Luke 8–9

Mary (called Magdalene) from whom seven demons had come out; Joanna the wife of Chuza, the manager of Herod's household; Susanna; and many others. These women were helping to support them out of their own means.

—Luke 8:2–3

I can clearly see how my understanding of these chapters changed as I got older. When I was young, all I heard was the story of the sower and the way seeds on different grounds either did or did not grow—a simple explanation that satisfied a child. As I grew older, I thought this reading was all about spreading the message and how some respond positively to it, and some do not.

As I studied the whole Bible more, gaining insight from the Old Testament books as well as these New Testament readings, I found the significance of mentioning the women at the beginning of the reading more important than at first glance. These women had been cured of evil spirits and diseases, and then, having experienced healing and transformation, they became active supporters of Jesus' ministry, staying with him to the end. They took on a significant role in making his ministry possible, supporting him and the disciples financially, practically, emotionally, and physically.

The role of these women underscores the diverse group of people who were deeply touched by Jesus' teachings and responded in gratitude and service in ways I still see today. My mother and godmother constantly worked in our church in London in ways I can only imagine now.

Here in Ferguson, I see women working in the church every day to make it relevant to our community, anticipating its needs, its hopes, and its dreams. I see them engaging in active listening, understanding and applying Jesus' teaching every day as they open their hearts to everyone they can. I've seen it in the starting of not one, but two homes for women, to be cared for, protected, and given a place of safety, healing, and peace.

Day 301

Read: Luke 10–11

Father, hallowed be your name, your kingdom come. Give us each day our daily bread. Forgive us our sins, for we also forgive everyone who sins against us. And lead us not into temptation.

—Luke 11:2–4

I asked my father why our words in the *Lord's Prayer* were not the same as the words in Luke's gospel. He spent quite a while explaining that in the translations from different languages over the years, someone thought the version we now had was clearer.

I wondered: *Clearer to whom?*

I asked questions a lot. Fortunately, I had parents, particularly my father, who liked that I did and would spend time talking with me. Much later, he shared that because he had not been around his father after he was ten years old, he didn't really know what a dad was supposed to do. So, when I started asking questions, he thought answering them was what he was supposed to do.

My father encouraged me to look behind the stories, to read deeper into them, to search for what the storyteller was trying to share. And it was my father who pointed out to me, when I was still young, that all the Gospels had been written many years after Jesus lived. Some scholars thought the Gospel of Luke had been written over one hundred years after Jesus died.

Years later in seminary, various Bible scholars shared their assessment of when the gospels had been written and the influence of other writings, such as the gospel of *Q*, which influenced Mark, Matthew, and Luke. They discussed what books had been compiled into the Bible and what writings had been left out. Shortly before my father died, I shared with him I still liked the prayer Jesus gave us in Luke better than the one the church would have us learn by rote and say every Sunday.

He smiled and simply said, " I agree."

Day 302

Read: Luke 12–13

"Woman, you are set free from your infirmity." Then he put his hands on her, and immediately she straightened up and praised God.

—Luke 13:12–13

When I started working at the BBC World Service, I could choose whether to work on a Sunday or not. However, the pressure was clearly on us to work on Sundays and at night. At that time, the BBC World Service broadcasted twenty-four hours a day, seven days a week, in thirty-nine languages, all over the world. Within a few months, it seemed quite normal to be working at night or over the weekend, including Sundays. I did not have a day dedicated as a Sabbath day, or a Sunday, or a special day for my relationship with God.

My journal showed a change in how I thought about my relationship with God and with the church. I valued a "moment in time" at the end of a night shift when I stepped out of the building into the dawn over London. I have fond memories of having breakfast for dinner early in the morning in a pub that stayed open for workers who were either finishing or starting work, or for others just waking from homelessness. Some of those morning conversations were every bit as healing as a doctor's visit in the daytime or a priest's words in a church on a Sunday. I learned to sit, listen, and share.

Near where I worked at the BBC World Service was a church, St. Stephen, Walbrook, in which the priest had started a ministry to help people considering suicide. It did not matter when help was needed; it was always available. They had a dedicated phone number offering a non-religious, non-judgmental, empathetic ear to listen to a caller. Their ministry gave me a unique perspective of church, and over the years, I encouraged many people struggling with life to phone the "Samaritans."

The Samaritans organization has been training volunteers to provide emotional support to people struggling to cope for over seventy years.

Day 303

Read: Luke 14–16

This man welcomes sinners and eats with them.

—Luke 15:2

A journal gathers all sorts of thoughts and memories. I have mentioned this before, but with this particular scripture, the memory of a Christmas working at the BBC World Service came flooding back. Christmas was different as we were working with a skeleton staff and ate a delicious meal in the cafeteria served by a wonderful down-to-earth woman and her staff who worked hard to make us all feel loved, and thanked, for working at Christmas. That year, I worked right up to and through Christmas. I knew I would not see my twin boys as they were with their mother and her family. It was too far for me to travel to my parents in Scotland where my siblings were gathering. To say I felt sorry for myself for being on my own was an understatement.

On the day before Christmas, I mentioned this to the landlord of my local pub, and he invited me to join them on the day after Christmas at their family gathering at the pub. I started to say that was nice, but I wanted to respect their family, when he interrupted me to say, "Didn't anyone tell you? Your great-grandmother was my great-grandfather's sister, which makes us cousins, and we want to make sure you feel one with us, one of our family. We see you as a lost sheep of our family, and now you are found, so come and join us."

I was stunned and amazed to find this flock I did not know I had and rejoiced with them all the following day, sharing stories of their lives, and sharing stories of our lives too. I thought I was going to be alone and sad over that Christmas; instead, I found love and new roots of my family instead.

Day 304

Read: Luke 17–18

Let the little children come to me, and do not hinder them, for the kingdom of God belongs to such as these.

—Luke 18:16

One passage or another jumped out to me through these two chapters of Luke. I clearly see how it addresses themes of faith, gratitude, humility, persistence in my prayer journey, and the challenges of people with wealth who still want to find the way to God. It is no mistake the early followers of Jesus talked of following The Way. Sitting in the quiet of an empty church in a small border town in Scotland, or looking out over a sunrise on Hampstead Heath, or standing at the back of a packed church funeral—these were all moments in time when the joy of my faith hit home. Simple moments in time on different days, and different years, with very different feelings, yet simple moments all the same.

Like a child discovering a new treasure, I have found moments of joy breaking through in unexpected places. I first must get out of my *head*, stopping myself from intellectualizing both the Bible and my relationship with God and Jesus, to truly feel closer to God. I need to share the feeling and excitement I experience in these moments with others, so they, too, can experience a relationship with God in their own unique way.

One of my journal entries for this scripture affirmed my source of self-worth that helped me feel confident and empowered at a moment when I had felt anything but. The text reminded me that God accepted me just as I was—perfect in God's eyes, God's creation. My worth came from within: who I was, my uniqueness, and my relationship with God. I had value for the world and could have a positive impact on others wherever my life took me.

Day 305

Read: Luke 19–20

Jesus said to him, "Today salvation has come to this house, because this man, too, is a son of Abraham. For the Son of Man came to seek and to save the lost."

—Luke 19:9–10

How many times did I read these words and give thanks that it opened up a door, a window, or a pathway to follow to make my life possible? My brother's best friend took his own life when I was still in high school. He used the official uniform tie from the school we both attended to take his own life. My brother was visibly shaken for a long time.

As his friend's story unraveled, it was clear it was his choice, and somehow, he had gotten lost. No matter how much we prayed, talked, soul-searched, or went over things, we could not find answers. We never did. For many years, as I prepared each morning to go to school, I tied my school tie and said a prayer for him, his mother, his father, my brother, and all his other friends who missed him deeply.

As I went through life, I was more aware of others who might be quietly slipping through the net. I developed a habit of listening more and sensing the strength of silences. Reaching out to others became a hallmark of who I was, who I am. I reached out to help them see how unique they were. God looks deeper inside of us than any one person ever can, and deeper, below the surface, there is potential in everyone waiting to be unlocked. I found many new friends over the years because I always looked to see where God was within them, remembering the words I had heard as a child from the two priests who changed my life, Trevor Huddleston and Desmond Tutu.

Always look for God in every person you meet, and search with an open heart, because then you will find what you seek.

Day 306

Read: Luke 21–22

All these people gave their gifts out of their wealth; but she out of her poverty put in all she had to live on.

—Luke 21:4

My grandmother's influence on me in my teenage years was significant. After my grandfather's death, she sat down with my parents who wanted to make sure she would be all right financially. Quickly, it became clear she did not have enough to live on her own anymore. She had survived week to week by what she earned cleaning houses for others. My parents thought her health was not so good, so she should stop cleaning others' homes and come live with us. We shuffled our rooms around, and my brother and I moved into a smaller bedroom, leaving the largest bedroom clear for my grandmother to move some of her furniture in with her.

She had a small state pension and a small pension from my grandfather's last employer. Every week, she would go and get her pensions in cash, bring them home, divide them up, and put the money into different jars: one for food, one for each of her children, one for her contribution to the home's utility bills, and one for God. For each of her children, she used the money to buy Christmas gifts, and she bought birthday cards for her siblings, her children, grandchildren, and great-grandchildren. Her food money was spent carefully on what she liked to eat, and she would shop every couple of days, more to get out and about than because she needed to shop that way. My parents said they really didn't need her to contribute to the utilities but accepted her money for her sense of pride, then quietly put it in savings bonds for her to use another day. Every week, my mother made sure Grandmother's envelope was in the plate on Sunday. She didn't have much, but what she had, she gave away.

Day 307

Read: Luke 23–24

When he was at the table with them, he took bread, gave thanks, broke it and began to give it to them.

—Luke 24:30

No matter how many times I read the Gospel of Luke, these words jump out to me. They resonate with me no matter where I am on my life's journey. My earliest journal entries reflected this as I sat at a dinner table and watched Father Trevor Huddleston break bread following his return from South Africa. Such a simple thing to do, break bread and share it with others. He shared many things with my parents about his time in South Africa—the hardships of the people, the struggles of Apartheid—but it was the breaking of bread, a moment of quiet, that captured the memory of the small child sitting at the Sunday dinner table.

Several years later, I reflected on this evening as I visited my sister's godfather, a benedictine monk, as he, in turn, visited with a priest in London for his holiday. It wasn't the conversation about art galleries or concerts that stuck out for me. It was the breaking and sharing of the bread in a quiet moment that I reflected on. *In remembrance of me* took on a life of its own.

As I grew older, I wrote about sitting with people in hospital, in hospice, in their homes, as a chaplain and as a friend, and I wrote about the words, the quietness, and the silences in the breaking and sharing of the bread that brought the presence of God into the space in ways I can still not clearly define. I feel this same presence every week as I receive communion in the eucharist at church. The simple remembrance of Jesus at that moment—not his life, his death, his healings, or his love, but his very essence—somehow stirs up my feelings.

Day 308

Read: John 1–2

The light shines in the darkness, and the darkness has not overcome it.
—John 1:5

As I grew up, I developed a better understanding of our world, our planet, our lives, and I asked more questions. With space travel a reality, not just a story written by Jules Verne, our knowledge of a world beyond our imagination grew as did my understanding of the Gospel of John. When I was a child, I sort of understood John's Gospel from the simple things Jesus talks about. Jesus describes himself using the things common to the people he lived around in Palestine at that time—everyday items, such as light, dark, water, bread, a vine, a shepherd, or a gate. I stopped and looked more deeply at commonplace items I took for granted.

As a child, I wrote about a flower I picked and pressed in my journal, describing it in detail and trying to draw a sketch of it. The petal and the leaf were so simple, yet when I looked at them closely, they were amazing.

Often, I've found the words from this scripture comforting, especially verse five: "The light shines in the darkness, and the darkness has not overcome it."

These words comfort me whether I'm sitting on my own in a chapel in the middle of the night struggling to understand why my marriage had failed or sitting with a parishioner as her husband slips away from life, takes his last breaths, and passes peacefully. So many times, when the darkness threatened to overcome the light, I remember light overcomes darkness.

Day 309

Read: John 3–4

For God did not send his Son into the world to condemn the world, but to save the world through him.

—John 3:17

The person who understood me at the deepest level was my father, and yet conversations with my father tended to revolve around the *why* questions: *Why did Jesus have to die for us to have eternal life?* We went back and forth about this, and I eventually understood what my parents believed. They accepted that even if we didn't deserve it, even if we were sinners, even if we hadn't gotten our lives cleaned up, Jesus gave his life for us, for me, faults and all. I struggled with this for years and finally had to let go and accept this. To accept that this gift of love was not just for me or a select few but for everyone—every tribe, every race, every person—was incredible and hard to do. Yet, this reality lies at the root of God's love for us, this limitless, boundless love.

There were difficult days when these chapters challenged me to think about someone who had hurt me or others, and I called on myself to still love them. I didn't condone what they had done, but I could still love them and forgive them. None of us are perfect, except in God's eyes, and it was good to remind myself of this each year when I read this passage. Forgiveness frees the forgiver as well as the forgiven, and I found the truth and love of that in my journal again and again.

Some people who knew me well saw me forgiving others and seemed eager to understand how my faith could help me in times like those. Some of them started reading the Bible along with me, talking and sharing about how it could help them in their lives too.

Day 310

Read: John 5–6

Then Jesus declared, "I am the bread of life. Whoever comes to me will never go hungry, and whoever believes in me will never be thirsty."
—John 6:35

We had hosted a free meal for local people in our community with no expectations of any results except the hungry would not be hungry for one evening. One of our guests had complained about the amount of food and what we served that evening. He complained he didn't like what we served. Then he complained about how much he had been given. Then he complained that he only got one second serving as we ran out of food. Then he complained about the dessert. He didn't like it, but he ate it anyway.

He kept on complaining for about an hour, so I sat down with him. I sat and listened to him as he complained some more. Then, he started to talk about his life and how unlucky he had been. For the next few hours, he shared his life story and all the decisions he had made that led him to where he was that day, living on his own on the streets.

Suddenly, he stopped. He said he guessed I'd want him to come to church properly if he kept taking our free food. I told him we wanted to make sure he wasn't hungry. Coming to church was his choice, always. I asked him if we could pray together right then, and he said yes. I took a small bread roll and broke it and gave it to him, sharing the eucharistic prayer, and gave him some water to drink. I prayed for him to be all he could be and have all he needed in his life. I put my arm around his shoulder, and we sat in silence for a minute or two before I started to clear up after the meal.

Day 311

Read: John 7–8

Let anyone who is thirsty come to me and drink. Whoever believes in me, as Scripture has said, rivers of living water will flow from within them.

—John 7:37–38

As a chaplain, I became quite adept at finding moments in the day when I could sit and read just a verse or two from scripture. It was easy to pick up where I had left off the day before. My method of reading through from beginning to end each year was different from the traditional methods of Bible study. I wanted to share my excitement when I heard verses like this one from John. I wanted to scream out: *If you are thirsty, then Jesus is here to give a drink of the Spirit, which will amaze you.*

On several occasions, I had written: our lives are touched by the *divine.* Sometimes underlining the word <u>divine</u>, or capitalizing it, DIVINE. I can't explain the divine and sometimes do not understand it. Yet somehow, I know when it moves inside me and my mind, becomes part of me, making me aware of gifts inside myself—love, joy, peace, kindness, generosity, faithfulness, gentleness, and self-control, as Paul would say in a letter to the Galatians.

I wrote many times how this type of passage brings a different Jesus to life in my heart. One who is not just a memory or a story or an idea, but a living presence in my life and the lives of everyone else. The Jesus of history, the Jesus who walked the dusty roads, the Jesus who taught and healed and guided his disciples. This Jesus is suddenly very real to me, and the presence can be truly felt. As I went through difficult or good times, I felt that presence walking with me, so I was never alone.

Day 312

Read: John 9–10

I have other sheep that are not of this sheep pen. I must bring them also. They too will listen to my voice, and there shall be one flock and one shepherd.

—John 10:16

When I was young, these passages led to a lot of discussion with my parents. Even then, I could sense the conflict between one way to find God and the fact that our neighbors were Jewish, Buddhist, Islamic, Sikh, Roman Catholic, and Greek Orthodox. I questioned if that meant that the Church of England might not be the only way. I found friends at school who were Roman Catholic, Church of Scotland, Presbyterian, Methodist, Baptist, Pentecostal, Quakers, and many other beliefs. I challenged myself to find a way to be open to the possibility my faith I was raised in was not the only way.

When I came to America, I was taken aback by the huge number of alternatives that presented themselves as Christian. Apart from the vast number of options on TV and radio—and now the internet—the number of churches was huge. This text was used by different churches in different ways. Some of them seemed to welcome anyone who wanted to come to church, and they would welcome people to be part of their community, to come through their gate, and be welcome. Others used the gate to keep people out who didn't fit the mold of the church, or the style of whom they wanted to let in the fold. Some of the churches threw up artificial barriers, and some tore them down.

As I explored my own beliefs in the first years of seminary, I knew I was where I was supposed to be. I was with the church that allowed me the freedom to worship as I did, with all the love in the world for myself, for others, and for God.

Day 313

Read: John 11–12

Then Jesus said, "Did I not tell you that if you believe, you will see the glory of God?"

—John 11:40

Over a period of nearly twenty years, I spent many days and nights sitting with people as they died. I also spent many days and nights sitting with those who lost their loved ones, friends or family members. Every single time, I experienced a moment of grace that was different, some different sound or sense. When I retired, an administrator at the hospital told me I had been present with over 2,000 people as they died. Every single one was different. Every single one etched into my memory. All of them are remembered in my journal on the day they died.

When I looked back over these same years, I also saw the babies who had been born, and the patients who had survived. I saw those who had been knocking at death's door and recovered. Those who slipped away. The babies who had come prematurely, born no bigger than a can of soda, yet survived. Those babies who had come early and breathed a breath for a few moments—long enough to be baptized, held, and loved—before letting go and dying. I saw the lives of people I would never know other than in the moments before they died, as they faced death alone except for the presence of the hospital staff and myself.

Often the bond made in those last moments was a moment of presence, a moment of peace, a moment of joy, even as life ended. In my journals, I processed my experiences of sickness and health, of life and death. I learned to breathe in and pray, *God within me,* and to breathe out and pray, *God around me,* as I processed these moments in the lives of those I was privileged to share for a moment in time. All I could do was show up, listen, and be present.

Day 314

Read: John 13–15

After he had said this, Jesus was troubled in spirit and testified, "Very truly I tell you, one of you is going to betray me."

—John 13:21

The first time I experienced betrayal, I noted in my journal that I could not believe it. *How could she? Why was I not enough for her? What had I done wrong?* I went into full-blown guilt mode, self-analyzing every word of our conversations, every action we had taken. I looked for any signs the betrayal would happen—not only the betrayal of my wife but the betrayal by a friend from high school too. How hadn't I seen it happening?

The questions written down in my journal went on and on and on. It was as if a flood gate opened and poured out onto the pages. When a similar scenario played out thirty years later in my second marriage, my entries reflected: *Not Again!* With incredulity, I sat and wrote in my journal how hurt I felt by the betrayal of my wife and a friend. This second time, though, I called both a priest friend and made an appointment with a therapist to sit down and talk, so that I didn't just bottle it up or empty myself into my journal. Sharing the betrayal with someone else was an important part of healing. Healing my relationship with my wife as we divorced. Healing the relationship with my children by providing them with safe spaces to grow up in.

This second time, I lost my wife, my home, and my job all in the same betrayal. Yet, by giving it all up, I was able to find myself and my call to ministry as a chaplain. I had very little money, yet with help from friends and church, I found a way to secure a roof over my head, a home for my children, food on the table, and hope in my heart.

Day 315

Read: John 16–18

My prayer is not for them alone. I pray also for those who will believe in me through their message, that all of them may be one.

—John 17:20

One of my friends writes of the indigenous tribes in America who sit in the winter and share stories of the spirits who guarded and protected them. The children listen and store the memories to share with their children as they grew up. Another friend shares how the children in their school in Africa sit on the ground while the storyteller shares the words which bring comfort and love to their souls.

In each case, a person shared the story of their faith and belief with others. How the hearers choose to experience these words, how they act on these words, is their choice. The one thing that stands out in my memory more than anything else is listening to the storytellers of my childhood. The priest from Africa shared that he had become a priest because of the experience of meeting and being seen as a human being by a white priest. The words and stories were explained to me as a child by my godmother, who sat and shared the stories from the Gospels in ways I could understand. My mother shared her understanding of life and how to live it with young mothers across the poorest parts of London while I sat beside her as a child. My father shared his stories of loss and love, the stories of his own life—the death of his mother, his father, and his journey to England and finding a church, my mother, and a new beginning. All these stories happened because a man named Jesus said a prayer before he died, asking for us to believe in him through the message the disciples would share with others.

Day 316

Read: John 19–21

He said, "Throw your net on the right side of the boat and you will find some."

—John 21:6

I can't help everyone I want to; I can't fix everything that is wrong in the world. Life isn't like that. It is the normality of this moment that always gets to me about these words. So many times, I have felt I am a failure or a loser, so I turned it over to God, praying about it. By doing this and letting go, I experienced a course correction in the same way Jesus told the disciples to throw their net on the other side of the boat, which made all the difference.

When I follow the new direction given to me, like the disciples, it fills my net, so I won't go hungry, physically or spiritually. Authoring this book has been a bit like that. I felt called to do this task, called to pour out myself from my journals to the page. Realizing this book is not about me was a gift that came as I wrote, discovering it as a safe space for others to grow into.

In many ways, these pages continue the line of sharing and giving that started with calling fishermen on a beach to follow, and three years later, cooking fish and breaking bread together. As I have poured out myself into the pages of this book, texts have jumped out at me; memories have burst onto the page. Yet consistently, there remains a presence, a spirit, watching over and guiding my thoughts and memories to share with hope and love, none more evident than in the reading today.

I know my job is not finished and there is still more to share, but this text is a bridge from the past to the future—honoring the past and welcoming the future, wherever it leads.

Day 317

Read: Acts 1–3

All of them were filled with the Holy Spirit and began to speak in other tongues as the Spirit enabled them.

—Acts 2:4

My journal noted the day I started to work at the BBC World Service. As a group, we were together for a two-week training, and this was the day we were shown the inner workings of the BBC World Service. A dozen of us walked through the building together. We were taken to see studios we would become quite familiar with, the Newsroom, a hive of activity with a noise level far higher than any of us expected, and important places like the cafeteria and the bathrooms. As we lined up to get some food and sit down, I experienced a sound that became familiar to me over the next ten-plus years—the buzz of voices. Sitting at tables were people who talked in thirty-nine different languages, all talking at once and all talking about the same stories of the day. Sometimes, they would turn from one table to another and change the language they were speaking, yet continue the same topic.

What was amazing was they shared the same stories and would share those stories over the radio that day or night as the building worked around the clock, twenty-four hours a day, seven days a week. I knew listening to them talking that—though I only understood a little that first day—I would learn and know them as friends and colleagues. We would share the good news together, maybe the world news, maybe stories from around the world, but underneath it all, I knew we would share the love of each other as "Nation shall speak peace unto Nation."

Day 318

Read: Acts 4–6

Jesus is the stone you builders rejected, which has become the cornerstone.

—Acts 4:11

Listening to people from other countries was enlightening to say the least. The range of stories, of lives lived, of childhoods lost, was incredible. The people from other countries had often held high office in their country of origin, then with a change in government in their country, they became exiles and found safety and a home with the BBC.

On Saturdays, I often walked with one or another of them up to the corner of Hyde Park. The first time, I was actually walking home, and two people from the German service walked with me. When we got to the corner of Hyde Park, the day speakers were standing at the corner speaking their minds from the boxes they had pulled up to use as podiums. They were demonstrating an old British custom of free speech.

The members of the German service were amazed the people could stand on a box and say whatever they wanted, and nobody was stepping up to arrest them or drag them away to prison. People in the crowd shouted at them every now and again, disagreeing with what they were saying, or agreeing. Some of the speeches were anti-government; some of them were pro. Some wanted the listeners to worship God, and someone else wanted them not to. One man with a clerical collar, standing on a box, wanted us all to repent and come to Jesus, so we would be healed.

This phenomenon is something unique to London, unique to Speaker's Corner, and echoed the voice of Peter speaking in front of the Sanhedrin and asking them to believe. I walked back this way many times over the next few years, and the voices in the wilderness kept shouting out and sharing their beliefs every week with whoever would stop and listen.

Day 319

Read: Acts 7–8

"Look," he said, "I see heaven open and the Son of Man standing at the right hand of God."

—Acts 7:56

My godparents made sure I knew the story of Stephen, inside out and back to front. Stephen gave a long history lesson to the Sanhedrin, the Jewish court, explaining how they had arrived in their current situation. However, even though he was well-researched and knew his stuff, they still killed him.

In one of my journals, I wrote about two fellow students and I entering a competition to design a new school extension. We visited the school many times, sitting in classrooms with the children who would be using it. We sat, played, and listened. Most of the children were handicapped in some way. Several of them had physical difficulties; several had autism and similar conditions.

We came up with a great design for these children, which everyone laughed at because it was huge. So, we went to the company building the extension and talked with them about the children and their needs. Then, a lightbulb went off. The company was transitioning from measuring everything in imperial sizes, in feet and inches, to measuring everything in metric as part of a national metrification program that was starting to affect the building industry. Because they were transitioning, we were able to double our volume of older imperial measurement components, doubling the space we could build at the same cost.

We then built a model the judges could physically sit inside to see how it felt and how the spaces worked for the children. We were thorough, knew our stuff, and won the competition. The building was built, and the children won. We spoke out for the children. We got their voices heard despite everyone discouraging us. We did not leave the children voiceless.

Day 320

Read: Acts 9–10

When he came to Jerusalem, he tried to join the disciples, but they were all
afraid of him, not believing that he really was a disciple.

—Acts 9:26

I noted: *I don't know the answer.*

I didn't say what the question was, just that I didn't know the answer. This entry was written at a time when I was going through a lot of soul-searching. I understood how Paul might have felt. One minute, he was convinced he should be persecuting Jesus and the followers of The Way wherever he could find them. All his training in scripture and the laws of the Sanhedrin told him Jesus was a fake. The next minute, the next second, he believed in Jesus!

I did have the wisdom to say, *I don't know.* When I looked back for the same scripture in a different year, I found this questioning had come up before. I spent time waiting, listening, and praying for the answer—emptying myself of preconceived ideas and making space within for the answer to come. The answer came when I admitted I didn't know something, because then I was open to possibilities.

As I became more comfortable with who I am, I realized I didn't need to pretend to be something I was not or have knowledge I didn't. Over time as I read this story of Paul, I found myself growing more and more confident in admitting who I am, in knowing what I know, and in knowing what I don't know.

I went right back to my childhood with my father. I thanked God my father always pushed me to answer questions with more questions and to respond with an *I don't know* when I didn't know.

Day 321

Read: Acts 11–13

I have made you a light for the Gentiles, that you may bring salvation to the ends of the earth.

—Acts 13:47

I am reminded we cannot do everything on our own. This truth is hard for me to hear as I am introverted and want to do things on my own. After all, if I do something on my own, there is less chance it will get messed up. If it does, there is no one to blame but myself. All through my life, there were people who supported me through thick and thin. Initially, it was my parents, sometimes my siblings, then my godparents and neighbors, and members of church. As I grew up, people helped me do the things I was best at, from singing in the choir, to drawing, to growing flowers and vegetables, or simply to being everything I could be and following my dreams.

As I grew older, those supporters became people who helped me through the challenges life threw at me from divorce to bankruptcy, giving me the strength to carry on against the odds. This was a two-way street, and as I was able to mentor and support others, I gave the very support I received to others who needed it.

I became aware of this particularly when I was called to be a chaplain. I sat with people through some of the most difficult moments of their lives, being present with them—not talking or fixing, but bringing the light to a place of darkness in their lives. I worked to bring the Spirit to them in a way they may never have experienced before, often by sitting and praying silently. I prayed they could receive my prayers and that those prayers would help them build a new relationship with the Spirit, so they could also share God's love.

Being the light in a time of darkness.

Day 322

Read: Acts 14–15

We believe it is through the grace of our Lord Jesus that we are saved, just as they are.

—Acts 15:11

My first journal was a simple little blank book with lines in it, small enough to write a few words down, yet it looked like a vast ocean to me at the time. In it, I wrote questions I was thinking about at the end of a day. I had lots of doubts about things, lots of doubts about myself. I'd write I couldn't do this or I couldn't do that, but I did not write a lot about any dreams, thoughts, or wishes.

I'm not quite sure when that changed, but I was writing in a larger journal and over several pages. My dreams involved what was possible and wondering what my role would be. Some entries reflected on what was happening with others in my family. The drama my sisters and mother brought in on a daily basis could have been created for a TV sitcom. I started to write my thoughts about what I was reading or what my father had read to us from the Bible. Early on, I understood the difference between what we thought it said and what it *could* say.

My journal came alive with my thoughts, dreams, and prayers, and took on a life of its own. Understanding the Bible was written by our religious ancestors—humans like us—helped me understand it wasn't perfect, and, in turn, my imperfections were acceptable too. Realizing God did not discriminate between us but loved us all equally was a mind-opening thought I put in my journal when I was still a teenager. Years later, reflecting on the same scripture, I understood I didn't need the extra weight on my shoulders. I could open up other hearts and minds to see the same way to faith I had found.

Day 323

Read: Acts 16–17

For in him we live and move and have our being.

—Acts 17:28

I noted the first time I stood at the pulpit and spoke. I didn't speak at once, but rather I stood with silence before the words would come out. "Be silent and know that I am God, said Jesus." Even in the silence, words not spoken are from God. My fears about sharing myself with this body of people disappeared as I spoke from my heart to evoke, to encourage, to dream of what might be, to think about what could change. I used my words in a prophetic and truthful way to stir the memories, longings, and instinctive feelings of the congregation in front of me. I reached for the feelings we all starve and long for, even without knowing we do.

It was a first step for me, which led to many years of sharing, listening, and leading studies of scripture and encouraging others to open their hearts and minds to what scripture meant in their lives. This congregation of people who made up the body of this church thirsted for something more, hungered for more. We met around a table together. This congregation grew. At first, they were a group of people who met together on a Sunday morning, sat and listened to a sermon, gathered to receive communion, and then shared their lives over coffee afterward. They became followers of Jesus who didn't compartmentalize church into one hour a week in one location. This congregation made a greater commitment every day to teaching, fellowship, the breaking of bread, and praying together—and not just at church, but in homes, in hospitals, on the streets, and at the market on weekends.

Every day in every way, we grow closer to God.

Day 324

Read: Acts 18–20

Paul said, "John's baptism was a baptism of repentance. He told the people to believe in the one coming after him, that is, in Jesus."
—Acts 19:4

Each man had a Bible in front of him, different versions, some more worn than others, but all of us turned to the pages in Acts we were studying. I sat in the silence at St. Stephen's church for a moment, then shared the words of Paul: "John's baptism was a baptism of repentance. He told the people to believe in the one coming after him, that is, in Jesus."

I sat in silence again for a moment before saying *Amen*, which they echoed. One of the men then read an entire verse, another the next, and the next one followed on. When we had four verses read, we stopped, and I asked them what they thought of this story from Paul. Within moments, they were sharing stories of crashing planes in World War II, of building planes in World War II, of fighting in the jungle on islands in the Pacific, of crossing the desert of North Africa, or of holding down the home front while friends were summoned to serve.

Each of them had memories to share that were triggered by these verses. All uniquely different, yet all the same, they shared how they came to believe in Jesus. As each of them had faced issues that had changed their lives, they felt closer to Jesus. They found Jesus was the only person they could trust in their time of need. Each of them was sure Jesus heard them and poured the Holy Spirit on them to get them through their struggle. One in particular shared his story of being adrift in the North Sea after his plane crashed. The survivors floated in a small rubber raft for seventy-two hours until they were saved, but he never doubted they would be saved, never.

Day 325

Read: Acts 21–23

And at that very moment I was able to see him.

—Acts 22:12

Gathering this same group of men each Saturday at St. Stephen's to share reading the Bible and the experiences they'd lived was an amazing gift. I noted how memories of my grandfather, my mother's father, came back to me as I sat with them. Unlike them, he had served in the First World War and had seen the senseless butchery it involved. He carried around a piece of shrapnel that had never been removed, That shrapnel ultimately killed him when it moved inside him later in life. He also caught malaria, a disease that continued to torment him the rest of his life, making it almost impossible to hold a steady job other than as a night watchman at a brewery and then at a candy manufacturer.

Despite his ill health, my most memorable moment with him was being carried on his shoulders to watch the Arsenal team play football at Highbury Stadium in Islington. I spent a whole ninety-plus minutes sitting on my grandfather's shoulders, seeing over the heads of everyone around me when I was only five years old. Tucking my feet around his neck and under his armpits. Secure, yet dangerous. Exciting, yet scary. Pressed on by the crowd, yet safe, knowing my grandfather held me.

For the first time, I saw what he could see, what others could see, what I would see as I grew to be over six feet tall. I looked above the crowds at a whole new world out there—a place to excite, to challenge, to see. On that day, he gave me a glimpse of another world, a world all around me, hidden from view—until it wasn't. At that moment, I could see, and what I saw was the world God created.

Day 326

Read: Acts 24–26

I have appeared to you to appoint you as a servant and as a witness to what you have seen and will see of me.

—Acts 26:16

The ink was smudged. I looked at it for a while, remembering the tears shed writing at the end of that day. The bullying I experienced cropped up several times in my journals. I was the youngest boy in our year, not yet sixteen; my voice had not yet broken. I sang the soprano solos with our school choir and in school concerts, and several of the teachers called me by my first name because of that. I was also involved with Youth & Music, an organization focused on classical music that helped arrange trips to classical concerts around London. Several teachers were involved with that too.

The bullies made me stand at the front of the room while they created a *mock court*, with several boys becoming my *jury*, and one boy becoming the *judge*. My main protagonist angrily shouted out the charges and the evidence. Before I could say anything, a boy who stood at the doorway said he wanted to be my defense. It was a Jewish boy who had recently lost his father. I had sat with him when he was upset and traveled with him on the subway back to Golders Green, visiting with his family to grieve their loss.

He stood up and argued every point they raised, making them appear ignorant about biology and classical music, and comparing their kangaroo court with Germany's fascism before the war. When he sat down, it was quiet until my prosecutor shouted out he wanted a decision, and he wanted it *now*. The judge turned to the jury and asked for a verdict.

"Guilty!" they cried.

Uproar followed, with the prosecutor demanding I be *Sent to Coventry*, his voice lost in all the shouting. I looked at my new friend who had defended me and mouthed, *Thank You.*

Day 327

Read: Acts 27–28

Otherwise, they might see with their eyes, hear with their ears, understand with their hearts and turn, and I would heal them.

—Acts 28:27

There were lots of days when tears flowed over the pages as I wrote under the covers in bed at night. I started slipping the journal under my pillow to not let it sit out where my parents, or my siblings, might read it. To say I was unhappy was an understatement. Two or three of the boys in my class now saw it as their mission in life to torment me every day. Getting changed for any sport became a nightmare. Tripping me up as I walked in class or along the halls of the school was a daily occurrence. Being pushed, being shoved became my daily life. Taking my books and schoolwork and destroying them became their daily sport.

Eventually, I created reasons not to go to school—an upset stomach, a fever, anything to avoid going. Until the day when one of the boys pushed me too far, and we fought. I had never fought anyone, but that day, I fought back. The boys in the classroom initially were cheering him on, but I slowly got the upper hand as I saw red! At some point a teacher separated us, and I was pulled off him. I was sent to the headmaster's study, and the whole story of their bullying came out. The headmaster spoke with many of the other boys and teachers, then called a full assembly. He addressed the issue of bullying, saying he had zero tolerance for it. My parents were called, and my father came from work to get me. I was ashamed of fighting, but my father was upset I hadn't shared the bullying with him or my mother. That evening, we prayed together as a family, and my parents hugged me.

Day 328

Read: Romans 1–3

This righteousness is given through faith in Jesus Christ to all who believe. There is no difference between Jew and Gentile.

—Romans 3:22

To say that my experience of school for several years had been a hostile environment is probably British understatement. It had been horrible. My father insisted on traveling with me to school each day for the following week, riding with me on the underground, walking up to the school with me, and saying goodbye at the school gates before walking back to the underground and going in to work himself.

I was nervous that first week after all this happened. However, several of the teachers went out of the way to say hello directly to me. My friend who had defended me in the kangaroo court fiasco made a point of sitting next to me and chatting about stamp collecting, a hobby we both shared.

One of our teachers, who taught math and ran the chess club, stood up in class at the beginning of his first lesson that week and started the lesson in silence. He stood looking at us all and paused until we were fully silent. After a few minutes of silence, he took his jacket off and turned back to the class, then slowly and purposively, he rolled his sleeves up on his shirt exposing some numbers tattooed on his forearms. He held them up so we could all see. Then he said, "These numbers were tattooed on me as a young boy, no older than you are now, by German soldiers as they sent me to the death camp. I prayed constantly and survived by God's intervention of the allied troops. We do not groom bullies in this school."

The silence continued as he rolled his sleeves back down and turned to the blackboard to start the lesson—a lesson he had already shared with every boy in the room!

Day 329

Read: Romans 4–7

Because we know that suffering produces perseverance; perseverance, character; and character, hope.

—Romans 5:3–4

I wrote, *experiences can color everything.* Things that happened long ago feel as if they were in a time far, far, away. However, those events seem to still affect how I see my life now and what I chose to believe about the world I live in. My past experiences influence my reactions, physical and emotional, to the everyday things that surround me. However, I discovered along the way I could change my reaction to circumstances. As I learned to pray more and stayed faithful in my beliefs, I was able to navigate through many difficult times in my life.

I still sometimes initially react the way I did as a child—shutting down, bottling up my emotions, putting up screens and barriers to anyone who might make the hint of helping me. I discovered there is a moment in time, between the stimulus of the incident and my reaction to it, when I can think and bring into focus my experiences from the past and how I reacted before. By taking those memories and considering them in a whole new light, a positive and pragmatic way, I can respond differently than I did as a child.

Gradually, I found with prayer I could establish an even keel for my life. My negative thoughts were replaced with more positive ones, and those, in turn, led me to making healthy decisions when faced with similar problems. In my journals, there are times when that strategy worked better than others. Certainly, reading Paul's letters to the Romans got me going round and round in circles sometimes, looking at the minutiae of the situation in the way only Paul could confuse. With each situation, as I persevered, there was new hope.

Day 330

Read: Romans 8–10

For those who are led by the Spirit of God are the children of God.

—Romans 8:14

My first wife admitted to sleeping with one of my friends and said she was not sure if we should stay together. She moved out, and I was left sitting alone. My father came over to be with me, and we sat quietly together as I shared with him what had happened. I also shared with him that several years before she had had an abortion. Her parents knew, but I didn't until it was too late to stop it. I cried as I shared this with my father. Suddenly, he was crying too. We both just sat and cried. He said he was sad I hadn't shared it with him several years before when it happened, that I had carried this on my own.

We talked about it, and through it all, I felt his compassion for me, my wife, and her parents. My father said he had never faced a situation like this. He had barely known his father, having been sent away to boarding school when he was only ten years old. He never saw him again, as he had died when my father was eighteen years old. He married my mother when he was twenty-six, and then they had to survive World War II almost immediately.

My father spent time with me just sitting, sharing his story, hearing my story, and praying together for whatever God wanted to show us we should do. As the months and years followed, I often remembered that day and how we supported each other. Through it all, we felt a presence with us, helping us, guiding us, comforting us, steering us toward what we needed to do. Life wasn't fixed, but it was shared, and *A problem shared is a problem halved*, my father would say.

Day 331

Read: Romans 11–13

Do not conform to the pattern of this world but be transformed by the renewing of your mind.

—Romans 12:2

No one else could hear the struggles in my head as I had to deal with life's experiences—from the birth of my twin sons to the almost immediate infidelity of their mother with a friend, to our divorce, to finding myself homeless and alone, though still employed and earning just enough to get by. I moved from multiple fleeting and often meaningless relationships to finding someone I truly believed I loved. However, because of my fear of commitment, she left me and left me empty, confirming my worst thoughts about relationships. I rebounded into a relationship that took over my life, consumed me, took me to a new country and a new life, different from anything I had experienced before. Through it all I struggled: *Where was God in all this?*

I wasn't sure for a while. As I settled into a relationship with my new church and made new friends and colleagues, I started to think more and more about whether I was living my life as God wanted me to do. One of my work colleagues questioned whether I could accept everything that corporate America was asking of me. I was using my skills, knowledge, and expertise to help people who didn't live their lives in the way I believe God wanted. Instead, they were focused on making more and more money, worshipping the mighty dollar. I found myself increasingly praying at work as well as at home about what it was that God was asking me to do. What should I be doing with the talents given to me? I found myself seeking God's will for me. Not my will, but how God's will could be done.

Day 332

Read: Romans 14–16

I urge you, brothers and sisters, to watch out for those who cause divisions and put obstacles in your way that are contrary to the teaching you have learned.

—Romans 16:17

I thought working at the BBC with the World Service would answer my need to be called to something greater than myself, and I worked with lots of different divisions and programs, constantly searching for something I could not find. Then I was offered the opportunity to accept another challenge, working for Prime Minister Margaret Thatcher to help her win her third general election in 1987, a great challenge and privilege. I was then offered the opportunity to spend two years running for office myself as a candidate in the 1989 European election. While this endeavor filled me emotionally, it did not fill my spiritual needs.

The subsequent challenge of helping the UK water industry regain its image with the public was something I thought might meet those needs, but I discovered the people who ran the companies were taking advantage of their customers by making as much money for themselves as they could. As I transitioned to working in America, I believed I could adapt to working in corporate America, and there, I would find the answer. My father-in-law and I talked about it, and he encouraged me to find a balance between the work in the corporation and lay ministry with the church. Several of my bosses in the company praised my work almost daily, but I found the work was all about boosting profits.

When the opportunity came to retrench what I was doing with my life, I realized God did indeed have a plan for me and probably always had. This shift coincided with my second divorce, and I was open to making my life as a father and a follower of The Way, both core tenets of my life going forward.

Day 333

Read: 1 Corinthians 1–4

Who has known the mind of the Lord so as to instruct him? But we have the mind of Christ.

—1 Corinthians 2:16

My journals over the years reflect on many things, yet through it all, I consistently was searching for answers to what was going on in my life. I searched for what God or the Spirit or Jesus was calling me to do, calling me to be. The more I left myself open to what the Spirit was speaking to me, the more I could learn about what my calling might be.

When I was younger, I felt the life the Spirit was calling me to follow was not for me. I just couldn't imagine doing it. As I grew older, I could hear the Spirit, feel the presence of the Spirit, and experience the call to minister pastorally to others.

One of the ways this manifested was in entering a process my church called discernment. I opened myself—my inner thoughts and feelings—to a small group of people, who in turn, were called to discern my calling with them, with our congregation, and with the church as a whole. I met with them regularly, with my priest, and with my counselor. Each played a role in discerning my call and what it meant. More than anything, though, spending time in meditation and prayer opened me to hearing the Spirit, and through that, hearing the mind of God.

It is hard to explain what happens until you try it yourself. Reading scripture every day was something I had done for years. Journaling almost every day was also something I had done for years. Realizing that this was all going somewhere, leading to something bigger than myself, was an eye-opener. Discovering I had a calling in my life, a purpose in my life beyond everything I had done up to that point, was enlightening—and a bit scary.

Day 334

Read: 1 Corinthians 5–8

"I have the right to do anything," you say, but not everything is beneficial.
—1 Corinthians 6:12

My mother struggled with the judgmental nature of a lot of the things Paul shared with us in scripture. I began to understand how the scriptures had been written by men for men and from a man's point of view, not a woman's. As my mother and I would discuss Paul, my grandmother would sit quietly and listen to us talk.

One day, I noted my grandmother's sudden comment, which cut through our discussion. "Paul was only a man; he only knew what he knew. He wasn't Jesus, and Jesus is different. He loves everybody, no matter what they do, or who they are. He didn't judge people, and Paul was not right to do so. You're supposed to love them, no matter what."

Both my mother and I sat quietly and took in the moment as the least formally educated person in the room understood the message of scripture Jesus brought us. We talked into the evening about how we could live our lives, what made sense of what Paul shared, and what didn't. We didn't believe we could pick and choose what to read. We needed to think for ourselves about where we were in our lives and apply scriptures accordingly.

Several years later, as the church I am part of changed its position on woman clergy and same-sex relationships, I had to evaluate where I stood on those issues. I was raised one way, to think a set of things to be right and wrong, yet I understood what my grandmother had shared so many years before. The Way is all about love in the purest and most amazing way, the way Jesus shared with us.

Day 335

Read: 1 Corinthians 9–11

This is my body, which is for you; do this in remembrance of me. This cup is the new covenant in my blood; do this, whenever you drink it, in remembrance of me.

—1 Corinthians 11:24–25

My colleague at church had asked me to practice, so I carefully took the chalice out of its case. I went into the quiet church as the afternoon sun shone through the stained-glass windows, casting a warm light. I set the table with the chalice, purificator, paten, bread, pall, corporal, and burse, then placed two cruets, one with water and another with wine, next to them. I lit some candles at the altar, placed the chalice to one side, placed the corporal to one side, removed the veil, removed the pall and patten and while saying a prayer, placed bread on the patten. Again, saying a prayer, I poured wine in the chalice and added a small amount of water. Then, I quietly and carefully prayed the Great Thanksgiving and the Eucharistic Prayer.

Something happens. It is impossible to put in words. Something happens. I was only practicing, yet something happened. I remembered the priest who stood at the altar when I was a child on holiday with my parents, brother, and aunt. He was an older priest, and all his moves at the altar were slow and deliberate. He had just finished consecrating the host when he suddenly collapsed to the ground. There was a moment of shock, then my father ran forward. He and my aunt lifted the priest to one side of the altar and helped him lie down on a pew. He spoke to my father, and my father asked us to come forward to receive communion, which we all did. As we finished, my father turned and gave communion to the priest, who made the sign of the cross and died. We were all in shock.

In my journal, I wrote the words: *The priest died saying, "It is finished. I am complete."*

Day 336

Read: 1 Corinthians 12–14

And now these three remain: faith, hope and love. But the greatest of these is love.

—1 Corinthians 13:13

My journals span the years from when I could first write words into a book to today. *When I was a child, I talked like a child, I thought like a child, I reasoned like a child* was a phrase I often heard as I went through life. The memories of my childhood were at times challenging, yet through it all—was love.

It has been a strange journey. Believing in God has been more of a relationship with God than simply realizing there is a God. Somehow in my life, I kept running into God in all sorts of people and places. I ran into God listening to our deacon at church when Desmond Tutu shared his life in Soweto and South Africa. His stories seemed so far away from our lives in a suburb in the North London, yet so close because we could feel the presence of God in every word he shared.

Years later, as I sat with a mother who had just lost a child, I was able to hold her and comfort her, sharing the presence of God with her—a God who loved her and her child. As a child, I couldn't imagine sitting with a mother who had lost her child. Nothing really prepares us for such a moment, except a love of God and knowing God loves us. Paul describes love as being patient, kind, and enduring, contrasting it with the temporary nature of prophecies, tongues, and knowledge. I realized being a chaplain was exactly where I was supposed to be.

And now these three remain: faith, hope and love. But the greatest of these is love.

Day 337

Read: 1 Corinthians 15–16

But someone will ask, "How are the dead raised? With what kind of body will they come?"

—1 Corinthians 15:35

I held the baby in my left hand. Smaller than a soda can, dwarfed by my hand. I anointed her, I blessed her, I kissed her forehead, and I named her. Her mother smiled at me through her tears—her exhaustion, sadness, and loss showing on her face. Yet, her thanks at my presence and actions showed in her eyes. Neither of us asked or said anything about resurrection at that moment. I held the baby while its life was slipping away. I laid the baby in her hands against her body. Holding it tenderly, she smiled down at the face of the child who might have been—the child who would always be part of their lives, yet always apart from their lives.

Her husband sat on the edge of the bed with his arm around her and the child, stroking its head as it breathed its last. No talk of resurrection here. The Spirit was present in this moment in time. I stepped back, standing with the medical team who had worked so hard in attempts to save this child but were now grieving with the mother and father at their loss. It was quiet in the room except for a gentle bleeping from a machine off to the side. The sun was, at last, creeping into the room. The light settled on the mother and father and child. They asked me to hold the child again while they comforted each other. I held the child, whom I had named moments before. I looked down at the child with its eyes closed, her breath ending. The beeping stopped, and I wept.

Breathe in, God within you; Breathe out, God around you.

Day 338

Read: 2 Corinthians 1–4

We always carry around in our body the death of Jesus, so that the life of Jesus may also be revealed in our body.

—2 Corinthians 4:10

I am thankful for the opportunities to bring the presence of God into the lives of others. I struggled in my life to be perfect until I realized that one of my goals in life is to *not* be perfect. I found life was about experimenting, struggling to learn from my mistakes, and staying in the moment so I could experience the presence of God. Working as a chaplain, serving others, drained me and left me needing time to just be—time to sit with the events of the previous day or night and process the experience.

I began spending a small amount of time in the hospital chapel before driving home or on to another task. The moments I spent sitting with my thoughts and prayers became essential for me to be present to others. So often I felt I was not enough, yet I realized by simply being present with people, I was enough to those around me. I was not aware of how my presence, my energy, my spirit, affected the people around me in numerous ways and moments.

As the years have gone by, I have realized how my presence reached out and touched many lives, and through them, touched the lives of many others. Each time one of them reaches back to me for comfort or advice, I am aware of how much the ministry of presence makes a difference in all our lives. How much our lives are like a ripple caused by a pebble tossed into a pond, or a seed planted in the winter that lies sleeping to wake and bloom in spring.

Day 339

Read: 2 Corinthians 5–9

We are therefore Christ's ambassadors, as though God were making his appeal through us.

—2 Corinthians 5:20

I have heard this scripture read in church many times as it is in the readings for Ash Wednesday. Each year when I read it myself, I remember different places, churches, and people who have impacted my life over the years, and memories of them come flooding back. Over the years, I have heard these thoughts of Paul coming from many different people with many different agendas, yet through it all, I hear another voice speaking through Paul's words, reminding me that one of my goals in life is to *not* be perfect. I often forget that.

Life is about experimenting, experiencing, and learning new things; therefore, a prerequisite of life is to be imperfect. When I sit with these words from Paul, memories come back of my grandmother, my mother, my father, my godparents, my siblings, my friends, my children, my loves. I remember how much I have learned from all of them. They helped me realize the world is a loving place, and in realizing that, I learned it's okay to be imperfect.

I can still, however, strive to do my best. To persevere. To love God for God's sake. To search my most hidden thoughts and find the way, the truth, and the life. To name the very things that separate me from God. To open myself to reconciliation with God and everyone.

Day 340

Read: 2 Corinthians 10–13

For though we live in the world, we do not wage war as the world does.
—2 Corinthians 10:3

Since 1951 when I was born, there have been wars somewhere every year of my life. I almost can't believe it, but it's true. My father was a conscientious objector in World War II and was removed from his job working for the London County Council as he could not be employed by the county council if he was a conscientious objector. As a chemical engineer by training, he was sent to work for a small company providing paint to the Merchant Marines and the Royal Navy for ships decks.

After a short while he invented, then patented products, which when added to the paint, increased its friction content when wet. This improvement meant ships decks could get wet, yet the sailors didn't slip as much. After the war, it was used for large cruise liners with Cunard and P & O and oil tankers, as well as footbridges and industrial plants. A variation of it was added to road tarmacs to make roads safer, particularly before traffic junctions.

He once said to me that he did not believe in war except that he could use the weapons God gave him, his intellect and belief, to fight the enemy and defeat the Devil wherever he might be. His pacifist view of fighting was refreshing to me and showed how his faith set him apart from others, yet his faith also enabled him to save thousands of lives and continues to do so today. He believed the work he did was aligned with his faith. He used God's mighty weapons to knock down the Devil's strongholds in ways that no one could have imagined until he did it.

Day 341

Read: Galatians 1–3

There is neither Jew nor Gentile, neither slave nor free, nor is there male and female, for you are all one in Christ Jesus.

—Galatians 3:28

The followers of The Way can come from any position in life, Jew or Gentile, rich or poor, male or female, slave or free. Sadly, over the centuries, that has not been true, especially after Christianity became an integral part of the ruling class, the empire, and later a part of the state and government. When I was young, I was comforted by knowing the rules surrounding attending church, but as I grew up, I challenged them more and more. The rules often seemed petty and immaterial to actually worshipping.

Personally, this distinction helped me on my journey to *believe God*, different from believing *in God*. Believing God deeply affected who I am and what I needed to do with my life and also woke me to be everything I have become. I chose to believe God. I can't pinpoint the exact moment, yet I experienced a sudden change in the way I looked at my life and purpose. I think I ran into God in a way, giving me an understanding that I couldn't reach otherwise.

This insight required a time when I had lost everything that gave me safety— a home, a job, a position in life—and showed me a way forward believing God in a way I could never have experienced before. I wrote about this, and in later years, the experience grew stronger as I spent more time in prayer and studying scripture. Opening myself up to reading through the Bible by reading a few verses every day has helped me focus and understand this much clearer than I could have when I was younger, and this process goes on every day.

Day 342

Read: Galatians 4–6

*Whoever sows to please their flesh, from the flesh will reap
destruction; whoever sows to please the Spirit, from the Spirit will reap
eternal life.*

—Galatians 6:8

My life had been turned upside down by the betrayal of my first wife
and a close friend, which sadly led to our divorce and a broken relationship
with my twin sons. I couldn't understand how—when I had worked so hard
to provide a home and a great place to live—my wife turned to someone
else for a sexual relationship. She truly had turned to someone else, my
friend, to satisfy a sexual need. I couldn't understand how our relationship
had not been enough.

I sought help from counseling and spent several years struggling with
this. Nearly thirty years later, married and living in America, I was faced
with an almost identical situation. I wrestled with watching my life repeat
with a divorce and a betrayal, and a sense of not being enough in so many
ways. Fortunately, I was able to sit with both a counselor and, separately,
a priest, who worked through this with me.

At the end of the day, I was able to make myself whole again, not
harboring resentment toward my ex-wife or my friend. It was not easy.
I found my faith helped guide my actions, my relationships, and my life
going forward. My faith, my ability to be a blessing to others, was driven
and guided by my faith. As I opened up and listened to others as a chaplain,
I was able to walk with others in their times of trouble, to be present to
them in their hour of need. In turning to my faith for guidance, I could
draw on strength from my faith, which I could share, in turn, with others.

Day 343

Read: Ephesians 1–3

. . . and to know this love that surpasses knowledge, that you may be filled to the measure of all the fullness of God.

—Ephesians 3:19

While on retreat with the brothers at the Society of St. John the Evangelist in Boston, I prayed to understand God's love for me and for help learning to share that love with others. Before I could share it with others, I needed to be sure I loved myself. The brothers were great at asking gentle questions that prodded my thoughts and delved deeper into my feelings. I had locked away my feelings after my two divorces, and they helped me open up and truly experience God's love for me—an unconditional love I could share with others. As I sat with my thoughts at the monastery, I felt God's spirit enter me in a way I still find hard to put in words.

Suddenly I knew the unconditional love of God and how I could share that gift with others. God's love extends deep into us; as a plant puts roots down into rich soil, good roots bring forth a strong and healthy plant. We see this explained in the parable of the mustard seed and in many other stories in the Bible. By creating a strong foundation, I was able to build and share this love with others, helping them experience what I had, the unconditional love of God.

When I started sharing the Bible-365 program with the groups at church, in the small group of the house church, and through the internet, I saw these roots bloom, and I felt God's love make itself known in their lives as they immersed themselves more and more in sharing the Bible and their experiences with each other.

Day 344

Read: Ephesians 4–6

Do not let any unwholesome talk come out of your mouths, but only what is helpful for building others up according to their needs, that it may benefit those who listen.

—Ephesians 4:29

What I hadn't expected to unpack was the depth of hurt and pain suppressed in the members of the Bible study group gathered in a parishioner's home. Several of them spoke about being judged or criticized by other members of the church, and in the process, they had criticized others. They realized they had spoken unkindly about others. By being sarcastic or mean, they tore down others in the way they felt torn down.

One woman had said things to her closest friend at church, and she could feel the pain she was causing both to her friend and herself. We talked about this, and I suggested when we wanted to say something hurtful, we needed to find a way to deliberately reach into ourselves and find kind and encouraging words to build each other up instead. We will always have times of conflict, irritation, or frustration; how we handle those moments is what makes us different.

Our group spent a long time discussing this. I shared the hardest similar situation I'd dealt with was the broken relationship with my second wife. There was so much hope when she brought me to America and into the circle of her family and friends. To then be so deeply hurt by her left me feeling betrayed, so it was easy to say hurtful or mean things about her. Knowing her well, I knew what would hurt her. By releasing my pain and opening myself to love, the Spirit moved me to only say things from love. I was able to give grace to her in a way I could have only imagined a few years ago.

Day 345

Read: Philippians 1–4

Rather, he made himself nothing by taking the very nature of a servant, being made in human likeness.

—Philippians 2:7

For many years, I worked with people who, by all normal standards, were celebrities. It wasn't until I visited my parents in Scotland that that fact hit me like a bolt out of the blue. My mother and I went down to the local shops for some groceries. The village still had all the individual shops: a butcher, a baker, a fish monger, a greengrocer, a newsagent, a pharmacist, and several other small shops selling TVs, shoes, clothes, and tourist things. As we went from shop to shop, my mother tailored her introduction of me, depending on whom she was addressing. With one shopkeeper, she mentioned one celebrity, with another, a different one. She was proud of me and showed me off to her friends.

I felt she was putting me on a pedestal, and I didn't want to be seen that way. I was blessed by the opportunities I had to work with these celebrities, yet I also knew I was only a small cog in a large wheel, just a fly on the wall. As we walked back to their house, I shared with my mother how I felt. I loved she was proud of me, yet I wanted her to know that her and my father's upbringing had made it possible for me to speak authentically whether I was with a prince or a commoner, a prime minister or a priest. I was simply me, an empty vessel used in different ways to do what God wanted me to do. I wanted to be God's eyes, ears, hands, and feet, in whatever way I could be—to help others and be the best I could be.

Day 346

Read: Colossians 1–4

Bear with each other and forgive one another if any of you has a grievance against someone.

—Colossians 3:13

My journals are windows into my soul. At different times, in different years, my writings are excruciatingly honest about where I was and what I was experiencing. Both at a very personal level and at a macro level, I struggled all my life with the thoughts behind this text. How can I possibly accept the hurt and pain inflicted on me and forgive the person who inflicted it?

Invariably, someone I knew well and loved dearly was the person who had completely burrowed under my skin. This person knew how to hurt me, and in the relationship, I trusted them not to hurt me. Yet again and again, I found myself fuming in front of my journal, as I had been hurt by someone who knew me well.

Then, as I bared my soul in my journal, I remembered the words of Paul: to forgive as the Lord forgives me. These words always pulled me up sharply, like reining in a galloping horse, or throttling back on a racing motorbike. By sitting quietly, reading a few verses from scripture, reading through a psalm, or listening to a recording of a choir singing a hymn, I was able to de-escalate my feelings to a place of giving thanks for the learning experience. I thanked God for the opportunity to grow from that day forward.

Day 347

Read: 1 Thessalonians 1–5

We always thank God for all of you and continually mention you in our prayers.

—1 Thessalonians 1:2

One of the blessings I have experienced from reading through the Bible each year is the daily habit of not only reading and sitting with the text but also thinking of my family and friends and saying a few prayers for them. When I was very young, my notebooks—they could hardly be called journals—contained sweet simple prayers for my family. I would name each one, spelling out my mother and father, then my three sisters and brother, then my grandparents, then my aunts and uncles and their children, and then my godparents. The circle grew to include people from church, neighbors, friends from school or church, and people I knew in other ways. Gradually over the years, the list grew and grew.

When Facebook started, I realized I could pray for people who became friends through this social media, and I started wishing them *Happy Birthday* and sending them a blessing each year. Sometimes, I offered them a thought or prayer if I felt they were struggling with something in their life.

I will not be leaving any large sum of money for my family or friends. I don't expect any buildings to be named after me. I hope my legacy is my blessing for my children, my family, my friends and neighbors, and those I have reached out to over the years, praying with and for them. I pray they find and experience the same love I have found in God through my faith.

Day 348

Read: 2 Thessalonians 1–3

We constantly pray for you, that our God may make you worthy of his calling.

—2 Thessalonians 1:11

To say I was feeling totally inadequate and unworthy of even being on the same planet as everybody I knew was probably an understatement. Then a priest sat with me. He sat while I poured my heart out to him. He patiently listened as I shared I was unworthy of doing anything, of being anything, of serving anyone anywhere. After we sat in silence for a while, he shared that I was ready. Ready to truly serve God in ways I had probably never imagined I could.

He talked about the life he saw God calling me to. He saw me preaching and teaching, comforting and caring, serving God in hospital rooms and at bedsides, simply being with people who needed to hear the word of God. He knew I was a gifted communicator. God had need of that gift, he said, but also needed my actions and words. He helped me understand I had come to the point where everything else was gone, everything else had failed. At that point, God steps in through the Spirit and guides us to where we are really needed. Then God goes further and gives us everything we need to do what is necessary to succeed.

We prayed together for quite a while. It would be a long and trying journey to achieve what we shared that day, requiring several years of study and prayer. Praying humbly for guidance and asking for God's grace and faith to guide me brought me to chaplaincy. Through God's guidance, through faith, and through prayer, I was ready to hear God's call to become the chaplain I was called to be.

Day 349

Read: 1 Timothy 1–6

Watch your life and doctrine closely. Persevere in them, because if you do, you will save both yourself and your hearers.

—1 Timothy 4:16

Deciding to study to become a chaplain was one thing; not being seen as a chaplain by the people around me was another. There was definitely a core group of people who believed in me and heard my call. However, as this was also a time of divorce, separation, and change, there were many who struggled to see this call in me. People who had known me as the public relations person, or the broadcaster, or the political advisor struggled seeing me as a chaplain, pastoring to a church and in a hospital.

By working hard at my studies, expanding my reading, seeking out both spiritual and temporal therapy to help me understand myself better, and spending time on retreat with the brothers at the Society of St. John the Evangelist in Boston, I was able to grow in my faith and my call. Many people who had been friends before, were still friends, though different. They needed me to explain why I was doing what I was doing. It did not fit with the American way to focus on earning as much money as possible and live a life of expensive tastes. Instead, I looked to simplify my life.

I found I could reduce my spending and live within my means, within whatever I was able to earn as a chaplain. Gradually, everyone who knew me before could see the progress I was making, and new friends through the church in North St. Louis County saw every day how I was called to ministry—a ministry of caring, praying, and teaching with them and for them. The notes in my journal became lighter and brighter as if I had turned on a light. Indeed, that is what God had done.

Day 350

Read: 2 Timothy 1–4

All Scripture is God-breathed and is useful for teaching, rebuking, correcting and training in righteousness.

—2 Timothy 3:16

I can see now how my parents introduced me to the Bible, to not be afraid of it, and encouraged me to explore life with the Bible beside me. Reading the Bible regularly has led me to some lively exchanges with God, with both an opportunity to speak and to listen. My parents never insisted I follow their beliefs; rather, they encouraged me to find my own faith.

It was like riding a bicycle. They taught me how to ride, what to watch out for, the rules of the road, how to maintain the bike, then removed the training wheels and sent me on my way—with their hearts in their mouths praying I wouldn't crash and burn! I can see how again and again, I have turned to the Bible for answers, or to find more questions, enabling me to pass through life safely. At the end of the day, I hope to be in right relationship with God. By reading and praying the Bible regularly, I have found myself open to sharing the scriptures with others, helping them share my experiences. By trusting the Spirit to guide me, the actions I shared as a chaplain brought me closer to God.

My journals have guided my thoughts over the years, making me aware that as a follower of The Way, I live counterculturally at times. I watch people loving money, wealth, power, pleasure, and themselves, and not loving God. In recent years, I have pondered why our society is a world without love. Sometimes, I felt I stood alone in my difference from the world, as if God is saying, *Be yourself and love God.*

Day 351

Read: Titus 1-3

You, however, must teach what is appropriate to sound doctrine.

—Titus 2:1

Our local Public Broadcasting Station in America has been sharing the "Meet the Midwife" series on television. It takes me back to my mother traveling to visit young wives church-based groups in the East End of London. I was quite young and enjoyed traveling on buses and the underground to visit with these, what seemed to me to be, far-flung places. My mother shared with these groups of young women, with their children and babies, helping them do more than just survive as England came out of the aftermath of World War II.

We still had rationing, and when she walked through the streets of the East End, wheeling me in a collapsible stroller, we saw bombed-out buildings and the signs of the aftermath of the war all around us. She sat and talked with them, often with me on her lap or by her side, about everything from how to care for a baby to personal hygiene, from how to feed a family on a budget to how to make time for themselves. She shared examples of how to take care of the home, and how to take care of their man. It was still, despite everything women had done in the war, a man's world. Yet my mother showed them how they could be more than their mothers had been and gave them a glimpse of their future as times were changing.

My mother always seemed to bring God into her conversation and shared how her faith had given her hope during the war, raising three, then four, now five children. What I saw was she gave them hope when all around them was despair. She showed them unconditional love and that God loved them unconditionally too.

Day 352

Read: Hebrews 1–6

We have this hope as an anchor for the soul, firm and secure.

—Hebrews 6:19

We were in the First Gulf War. I was making a cup of coffee in my office in Whitehall. Earlier, I had taken my overnight briefing across to my colleague who was going into the Downing Street War Cabinet meeting. I walked across the Horse Guards Parade ground, past the mounted member of the household cavalry who was just coming on duty early in the morning, and back to my office. Suddenly, there was a huge explosion and all my windows facing the Horse Guards were blown out, and I was left sitting, surrounded by shattered glass and debris.

For several hours, our building and the whole area was locked down with no phone service and no way of telling anyone I was okay. At one point, a soldier climbed through the window to check if everyone was okay and told me to stay put until the area was cleared. The Irish Republican Army, the IRA, had attempted to assassinate John Major, the British Prime Minister, using mortar fire from a truck parked right outside my window. The truck's suspension broke with firing the first mortar and then exploded.

I sat among the rubble and prayed for God to protect those around me in the area, from the Prime Minister and the War Cabinet to the soldiers and first responders in the area. I think I lost my sense of security that morning. I clung to my belief that God had a purpose for me, even though it would be several years before God shared what that purpose was.

Day 353

Read: Hebrews 7–10

I will put my laws in their minds and write them in their hearts.

—Hebrews 8:10

Over the years, I heard all sorts of different versions and comments about this passage from scripture. To me, the text speaks of a wonderful sense of freedom. I met many people in my life who were shut in, or held back by circumstances or traditions, because *We have always done it that way* or *If it ain't broke, don't fix it.*

I wanted to scream from the rooftops, "It doesn't have to be that way!"

I noted one of my then bosses asked me to *stay in the box* for once, because I was constantly thinking outside of the box, and it was exhausting him. I surprised him by saying where other people saw boxes to stay in or think outside of, I didn't see a box at all. Similarly, my experience of religion in America has been different than what I expected to find. Religion in America tends to put God in a box; however, I saw God move to supply his own Spirit to live within us.

The new covenant talked about here moves on from the "City on the Hill" quoted by John Winthrop in 1630 as they founded New England or the various African American understandings and expressions of exodus themes in the context of slavery, emancipation, migration, and civil rights on towards black liberation, feminist, and gay theology. To say that the box was shattered into pieces reminded me of sitting in my office among the broken glass and rubble, wondering what was next, yet knowing God was with me, within me, around me, and still speaking.

Day 354

Read: Hebrews 11–13

And may he work in us what is pleasing to him, through Jesus Christ, to whom be glory for ever and ever. Amen.

—Hebrews 13:21

One amazing thing that comes out of reading a small amount of scripture every day is the closeness you gradually feel to God—who or whatever God means to you.

Sometimes, I barely hold my head above water. Other times I soar like an eagle. What I have witnessed in my journals is a growing relationship with God through the Bible—a human relationship beyond my level of comprehension, yet as human as you or I. When I realized I could be equipped to move forward in the form of ministry I was called to follow, the barriers that made it seem impossible fell away. The journey wasn't easy, but every journal entry confirmed it was the correct path.

To find God was working through me as I sat with a family of a parishioner who died or with the mother of a newborn facing life as a single mother or to sit in a small group studying the Bible, sharing their stories, hopes, and dreams is almost inexplicable. To find God working through me at those moments is only understandable by accepting God moves in mysterious ways. The more experiences I have, the more I know I have so much more to experience in life.

My journal gathers my thoughts about life and The Way, yet it never takes me far from that small child growing up in London, my parents, grandparents, godparents, and the cloud of witnesses who surrounded me almost every moment of my life. My journal has helped me realize I have a little five-year-old inside me, and I can talk to him now whenever I want to, because I finally see him.

Day 355

Read: James 1–5

Everyone should be quick to listen, slow to speak and slow to become angry, because human anger does not produce the righteousness that God desires.

—James 1:19–20

Growing up the last of five children, separated by thirteen years, I found at an early age if I didn't speak up, no one knew I was there. I was almost the opposite of this verse, and it was with great difficulty and help that I worked at overcoming this. Over the years, I have lost friendships or hurt friends that didn't deserve it. More than once, I felt regret at what I was saying as I said it, knowing I was hurting someone's feelings. As I worked at being slow to speak, alongside working toward my calling as a chaplain, God showed me a better way of handling friendships and situations.

In my years of recorded memories, I read about moments when I wished: *If only I had kept quiet for a few more minutes and held my words, then I would have seen their side of the problem.* If only I had walked in their shoes for a while longer and seen the depth of their problem from their point of view, I could have made a positive difference in their life instead of a destructive one.

Over the past few years, I have seen a change. I am quicker to listen to others and slower to speak. I don't listen so that I can plan what I will say, but I actively listen so when I speak, I respond from love, not from anger. I am a work in progress; I only have to look in my journals to see that. However, these words, thoughts, and prayers from James are a guide to improving and staying open to help from my faith.

Day 356

Read: 1 Peter 1–5

Not lording it over those entrusted to you but being examples to the flock.
—1 Peter 5:3

My father's name was Peter. I always felt he was the rock of our family, holding us all together with the glue of faith and love when we were struggling to stay a family and would have fragmented into separate lives. I can imagine him being with Jesus on the banks of the Lake of Galilee, or the banks of Lock Lomond, or the banks of the River Tweed in Scotland, where they moved to spend the last twenty years of their retirement. I can hear Jesus saying to him, "Feed my sheep."

Not long after my parents retired to Scotland, the bishop of their diocese asked him to visit him in Edinburgh. He asked my father if he would accept ordination under Canon Eleven (Si Quis) to enable him to provide priestly care for several small churches along the border of Scotland and England. He accepted, and for the next few years, he traveled between the churches, bringing communion to the flock, sharing scripture, and preaching short but memorable homilies to small congregations of Episcopalians.

He truly believed the church is where two or three are gathered, so he brought communion. After a few years, another full-time priest retired to the area, and he replaced my father. He and his wife became great friends with my parents and were with them as they aged, living nearby in the same village on the banks of the River Tweed.

In my journal, I wrote that when my father was called, he responded, and when he was replaced, he stepped back, making way for a new shepherd for the flock. His humility and grace were wonderful examples and lessons on how to *let go and let God* in any situation.

Day 357

Read: 2 Peter 1–3

This is my Son, whom I love; with him I am well pleased.
—2 Peter 1:17

Reading the Bible, understanding the stories, and listening to the prophecies is not like working at the BBC World Service, where every news story must have two or possibly three confirmed corroborating sources. Peter probably dictated this story as he knew he faced death. He wanted, perhaps, to ensure the stories he told in person would continue to be shared after he died. Peter believed God had done something special in Jesus, and if so, it was inconceivable that God would not allow the events and messages of Jesus to be preserved. Peter's accounts and all the stories were God's Word, written down to pass onward.

This made total sense to me as I looked around the cafeteria at broadcasters sharing the news in more than thirty-nine languages every hour of the day, seven days a week. Peter goes further, though, and as with the BBC World Service witnessing to the truth around the world, he witnesses to the transfiguration of Jesus as his deathbed testimony. His testimony—and the testimony of the apostles—about the resurrection made Jesus' crucifixion stand out among the thousands of crucifixions the Roman Empire inflicted on the world.

Peter's words also remind me of a journal entry about following the path of pilgrimage with my own Peter, my father, as we approached the Holy Island of Lindisfarne together in the footsteps of St. Cuthbert. We walked across the causeway instead of driving to experience the presence of the footsteps that had passed before. In the wind and the circling sea birds, we heard the words of prophecy from all the prophets who spoke for God as they were guided by the Spirit.

Day 358

Read: 1 John 1–5

This is how we know that we live in him and he in us: He has given us of his Spirit.

—1 John 4:13

The theme of my life, from when I was born to today, is love. Love is so integral to my life that it is almost the oxygen. My parents wanted me to be born as they moved into a new home and life in North London after surviving the Second World War. Love surrounded me as a child from my family, my church family, and my neighbors. I was loved by people from countries and places all over the world, receiving support from so many. At the time, I was probably oblivious to their love. Gradually, I recognized and found the different types of love that supported me through difficult times and decisions.

Ultimately, I understood God is love. When I realized this, the impact was huge, so huge I couldn't believe my thoughts for a while, so I just sat with the thought for days and days. God was no longer the white-haired old gentleman in the paintings and books of my childhood, rather God was something within me and within everyone I met.

This understanding took me back to the words of Desmond Tutu when he was the deacon in our church, asking us to look for God in everyone we met, no matter their race, color, or creed. I was taken back to the words of John Stott sitting in the candlelit chapel of All Soul's Langham Place, to the studios of the BBC World Service in the middle of the night, to the bedside of a patient in a hospital in Lake St. Louis, Missouri, to the streets of Ferguson. God is in everyone I see; I need only open my eyes and my heart and love them.

Day 359

Read: 2 John, 3 John, Jude

As you have heard from the beginning, his command is that you walk in love.
—2 John 1:6

To walk in love. Again and again in my journals, I came across this truth.

My mother shared so much of herself, at times I joked she cared more for others than her own family.

My grandmother had very little, yet what she had she gave away to us and to the church.

My eldest sister had not had a vacation for more than thirty years as she cared for her handicapped daughter when the local authority decided to step in and help with some respite care. So, what did she do? She took a vacation trip to Africa to visit with the community her church had been supporting for years, so she could give back to them in person.

When the youngest of my three sisters moved to Edinburgh, she was saddened by how many homeless people were on the street. So, she started by giving them breakfast, then recruited help to take over a vacant church and serve them not just breakfast but provide them with a warm place to be. When her own ill health stopped her, she handed it over to the local authority, who expanded it to include mental care.

My brother started a program to help people who had lost their jobs, who needed to retrain on computers. With several friends, he developed a program to make help available.

I was growing up, getting married, getting divorced, getting remarried, moving to America, getting divorced again, and only then did I realize my call to help others. As I committed to chaplaincy in hospitals, homes, and church, I realized I loved God with my whole heart as my mother, father, sisters and brother had always shown me.

Day 360

Read: Revelation 1–3

You have persevered and have endured hardships for my name and have not grown weary.

—Revelation 2:3

When I first started in chaplaincy, it wasn't easy. The first stage was taking a class in clinical pastoral education, known as CPE, which I took at a local hospital. My supervisor was dealing with some personal issues during the course, and we clashed several times. However, we found a way to work together, and I was able to complete the unit in a positive, loving manner. Through the unit, I realized I needed to let go of a lot of my preconceived ideas about being a chaplain and listen to others' feedback.

When I took my second unit, I was with a different hospital and supervisor, and it went smoothly and was an incredible loving experience. I guess I was more open to everything by then. I also had experience being a chaplain, particularly in a hospital setting, for several years. In the process of this educational unit, I had a real breakthrough about being with a patient who was nonresponsive when a stroke left him with *Locked-in syndrome*(LIS). We shared a book and movie called, *The Diving Bell and the Butterfly*, by Jean-Dominique Bauby, and my whole way of being with patients in this situation was transformed. This story changed my view so much, I shared it with several key nurses and doctors at the hospitals where I worked.

Every day, I worked on being focused and present with patients because I learned that in being present with patients spiritually, I was bringing the healing power of *presence* to them and their family. I became aware my role in health care was more than medicine; it was to help bring the patient to God's presence and to know God's love.

Day 361

Read: Revelation 4–8

You are worthy, our Lord and God, to receive glory and honor and power, for you created all things, and by your will they were created and have their being.

—Revelation 4:11

My mother wanted me to be aware of how much everything I did, everything I achieved, everything I could be was a gift from God. When two other students and I won the Royal Academy Award for Architecture awarded by the British Institution, I was able to stay grounded and give thanks that we made a difference in the lives of the severely handicapped children whose education needs were not currently being met. It wasn't about us; it was about them.

When our church was closing in London, and we won our court case to decide whom our church would be sold to, we were able to gift it to the Church of Antioch and the Orient. They changed it to their cathedral for the whole of the United Kingdom. It was not about us, a handful of parishioners; it was about God's work in the world and helping the church grow in a new way.

I was in delivery with a young couple whose baby suffered a disease that would take its life. I baptized their child while it still lay in the womb, before it was gently lifted out by careful, loving hands to live for a brief moment before going to be with God. Our team cared for the mother, father, and child, bringing the presence of God to them, laying down our best efforts and ministry in worship that day.

Day 362

Read: Revelation 9–12

The great dragon was hurled down, that ancient serpent called the devil, or Satan, who leads the whole world astray.

—Revelation 12:9

There were times when I was tempted by the influence of wealth, glory, or fame, and I realized, through prayer, they were fleeting and not what God called me to. Several times in my work, I was being offered more, yet each time it took me further away from having God at the center of my life. I was tempted to accept an inflated salary, because everyone was doing it, but fortunately, I was influenced by others to whom money wasn't the goal in life.

I learned this lesson from John Stott who, rather than accept the money his books were making, shared the royalties with his foundation to promote the Gospel through the Langham Partnership. His example stuck with me, and when I accepted the call to be a chaplain, I knew it would not be easy, financially or in the status within my community.

In fact, my community at the start of this journey couldn't believe what I was doing. Several thought I must have a secret source of funding to be able to afford the call. Instead, I trusted in God to help and guide me. I was blessed with help at times when I needed it from friends through church, and they have continued to support my ministry.

I can live comfortably, safely, and able to make ends meet most of the time. I have had enough. Trusting God is a life-changer in so many ways. Being open to God's love is even bigger.

Day 363

Read: Revelation 13–16

For you alone are holy. All nations will come and worship before you, for your righteous acts have been revealed.

—Revelation 15:4

I was a child when we were visited at church in London by Desmond Tutu, who had come to study at King's College, in London. While completing his studies for ordination, he came to be a deacon in Golders Green, where his mentor Trevor Huddleston had worshipped with his aunt. I had no idea who he was, or that he was coming to visit; however, when he preached at church, everyone listened as he shared his experience of South Africa. When he finished his sermon, he stopped and asked all the children and young people to come forward.

We gathered at his feet as he shared his joy of being with us and how he hoped we would hold the love of God in our hearts and find it in everyone we met. Later, over lunch, I heard my parents talking about a dream I had shared of sitting at Desmond Tutu's feet, asking me if I knew he was coming to visit. I didn't. When I was young, I could open my mind and my heart through my dreams and invite guidance into my life. As I grew older, I rarely could do this.

As I grew in my understanding of my call to chaplaincy, I found in prayer, meditation, and sleep, I could again open my mind and heart to be ready for God. Some might describe this practice as being open to the universe; to me, it is being open to God. Not everything I see and hear are signs from God; however, my intuition guides me in my thoughts and in being present to others in need. I have learned to be patient, receptive ,and thankful to God from whom all blessings flow, as the dust of the earth is washed away from my eyes.

Day 364

Read: Revelation 17–19

But the beast was captured, and with it the false prophet who had performed the signs on its behalf.

—Revelation 19:20

Christmas always has the stories from the Bible that are so familiar about shepherds, wise men, sheep, and a special birth. Yet for years I also found myself reading Revelation and experiencing God's positive purpose for humanity. Revelation is not pleasant to read; it shares an amazing gift to us.

Christmas has been both the best of times and the worst of times in my life. It was a moment of joy when our visitor at church in London from Sri Lanka came to our church one Christmas Eve, came home with us, gave birth in my parents' bed with us all gathered around her, and brought her child to church the next day to be baptized.

It was a moment of emptiness when I sat on my own outside the church of St. Margaret's, Westminster on a cold Christmas Eve, listening to the sounds of the service inside in the warmth with friends singing in the choir and in the pews, yet not feeling worthy enough to go in and pray. I felt too broken and unworthy to even set foot inside on such a night. I felt a total and utter failure in my life, my relationships, and my call to be something worthy of God's love. As the church emptied and people flowed by me, seemingly ignoring me sitting huddled on a bench, I discovered that God still loved me unconditionally as someone stopped to ask me if I was okay. A politician who would go on to be a great friend and mentor in my life invited me to walk with him and his wife as they walked back to their home across the road.

A moment of kindness, friendship, and resurrection in my life.

Day 365

Read: Revelation 20–22

The city does not need the sun or the moon to shine on it, for the glory of God gives it light, and the Lamb is its lamp.

—Revelation 21:23

My journal entries around Christmas each year often mention deeper thoughts about faith than any other days. I guess I had more time on my hands to sit, think, and write. This vision going forward is of the resurrected Jesus as our temple no matter where we are. Yet for centuries after this book was written, the established church built physical structures to gather and worship in. The faith of a few following The Way became an organized religion that spread across the world.

Yet, when I think back to the people whose lives have touched mine, their humility and faith didn't need a physical building to share the presence of God with me, with us. Many whose lives and love touched my soul helped me, over the last few years, to come full circle to the child I knew and can see now was always supposed to be in the ministry of caring and feeding God's sheep.

Through my journals, I often see and understand with hindsight what has guided me as I moved forward in life. Each year as I start anew, I find new meaning, new understanding, and new life. God is always changing things up and never allows us to sit still for too long as there are always new ways to bring God's word to others.

Each year as I reach the end of my readings from Gensis to Revelation, and as I explore my thoughts and emotions to support my self-awareness, I am reminded of what this journey is all about in one verse, Revelation 22:13: *I am the Alpha and the Omega, the First and the Last, the Beginning and the End.*

Bible Readings for One Year

Jan 1: Gen 1–3
Jan 2: Gen 4–7
Jan 3: Gen 8–11
Jan 4: Gen 12–15
Jan 5: Gen 16–18
Jan 6: Gen 19–21
Jan 7: Gen 22–24
Jan 8: Gen 25–26
Jan 9: Gen 27–29
Jan 10: Gen 30–31
Jan 11: Gen 32–34
Jan 12: Gen 35–37
Jan 13: Gen 38–40
Jan 14: Gen 41–42
Jan 15: Gen 43–45
Jan 16: Gen 46–47
Jan 17: Gen 48–50
Jan 18: Ex 1–3
Jan 19: Ex 4–6
Jan 20: Ex 7–9
Jan 21: Ex 10–12
Jan 22: Ex 13–15
Jan 23: Ex 16–18
Jan 24: Ex 19–21
Jan 25: Ex 22–24
Jan 26: Ex 25–27
Jan 27: Ex 28–29
Jan 28: Ex 30–32
Jan 29: Ex 33–35
Jan 30: Ex 36–38
Jan 31: Ex 39–40
Feb 1: Lev 1–4
Feb 2: Lev 5–7
Feb 3: Lev 8–10
Feb 4: Lev 11–13
Feb 5: Lev 14–15
Feb 6: Lev 16–18
Feb 7: Lev 19–21
Feb 8: Lev 22–23
Feb 9: Lev 24–25
Feb 10: Lev 26–27
Feb 11: Num 1–2
Feb 12: Num 3–4
Feb 13: Num 5–6
Feb 14: Num 7
Feb 15: Num 8–10
Feb 16: Num 11–13
Feb 17: Num 14–15

Feb 18: Num 16–17
Feb 19: Num 18–20
Feb 20: Num 21–22
Feb 21: Num 23–25
Feb 22: Num 26–27
Feb 23: Num 28–30
Feb 24: Num 31–32
Feb 25: Num 33–34
Feb 26: Num 35–36
Feb 27: Deut 1–2
Feb 28: Deut 3–4
Mar 1: Deut 5–7
Mar 2: Deut 8–10
Mar 3: Deut 11–13
Mar 4: Deut 14–16
Mar 5: Deut 17–20
Mar 6: Deut 21–23
Mar 7: Deut 24–27
Mar 8: Deut 28–29
Mar 9: Deut 30–31
Mar 10: Deut 32–34
Mar 11: Josh 1–4
Mar 12: Josh 5–8
Mar 13: Josh 9–11
Mar 14: Josh 12–15
Mar 15: Josh 16–18
Mar 16: Josh 19–21
Mar 17: Josh 22–24
Mar 18: Jud 1–2
Mar 19: Jud 3–5
Mar 20: Jud 6–7
Mar 21: Jud 8–9
Mar 22: Jud 10–12
Mar 23: Jud 13–15
Mar 24: Jud 16–18
Mar 25: Jud 19–21
Mar 26: Ruth
Mar 27: 1Sam 1–3
Mar 28: 1Sam 4–8
Mar 29: 1Sam 9–12
Mar 30: 1Sam 13–14
Mar 31: 1Sam 15–17
Apr 1: 1Sam 18–20
Apr 2: 1Sam 21–24
Apr 3: 1Sam 25–27
Apr 4: 1Sam 28–31
Apr 5: 2Sam 1–3
Apr 6: 2Sam 4–7

Apr 7: 2Sam 8–12
Apr 8: 2Sam 13–15
Apr 9: 2Sam 16–18
Apr 10: 2Sam 19–21
Apr 11: 2Sam 22–24
Apr 12: 1King 1–2
Apr 13: 1King 3–5
Apr 14: 1King 6–7
Apr 15: 1King 8–9
Apr 16: 1King 10–11
Apr 17: 1King 12–14
Apr 18: 1King 15–17
Apr 19: 1King 18–20
Apr 20: 1King 21–22
Apr 21: 2King 1–3
Apr 22: 2King 4–5
Apr 23: 2King 6–8
Apr 24: 2King 9–11
Apr 25: 2King 12–14
Apr 26: 2King 15–17
Apr 27: 2King 18–19
Apr 28: 2King 20–22
Apr 29: 2King 23–25
Apr 30: 1Chron 1–2
May 1: 1Chron 3–5
May 2: 1Chron 6
May 3: 1Chron 7–8
May 4: 1Chron 9–11
May 5: 1Chron 12–14
May 6: 1Chron 15–17
May 7: 1Chron 18–21
May 8: 1Chron 22–24
May 9: 1Chron 25–27
May 10: 1Chron 28–29,
2Chron 1
May 11: 2Chron 2–5
May 12: 2Chron 6–8
May 13: 2Chron 9–12
May 14: 2Chron 13–17
May 15: 2Chron 18–20
May 16: 2Chron 21–24
May 17: 2Chron 25–27
May 18: 2Chron 28–31
May 19: 2Chron 32–34
May 20: 2Chron 35–36
May 21: Ezra 1–3
May 22: Ezra 4–7
May 23: Ezra 8–10

May 24: Neh 1–3
May 25: Neh 4–6
May 26: Neh 7
May 27: Neh 8–9
May 28: Neh 10–11
May 29: Neh 12–13
May 30: Est 1–5
May 31: Est 6–10
Jun 1: Job 1–4
Jun 2: Job 5–7
Jun 3: Job 8–10
Jun 4: Job 11–13
Jun 5: Job 14–16
Jun 6: Job 17–20
Jun 7: Job 21–23
Jun 8: Job 24–28
Jun 9: Job 29–31
Jun 10: Job 32–34
Jun 11: Job 35–37
Jun 12: Job 38–39
Jun 13: Job 40–42
Jun 14: Ps 1–8
Jun 15: Ps 9–16
Jun 16: Ps 17–20
Jun 17: Ps 21–25
Jun 18: Ps 26–31
Jun 19: Ps 32–35
Jun 20: Ps 36–39
Jun 21: Ps 40–45
Jun 22: Ps 46–50
Jun 23: Ps 51–57
Jun 24: Ps 58–65
Jun 25: Ps 66–69
Jun 26: Ps 70–73
Jun 27: Ps 74–77
Jun 28: Ps 78–79
Jun 29: Ps 80–85
Jun 30: Ps 86–89
Jul 1: Ps 90–95
Jul 2: Ps 96–102
Jul 3: Ps 103–105
Jul 4: Ps 106–107
Jul 5: Ps 108–114
Jul 6: Ps 115–118
Jul 7: Ps 119:1–88
Jul 8: Ps 119:89–176
Jul 9: Ps 120–132
Jul 10: Ps 133–139

Jul 11: Ps 140–145	Sep 2: Ezek 13–15	Oct 25: Luke 4–5	Dec 17: Titus–Philemon
Jul 12: Ps 146–150	Sep 3: Ezek 16–17	Oct 26: Luke 6–7	Dec 18: Heb 1–6
Jul 13: Prov 1–3	Sep 4: Ezek 18–20	Oct 27: Luke 8–9	Dec 19: Heb 7–10
Jul 14: Prov 4–6	Sep 5: Ezek 21–22	Oct 28: Luke 10–11	Dec 20: Heb 11–13
Jul 15: Prov 7–9	Sep 6: Ezek 23–24	Oct 29: Luke 12–13	Dec 21: James 1–5
Jul 16: Prov 10–12	Sep 7: Ezek 25–27	Oct 30: Luke 14–16	Dec 22: 1 Peter 1–5
Jul 17: Prov 13–15	Sep 8: Ezek 28–30	Oct 31: Luke 17–18	Dec 23: 2 Peter 1–3
Jul 18: Prov 16–18	Sep 9: Ezek 31–33	Nov 1: Luke 19–20	Dec 24: 1 John 1–5
Jul 19: Prov 19–21	Sep 10: Ezek 34–36	Nov 2: Luke 21–22	Dec 25: 2John, 3John, Jude
Jul 20: Prov 22–23	Sep 11: Ezek 37–39	Nov 3: Luke 23–24	Dec 26: Rev 1–3
Jul 21: Prov 24–26	Sep 12: Ezek 40–42	Nov 4: John 1–2	Dec 27: Rev 4–8
Jul 22: Prov 27–29	Sep 13: Ezek 43–45	Nov 5: John 3–4	Dec 28: Rev 9–12
Jul 23: Prov 30–31	Sep 14: Ezek 46–48	Nov 6: John 5–6	Dec 29: Rev 13–16
Jul 24: Ecc 1–4	Sep 15: Dan 1–3	Nov 7: John 7–8	Dec 30: Rev 17–19
Jul 25: Ecc 5–8	Sep 16: Dan 4–6	Nov 8: John 9–10	Dec 31: Rev 20–22
Jul 26: Ecc 9–12	Sep 17: Dan 7–9	Nov 9: John 11–12	
Jul 27: Solomon 1–8	Sep 18: Dan 10–12	Nov 10: John 13–15	
Jul 28: Is 1–4	Sep 19: Hos 1–7	Nov 11: John 16–18	
Jul 29: Is 5–8	Sep 20: Hos 8–14	Nov 12: John 19–21	
Jul 30: Is 9–12	Sep 21: Joel	Nov 13: Acts 1–3	
Jul 31: Is 13–17	Sep 22: Amos 1–5	Nov 14: Acts 4–6	
Aug 1: Is 18–22	Sep 23: Amos 6–9	Nov 15: Acts 7–8	
Aug 2: Is 23–27	Sep 24: Oba–Jonah	Nov 16: Acts 9–10	
Aug 3: Is 28–30	Sep 25: Micah 1–7	Nov 17: Acts 11–13	
Aug 4: Is 31–35	Sep 26: Nahum 1–3	Nov 18: Acts 14–15	
Aug 5: Is 36–41	Sep 27: Hab–Zeph	Nov 19: Acts 16–17	
Aug 6: Is 42–44	Sep 28: Haggai 1–2	Nov 20: Acts 18–20	
Aug 7: Is 45–48	Sep 29: Zech 1–7	Nov 21: Acts 21–23	
Aug 8: Is 49–53	Sep 30: Zech 8–14	Nov 22: Acts 24–26	
Aug 9: Is 54–58	Oct 1: Malachi 1–4	Nov 23: Acts 27–28	
Aug 10: Is 59–63	Oct 2: Matt 1–4	Nov 24: Rom 1–3	
Aug 11: Is 64–66	Oct 3: Matt 5–6	Nov 25: Rom 4–7	
Aug 12: Jer 1–3	Oct 4: Matt 7–8	Nov 26: Rom 8–10	
Aug 13: Jer 4–6	Oct 5: Matt 9–10	Nov 27: Rom 11–13	
Aug 14: Jer 7–9	Oct 6: Matt 11–12	Nov 28: Rom 14–16	
Aug 15: Jer 10–13	Oct 7: Matt 13–14	Nov 29: 1Cor 1–4	
Aug 16: Jer 14–17	Oct 8: Matt 15–17	Nov 30: 1Cor 5–8	
Aug 17: Jer 18–22	Oct 9: Matt 18–19	Dec 1: 1Cor 9–11	
Aug 18: Jer 23–25	Oct 10: Matt 20–21	Dec 2: 1Cor 12–14	
Aug 19: Jer 26–29	Oct 11: Matt 22–23	Dec 3: 1Cor 15–16	
Aug 20: Jer 30–31	Oct 12: Matt 24–25	Dec 4: 2Cor 1–4	
Aug 21: Jer 32–34	Oct 13: Matt 26	Dec 5: 2Cor 5–9	
Aug 22: Jer 35–37	Oct 14: Matt 27–28	Dec 6: 2Cor 10–13	
Aug 23: Jer 38–41	Oct 15: Mark 1–3	Dec 7: Gal 1–3	
Aug 24: Jer 42–45	Oct 16: Mark 4–5	Dec 8: Gal 4–6	
Aug 25: Jer 46–48	Oct 17: Mark 6–7	Dec 9: Eph 1–3	
Aug 26: Jer 49–50	Oct 18: Mark 8–9	Dec 10: Eph 4–6	
Aug 27: Jer 51–52	Oct 19: Mark 10–11	Dec 11: Philippians 1–4	
Aug 28: Lam 1–3:36	Oct 20: Mark 12–13	Dec 12: Colossians 1–4	
Aug 29: Lam 3:37–5	Oct 21: Mark 14	Dec 13: 1 Thess 1–5	
Aug 30: Ezek 1–4	Oct 22: Mark 15–16	Dec 14: 2 Thess 1–3	
Aug 31: Ezek 5–8	Oct 23: Luke 1	Dec 15: 1 Timothy 1–6	
Sep 1: Ezek 9–12	Oct 24: Luke 2–3	Dec 16: 2 Timothy 1–4	

Acknowledgments

This is my first book with Seshat Press. What an incredible journey that started almost twenty years ago when I first heard Christine Kloser share about her new program, *Get Your Book Done*. Although I had written quite a bit with the BBC and throughout my careers in broadcasting, public relations, and ministry, I had not written a book since 1989. Along the way, several friends and family suggested that I should sit down and write a book. However, it was Christine who triggered my action three years ago to start seriously considering writing a book when she and her husband David discussed with me what I was passionate about writing.

Over the next two years, the *Get Your Book Done Team* coaches of Penny Legg, Ellen Monses, Carrie Jareed, and Jean Merrill encouraged me to write my book based on my journals that I now share with you. This last year has been focused on editing and fine tuning, which I could not have done without the guidance of my amazing editor, Karen Burton, who really understood where I was coming from. I am deeply grateful for all their support on this journey of reflecting on seventy years of my life—my early scribbling, writing, and memories. They were able to help me bring the connections to life as my daily habit of reading scripture tied into my daily journaling.

Most of us do not want a God who comes into our everyday life and interferes with our plans and decisions. Most would rather keep God at a distance. It was the friendship of several priests and colleagues over the years who guided me and reminded me of the influence of God in our ordinary lives. Several priests throughout my life have influenced my thinking about this: Athur Taylor, Trevor Huddleston, Desmond Tutu, John Stott, Warren Crews, James Purdy, Steve Lawler, Traci Blackman, and more recently, Bishops G. Wayne Smith, Jake Owensby, and Deon K. Johnson. They have all shaped my life and faith at different times when I was struggling or just coasting along, oblivious to the world around me.

Bringing it all into focus over the last few years has been small groups of prayer warriors, with whom I explored daily readings of Morning Prayer and reading the Bible from Genesis to Revelation together over 365 days. The power of daily prayer and readings cannot be underrated, and my thanks go out to Joe, Ginger, Wanda, Joyce, Ed, Tim, Tammy, Bob, Ginny, Erva, and Donna for their presence in my life.

Finally, I would like to acknowledge the immense input and support from Charles and Elizabeth, my children here in America, who have walked the walk with me over the last thirty years through thick and thin with great patience and understanding for their father who might have something to share.

References, Resources, and Readings

"A Covenant Prayer in the Wesleyan Tradition." 1989. *The United Methodist Hymnal: Book of United Methodist Worship.* Nashville, TN: United Methodist Publishing House.

Bauby, Jean-Dominique. 1998. *The Diving Bell and the Butterfly: A Memoir of Life in Death.* NYC: Vintage.

Borg, Marcus. 2014. "What the Bible Is." *The Marcus J Borg Foundation.* marcusjborg.org/posts-by-marcus/what-the-bible-is/

Brettler, Marc, Carol Newsom, and Pheme Perkins, eds. 2018. *The New Oxford Annotated Bible with Apocrypha.* 5th ed. New York, NY: Oxford University Press.

Brooke, Rupert. 1915. "The Soldier." *1914 and Other Poems.* London: Sidgwick & Jackson Limited.

Brown, Margaret Wise. 1942. *The Runaway Bunny.* New York: Harper & Brothers.

Brown, Margaret Wise. 1947. *Goodnight Moon.* Illustrated by Clement Hurd. New York: Harper & Row.

Lewis, C.S. 1950–1956. *The Chronicles of Narnia.* London: Geoffrey Bles.

Merton, Thomas. 1956. *Thoughts in Solitude.* New York: Farrar, Straus & Cudahy.

Milne, A.A. 1926. *The Adventures of Winnie the Pooh.* Illustrated by E.H. Shepard. England: Methuen & Co.

The New Revised Standard Version Bible: Anglicized Edition. 1995. The Division of Christian Education of the National Council of the Churches of Christ in the United States of America.

Norton, Mary. 1952. *The Borrowers.* London: J.M. Dent.

Potter, Beatrix. 1902. *The Tales of Peter Rabbit.* England: Frederick Warne & Co.

Ransom, Arthur. 1930. *Swallows and Amazons.* Jonathan Cape.

Shakespeare, William. 1603/2008. *Hamlet.* Edited by George Richard Hibbard. Oxford UP.

Stott, John. 1958. *Basic Christianity.* Grand Rapids, MI: Wm. B. Eerdmans Publishing.

Wells, H.G. 1895. *The Time Machine.* Henry Holt.

Wells, H.G. 1905. *Kipps: The Story of a Simple Soul.* New York: Charles Scribner's Sons.

About the Author

Stephen J. Robin was born in Hampstead, London, England, in September 1951 and grew up in a large family in the suburbs. He attended Orange Hill Grammar School before earning a B.Sc. (Hons) in Environmental Studies from University College London (UCL), where he was jointly awarded the 1973 Royal Academy Award for Architecture.

In 1974, Stephen began his career at the BBC, working as a studio manager, then producer, writer, director, and editor. He played a key research/producer role in launching the

first *Guinness Book of Records Hall of Fame* show with Sir David Frost and Norris McWhirter, featuring guests, such as Sir Paul McCartney and Billie Jean King. He also curated a BBC Overseas Service Radio catalog, championing the work of comedy greats like Tony Hancock, Morecambe and Wise, Benny Hill, and Monty Python, while producing live recording sessions for BBC Radio Two and Three, spanning big band, jazz, and classical orchestras.

In 1987, Stephen transitioned into politics, serving as a media and broadcasting consultant for Conservative Central Office during the British general election. Reporting directly to the Rt. Hon. Norman Tebbit, MP, he managed broadcasting operations, continuing in the role after the successful re-election of Prime Minister Margaret Thatcher. In 1989, he was nominated as the Conservative candidate for Strathclyde West in the European Elections, spearheading the successful *Spring into Europe* campaign, which doubled Scottish Conservative Party membership. That same year, he was appointed by the European and Social Committee of the European Community as an Expert on Broadcasting and Culture in relation to the European Broadcasting Directive.

Shifting to crisis communications in 1990, Stephen joined Weber/Shandwick Public Relations as a Senior Consultant, advising the British

Foreign Office during the Gulf Crisis and Gulf War (Desert Storm). He also developed crisis management strategies for the British Airport Authority (BAA) and led the first global investor audit for the Northern Ireland Industrial Development Board.

In 1991, as Director of Communications for the UK Water Industry and the Water Services Association, he implemented a national communications strategy that significantly improved public perception, earning high satisfaction ratings in European surveys.

Relocating to the US in 1992, Stephen joined Emerson Electric Co., where he elevated media awareness of its motor divisions, contributed to significant business growth, and led award-winning advertising and editorial initiatives. He also played a key role in consolidating Emerson's motor-related businesses into a unified group.

From 1999, he worked with the executive search firm Grant Cooper and Associates, managing high-profile recruitment and public relations efforts. Around this time, he also founded *Solutions Not Problems*, a consultancy specializing in branding, strategic planning, and communications for senior executives.

In 2004, Stephen pursued theological studies at Eden Seminary, earning a Master of Divinity. He served as a chaplain at Barnes-Jewish Hospital and St. Stephen's Episcopal Church in Ferguson, Missouri, providing pastoral care and support. In 2010, he became an Emergency Department trauma chaplain at SSM Healthcare hospitals in Missouri, retiring from full-time chaplaincy in 2013 to focus on parish ministry.

Since 2014, he has resided in Ferguson, Missouri, where he remains actively involved in his community.

www.ingramcontent.com/pod-product-compliance
Lightning Source LLC
Chambersburg PA
CBHW070545130626

46556CB00001B/25